FREEDOM, FEMINISM, AND THE STATE

An Overview of Individualist Feminism

edited by Wendy McElroy
foreword by Lewis Perry

ACKNOWLEDGMENTS

The extract from *Give Me Liberty* by Rose Wilder Lane is reprinted by permission of Sue Ford.

"Antigone's Daughters" by Jean Bethke Elshtain is reprinted from the April 1982 issue of *democracy* by permission of the publisher.

"Government Is Women's Enemy" by Sharon Presley and Lynn Kinsky, "Prostitution" by "Danielle," "Are Feminist Businesses Capitalistic?" by Rosalie Nichols, and "Protective Labor Legislation" by Joan Kennedy Taylor are reprinted by permission of the authors and of the Association of Libertarian Feminists, 435½ N. Van Ness Avenue, Los Angeles, Calif. 90004.

"If You Liked Gun Control, You'll Love the Antiabortion Amendment" by Beverly J. Combs is reprinted by permission from the May 1977 issue of *Reason*. Copyright © 1977 by Reason Enterprises, Box 40105, Santa Barbara, Calif. 93103.

"Women and the Rise of the American Medical Profession" by Barbara Ehrenreich and Deirdre English is reprinted from *Witches, Midwives and Nurses* by permission of The Feminist Press, Box 334, Old Westbury, N.Y. 11568. Copyright © 1973 by Barbara Ehrenreich and Deirdre English.

Library of Congress Cataloging in Publication Data

Main entry under title:

Freedom, feminism, and the state.

Bibliography
Includes index.
1. Feminism—United States—History—Addresses, essays, lectures. 2. Individualism—Addresses, essays, lectures. 3. Women in politics—United States—History—Addresses, essays, lectures.
I. McElroy, Wendy.
HQ1410.F73 1982 305.4'2'0973 82-22010
ISBN 0-932790-32-1

Printed in the United States of America.

CATO INSTITUTE
224 Second Street, S.E.
Washington, D.C. 20003

For George H. Smith

CONTENTS

FOREWORD

Reading this useful anthology, I found myself looking backward. In the mid-1960s Leonard I. Krimerman and I offered a collection of libertarian writings, *Patterns of Anarchy,* that was a result of an immersion in the radical culture of the universities. Our commitment to campus civil rights and peace movements had led us into study groups and earnest discussions of many topics and writers. The publishing industry was alert to an awakening of interest in political philosophy, and when we decided that the anarchist tradition included many writers who deserved to be republished, Doubleday was willing to bring out a large paperback edition. The purpose of *Patterns of Anarchy* was neither to proselytize for anarchism nor to display a past tradition as though it belonged in a museum; it was to stimulate thinking about liberty and the state. And for several years it was clear that our collection, along with other works on anarchism that soon appeared, was widely read and discussed.

As everyone knows, the student culture of the 1960s proved to be vulnerable to the designs of the faddists and advertisers who manipulate popular culture. Furthermore, new styles of social activism became so sensitive about "elitism" that they disparaged inquiry into traditions of political thought. The publishing industry, absorbed by international conglomerates, lost touch with intellectual discourse, which in turn became fragmented and ahistorical. Anarchism also took a disappointing turn. Too often it became a code word for antisocial or self-destructive behavior, or else it substituted career-oriented selfishness for traditional conceptions of community. Meanwhile students, pressed by vocational anxieties, had less time for eager reading.

I confess, then, to some nostalgia at the publication in the 1980s of a volume based on the premise that radicals must think seriously about individualism and political power, especially since the editor has turned to several writers who impressed Krimerman and me 20 years ago—for example, Voltairine de Cleyre, Emma Goldman, and the contributors to Benjamin R. Tucker's *Liberty*. But I should make it clear that there was too much foolishness and mindlessness in the 1960s for anyone to dream of a "return" to that decade. Only

Madison Avenue believes that the past can be manipulated so shallowly. The intellectual necessity now, as always, is to make sense of the present and to face the future with clarity.

But one kind of recovery may still be advocated: the recovery of historical consciousness in intellectual life. The problem goes beyond the submergence of history in high school social studies and university social science curricula. We may be on the verge of forgetting that intellectuals mature by thinking through and finding their relation to political and philosophical traditions. In the autobiographies of intellectuals of previous generations—I have been reading Lewis Mumford's *Sketches from Life,* but the same point holds for many of Mumford's contemporaries or for 19th-century writers—one is indeed struck by changes in cultural milieu from one decade to the next. But we also glimpse the ways in which intellectual voices gained force from grappling with classic expressions of individual rights and political responsibilities. Mumford, for example, speaks of his "master Emerson" and of his "lifelong intercourse" with Plato. This kind of historical consciousness is not dead. Without toting up too many recent examples, I think of Tillie Olsen's commentary on Rebecca Harding Davis, Lawrence Goodwyn's celebration of the Populists, or Henry Glassie's uses of John Ruskin. But its chances of survival diminish in an ahistorical system of education geared to prepare students for jobs in large corporations and in an economy that profits from rapidly shifting fads. There is no reason to expect the schools or pop culture to change their course, but it is encouraging to think that feminist movements could play a part in restoring a search for intellectual independence.

It may not be easy to come to terms with some of these writers. In some ways our milieu is less oppressive than that which the Harmans and Ezra Heywood describe in these pages. In other ways the power of modern international bureaucracies seems so enormous that 19th-century libertarian conceptions of liberty may seem almost quaint. In any event, I am inclined to argue with the authors of some of these essays. I am more of a believer in democratic politics than many libertarians, and they sometimes strike me as too insensitive to the viewpoints of the working classes. In my opinion, they are also too hostile to American religious traditions. But it should prove worthwhile to grapple with these champions of a continuing process of revolution. For feminists, the disastrous strategies of the ERA campaign and the floundering leadership of the Carter years ought to provoke a reexamination of goals and principles. Is it too rash to hope for a reexamination that goes beyond the exigencies of feminist politics and proceeds toward a new intellectual radicalism?

Lewis Perry

Lewis Perry is professor of history at Indiana University, editor of *The Journal of American History,* and author of *Radical Abolitionism* and *Childhood, Marriage, and Reform.*

INTRODUCTION

The Roots of Individualist Feminism in 19th-Century America

Wendy McElroy

"To me," wrote Voltairine de Cleyre (1866–1912), "any dependence, any thing which destroys the complete selfhood of the individual, is in the line of slavery."[1]

Charlotte Perkins Gilman (1860–1935) wrote: "To define individual duty is difficult; but the collective duty of a class or sex is clear. It is the duty of women . . . to bring children into the world who are superior to their parents; and to forward the progress of the race."[2]

These quotes illustrate two opposing traditions within feminism—individualism and socialism. Both believe that women should have the same rights as men, that women should be equal,[3] but the meaning of equality differs within the feminist movement. Throughout most of its history, American mainstream feminism considered equality to mean equal treatment under existing laws and equal representation within existing institutions. The focus was not to change the status quo in a basic sense, but rather to be included within it. The more radical feminists protested that the existing laws and institutions were the source of injustice and, thus, could not be reformed. These feminists saw something fundamentally wrong with society beyond discrimination against women, and their concepts of equality reflected this. To the individualist, equality was a political term referring to the protection of individual rights; that is, protection of the moral jurisdiction every human being has over his or her own body. To socialist-feminists, it was a socio-economic term. Women could be equal only after private property and the family relationships it encouraged were eliminated.

In order to appreciate the radical traditions within feminism, we must set the context of the mainstream movement. Currently, socio-economic equality is the dominant goal of feminism. Even moderate

[1]Paul Avrich, *An American Anarchist, The Life of Voltairine de Cleyre* (Princeton: Princeton University Press, 1978), p. 161.

[2]Quoted in Aileen Kraditor, *Up From the Pedestal* (Chicago: Quadrangle Books, 1968), p. 175.

[3]This does not include the small minority who believe women are naturally superior to men and that society should reflect this.

feminists, exemplified by the National Organization of Women, accept this form of equality by demanding legislation that would provide equal pay for equal work.[4] This has not always been the case. The roots of American feminism are individualistic. This introduction will trace feminism from these roots to the passage of the Nineteenth Amendment (1920), which incorporated women's suffrage into the U.S. Constitution. We will then compare the philosophy and relative contribution of individualist and socialist feminism.

The Roots of Feminism

As an organized force, feminism dates from abolitionism in the early 1830s.[5] Abolitionism was the radical anti-slavery movement which demanded the immediate cessation of slavery on the grounds that every man was a self-owner; that is, every human being has moral jurisdiction over his or her own body. It was the first organized, radical movement in which women played prominent roles and from which a woman's movement sprang. Abbie Kelley (1810–1887), an abolitionist-feminist, observed: "We have good cause to be grateful to the slave, for the benefit we have received to ourselves, in working for him. In striving to strike his irons off, we found most surely that we were manacled ourselves."[6] The modern historian, Aileen S. Kraditor, wrote:

> A few women in the abolitionist movement in the 1830s . . . found their religiously inspired work for the slave impeded by prejudices against public activity by women. They and many others began to ponder the parallels between women's status and the Negro's status, and to notice that white men usually applied the principles of natural rights and the ideology of individualism only to themselves.[7]

In the early 19th century, married women could not enter into contracts without their husband's consent, women lost all title to property

[4]A statement adopted by NOW's organizing conference (1966) reads, in part, "Discrimination in employment on the basis of sex is now prohibited by federal law . . . the Commission has not made clear its intention to enforce the law with the same seriousness on behalf of women as of other victims of discrimination."

[5]For background information see Lewis Perry, *Radical Abolitionism: Anarchy and the Government of God in Antislavery Thought* (Ithaca, N.Y.: Cornell University Press, 1973); and Blanche Glassman Hersh, *The Slavery of Sex: Feminist Abolitionists in America* (Chicago: University of Illinois Press, 1978). For an overview of women's participation in the American Revolution, see Linda Kerber, *Women of the Republic* (Williamsburg, Va.: University of North Carolina Press, 1980).

[6]Carrie Hapman Catt and Nettie Rogers Shuler, *Woman Suffrage and Politics* (Seattle: University of Washington Press, 1969), p. 37.

[7]Kraditor, *Up From the Pedestal*, pp. 13–14.

or future earnings upon marriage, children were legally controlled by the father, and women were often without recourse against kidnapping or imprisonment by husbands and other male relatives.

Within abolitionism, women's rights stirred hot debate. The strongest advocate of women's rights was the libertarian William Lloyd Garrison (1805–1879), editor of the *Liberator,* who insisted that anti-slavery was a battle for human rights, not male rights.[8] Many of the abolitionists who opposed Garrison on this agreed that women were self-owners but resisted mixing woman's rights with anti-slavery for fear it would hurt the latter cause; Theodore Weld (1803–1895) exemplified this position. Through his encouragement, Angelina Grimké (1805–1879), Sarah Grimké (1792–1873), and Abbie Kelley became the first women in America to lecture before an audience that included men.[9] Nevertheless, he admonished them to stop introducing woman's rights into their speeches. "Is it not forgetting the great and dreadful wrongs of the slave," he asked Angelina, "in a selfish crusade against some paltry grievances of our own?"[10] "The time to assert a right," she countered, "is the time when that right is denied. We must establish this right for if we do not, it will be impossible for us to go on with the work of Emancipation."[11]

In a speech before the Massachusetts Legislature on February 21, 1838, whereby Angelina Grimké became the first woman to speak before an American legislative body, she continued to mix the two issues:

> Mr. Chairman, it is my privilege to stand before you . . . on behalf of the 20,000 women of Massachusetts whose names are enrolled on petitions . . . these petitions relate to the great and solemn subject of slavery . . . and because it is a political subject, it has often tauntingly been said that women have nothing to do with it. Are we aliens

[8]Quakerism was another major influence. Quaker abolitionist-feminists included Sarah Grimké, Angelina Grimké, Lydia White, Lucretia Mott, Abbie Kelley, M. Carey Thomas, Elizabeth Chandler, and Prudence Crandall. The Quaker influence imbued woman's rights with a religious fervor, perhaps best exemplified by the lectures of Lucretia Mott. See Dana Greene, ed., *Lucretia Mott: Her Complete Speeches and Sermons* (New York: Edwin Mellen Press, 1980).

[9]A mixed audience was one composed of both males and females. This was such a radical break with tradition that the Grimké sisters were assured that no respectable man would marry them thereafter.

[10]Gerda Lerner, *The Grimké Sisters from South Carolina: Rebels Against Slavery* (Boston: Houghton Mifflin Co., 1967), p. 200. Weld also expressed concern over the fact that they felt themselves logically proceeding from "peace" principles to opposition to all government. For additional information on the Civil War period and feminism, see Ellen Carol DuBois, *Feminism and Suffrage* (Ithaca, N.Y.: Cornell University Press, 1980).

[11]Lerner, *The Grimké Sisters from South Carolina,* p. 201.

> because we are women? Are we bereft of citizenship because we are mothers, wives, and daughters of a mighty people?[12]

Sarah Grimké's tactics were similar to those of her younger sister. Her pamphlet, *Letters on the Equality of the Sexes and the Condition of Woman* (1837), used the individualist-feminist approach of comparing women to slaves. "If the wife be injured in her person or property," Sarah quoted Blackstone, "she can bring no action for redress without her husband's concurrence, and in his name as well as her own." Sarah observed, "[T]his law is similar to the law respecting slaves, 'A slave cannot bring suit against his master or any other person, for an injury—his master must bring it.' " She compared the Louisiana law that said that all a slave possesses belongs to his master with a law that said, "A woman's personal property by marriage becomes absolutely her husband's which, at his death, he may leave entirely from her."[13]

Through the efforts of the Grimké sisters, women's rights became a subject of controversy throughout America. Angelina wrote:

> We have given great offense on account of our womanhood, which seems to be as objectionable as our abolitionism. The whole land seems aroused to discussion on the province of women, and I am glad of it. We are willing to bear the brunt of the storm, if we can only be the means of making a break in that wall of public opinion which lies right in the way of women's rights, true dignity, honor and usefulness.[14]

To the Grimké sisters, who smoothed the path for future feminists by breaking social taboos, and to Lucretia Mott (1793–1880), who encouraged civil disobedience through her involvement in the underground railroad, equality meant equal protection under just law and the equal opportunity to protest injustice.

The Civil War and Feminism

To focus the discussion of pre- and post-Civil War feminism, we will consider four questions: What were the feminists' views of themselves, of blacks, of men, and of government?

Before the Civil War, feminists championed black rights, identifying

[12]Ibid., p. 183.

[13]Sarah Grimké, *Letters on the Equality of the Sexes and the Condition of Woman* (New York: Burt Franklin, 1837), Letter XII.

[14]Lerner, *The Grimké Sisters from South Carolina*, p. 183.

themselves with the plight of the slave. Their attitude toward men was generally cordial. In light of the harsh discrimination they often suffered, this was surprising. American women who journeyed to the 1840 World Anti-Slavery Conference in London, for example, were barred from sitting with the assembly; they were forced to follow the proceedings from balcony seats hidden behind curtains. Any anger they felt toward men may have been tempered by the actions of Garrison and several other male abolitionists who chose to sit with them in protest rather than to join the body of the conference.

The feminists' attitude toward themselves was largely a manifestation of the Quaker background many of them shared and of Garrison's influence in maintaining that the individual must act according to his conscience and be held rigidly accountable for his actions. The core of Garrisonian strategy was that a revolution in ideas must precede and underlie any institutional reform. Both of these influences tended to instill a moral pietism within these women which they carried over into feminism.

This had wide implications for the abolitionist-feminist view of politics and government. Quakers at that time repudiated political action, often ostracizing those members who engaged in it. Angelina Grimké exemplified the Garrisonian position on politics:

> Dost thou ask me if I would wish to see women engaged in the contention and strife of sectarian controversy, or in the intrigues of political partizans? I say no!—never. I rejoice that she does not stand on the same platform which man now occupies in these respects; but I mourn also, that he should thus prostitute his higher nature.[15]

Nevertheless, political feminism was on the rise. Elizabeth Cady Stanton (1815–1902), who attended the 1840 World Anti-Slavery Conference, was embittered by its treatment of women. With Lucretia Mott, she planned the 1848 Seneca Falls Convention to discuss women's rights and there introduced a women's suffrage resolution: "*Resolved*, that it is the duty of the women of this country to secure to themselves their sacred right to the elective franchise."[16] The resolution met strong resistance from Mott and other members of the old guard. It was passed by a narrow margin, the only resolution not to receive a unanimous

[15]Angelina Grimké, *Letters to Catherine E. Beecher, in Reply to an Essay on Slavery and Abolitionism* (Boston: 1838), Letter XII (East Boyston, Mass., 1837).

[16]Susan B. Anthony, Elizabeth Cady Stanton, and Ida H. Harper, *The History of Woman Suffrage*, Vol. 1 (New York: Fowler & Wells, 1881–1922), pp. 70–73.

vote. But by the 1858 woman's convention, political feminism had prevailed to the point that suffrage was a virtually uncontested goal within the movement.

The Civil War changed feminism. Individualism in America was dealt a stunning blow by war measures that included conscription, censorship, suspension of habeas corpus, political imprisonment, legal tender laws, and dramatically increased taxes and tariffs. The war also affected the popular view of government. With the cry of "no taxation without representation" still echoing from the recent past, government was viewed as requiring the consent of its citizens. "One of the fundamental principles announced in the Declaration of Independence," wrote Harriet Martineau, "is that governments derive their just powers from the consent of the governed."[17] Feminists capitalized on this by paraphrasing the Declaration of Independence to reflect their grievances against the government of men.[18] When the North refused to permit the South to withdraw its consent by seceding and when it imposed an unpopular government upon the South during Reconstruction, the consensual view of government was weakened. "One Union Under God" became a common sentiment.

Generally, feminists supported the war as a means of ending slavery, and, in devoting themselves to the war effort, they shelved the women's rights issue. After 1800, the legal disabilities of women had been changing slowly. In 1809 Connecticut gave married women the right to make a will. Texas (1840) and Alabama (1843) followed suit. After the war, however, feminists found that some legal rights had been lost to them. For example, the 1860 New York law granting women the right to equal guardianship of their children had been diluted so as to merely forbid the father from giving away the child without written permission from the mother. Moreover, the war had enfranchised neither blacks nor women. The freedom of blacks in particular was greatly jeopardized by post-war hostility, and many felt their rights would be secure only through an amendment to the Constitution guaranteeing enfranchisement.

[17]Harriet Martineau, *Society in America,* Vol. 1 (New York: Saunders & Otley, 1837), p. 199.

[18]The Declaration of Sentiments (July 1848) is perhaps the most famous feminist document. It begins: "When, in the course of human events, it becomes necessary for one portion of the family of man to assume among the people of the earth a position different from that which they have hitherto occupied, but one to which the laws of nature and of nature's God entitle them, a decent respect to the opinions of mankind requires that they should declare the causes that impel them to such a course."

Post-Civil War Feminism

After the war, the key issues for mainstream feminism were the Thirteenth, Fourteenth, and Fifteenth Amendments to the Constitution, all aimed at securing freedom for blacks. Although feminists were pulled in two directions, desiring rights for blacks *and* rights for women, they gave priority to black rights. Elizabeth Cady Stanton and Susan B. Anthony (1820–1906) organized the National Loyal Women's League, which collected 400,000 signatures on petitions supporting the Thirteenth Amendment. The Fourteenth and Fifteenth Amendments, however, were different matters.

The Fourteenth Amendment provided that if the right to vote were denied to any law-abiding male inhabitants of a state over the age of 21 (excluding untaxed Indians), that state's basis for representation in Congress would be proportionately reduced. Its purpose was to secure votes for black men and, in attempting to do so, it introduced the word "male" into the U.S. Constitution. The Fifteenth Amendment assured that the right to vote could not be abridged because of "race, color, or previous condition of servitude." It was objectionable to feminists because it made no reference to sex.

Male abolitionists almost universally rejected women's claim to suffrage, insisting that this was not the time to stress women's rights.[19] "As Abraham Lincoln said, 'one war at a time,' " counselled Wendell Phillips, "so I say one question at a time. This hour belongs to the negro."[20] Although Stanton had tirelessly worked for the Thirteenth Amendment, she was now skeptical. "Do you believe the African race is composed entirely of males?" she asked Phillips.[21] To Susan B. Anthony, she wrote: "I have argued constantly with Phillips and the whole anti-slavery fraternity, but I feel one and all will favor enfranchising the negro without us. Women's cause is in deep water."[22] Susan B. Anthony appealed to the male fraternity: "No, no, this is the hour to press woman's claims; we have stood with the black man in the Constitution over half a century . . . Enfranchise him, and we are left outside with lunatics, idiots and criminals."[23]

[19]Even Garrison, the all-weather friend of feminism, refused to support women's suffrage on the grounds that he was against voting altogether. This line of opposition to women's suffrage is relatively unexplored.

[20]Anthony, et al., *History of Woman Suffrage,* p. 59.

[21]Ibid., p. 60.

[22]Ibid.

[23]Quoted in William L. O'Neill, *Everyone was Brave: A History of Feminism in America* (New York: Quadrant Press, 1971), p. 17.

The catalyst to this situation was the 1867 Kansas campaign to secure votes for women in that state. As confirmed Republicans, Anthony and Stanton travelled from town to town within Kansas, publicly giving impassioned speeches and privately appealing to the Republican Party and Republican papers to lend them the promised support. This support never materialized. Later, Stanton wrote:

> The editors of the New York Tribune and the Independent can never know how wistfully from day to day their papers were searched for some inspiring editorial on the woman's amendment, but naught was there; there were no words of hope and encouragement, no eloquent letters from an Eastern man that could be read to the people . . . all calmly watched the struggle from afar and when defeat came . . . no consoling words were offered for the woman's loss.[24]

Feeling betrayed, Stanton and Anthony repudiated the Republican Party, thus breaking with many of their abolitionist friends. They began to court the traditionally pro-slavery Democrats and to associate with the prominent racist George Francis Train, who lectured with them and financed the initial issue of their periodical *Revolution;* its motto was "Men, their rights, nothing more; Women, their rights, nothing less."

Stanton and Anthony's activities split mainstream feminism in two. To the sharp criticism of their racist connections, Anthony replied, "Why should we not accept all in favor of woman suffrage to our platform and association even though they be rabid pro-slavery Democrats."[25] The association referred to was the National Woman Suffrage Association established by Stanton and Anthony in 1869. The antagonism this created was so great that Lucy Stone (1818–1893) and Henry Blackwell (1825–1909) founded the American Woman Suffrage Association in 1869. The rift lasted 20 years until the two groups merged to form the National American Woman's Suffrage Association which, after the passage of the Nineteenth Amendment, became the League of Women Voters.

Despite their protests, Stone and Blackwell were not above reproach on racial matters. In his address, *What the South Can Do: How the Southern States Can Make Themselves Masters of the Situation* (1867), Blackwell used white supremacist arguments:

[24]Catt and Shuler, *Woman Suffrage and Politics,* pp. 55–56. Parker Pillsbury, editor of the *Standard,* was an exception; he resigned his post in protest over the paper's refusal to print the woman suffrage point of view.

[25]Anthony, et al., *History of Woman Suffrage,* p. 95.

> If you are to share the future government of your states with a race you deem naturally and hopelessly inferior, avert the social chaos, which seems to you so imminent, by utilizing the intelligence and patriotism of the wives and daughters of the South.[26]

Even feminists who considered themselves true to their abolitionist roots were straying far from its spirit.

The feminist movement had clearly changed. Prior to the war, black rights were emphasized as part of every human being's right of self-ownership; the conditions of slaves and women were drawn as parallels. After the war, many feminists began to view black rights as hostile to those of women. "This republican cry of manhood suffrage," commented Stanton, "created an antagonism between black men and all women."[27]

The refusal of abolitionist men to support feminist goals created a suspicion of men among some prominent feminists. "We repudiated man's counsels forever," wrote Anthony.[28] The attitude toward political action had also shifted. Before the Civil War, feminists tended toward apolitical strategy. The new feminism focused upon enfranchisement almost to the exclusion of other goals.

The fundamental change, however, was feminism's attitude toward itself. Early feminism was a moral, pietistic crusade that refused to compromise an ideological context, which was broader than rights for women. It encompassed a view of human nature and of one's proper relationship to God and other human beings. In contrast, post-war feminism seemed narrow and pragmatic, almost evolving into a single-issue movement—the issue of women's suffrage. Votes for women became the overriding strategy on which other reforms were said to rely.

As suffrage increased in popularity and attracted ideologically diverse women, Stanton and other leaders began to compromise subsidiary issues. Feminism employed blatantly white supremacist arguments to further suffrage, pointing out that white women would add to the white vote since they were more likely to vote than minority women.

[26]Kraditor, *Up From the Pedestal*, p. 256. Although women's suffrage may have increased the white vote proportionately, the South was reluctant to endorse the right of the federal government to extend suffrage as this could be viewed as an endorsement of the Fourteenth Amendment.

[27]O'Neill, *Everyone Was Brave*, p. 17.

[28]Ibid.

This argument was adapted to counter the fear of enfranchising immigrant women. Feminists suggested that millions of native American women were more likely to vote than foreigners, thus softening the impact of foreign morals exemplified by Catholicism.[29] For similar reasons, the feminists called for an elitist, limited suffrage; even the former abolitionist, Elizabeth Cady Stanton, supported literacy tests as a prerequisite for the vote. As Susan B. Anthony and Ida Husted Harper commented:

> . . . the worst elements have been put into the ballot-box and the best elements kept out. This fatal mistake is even now beginning to dawn upon the minds of those who have cherished an ideal of the grandeur of a republic, and they dimly see that in woman lies the highest promise of its fulfillment. Those who fear the foreign vote will learn eventually that there are more American-born women in the United States than foreign born men and women; and those who dread the ignorant vote will study the statistics and see that the percentage of illiteracy is much smaller among women than among men.[30]

Moreover, as feminism grew it became increasingly "respectable" in its attitude and goals. Eugenics and social purity reform, both popular causes, became a staple of mainstream feminism. Social purity campaigns included raising the age of consent, the reformation of prostitutes, censorship of obscenity, and the advocacy of birth control through restraint. As Linda Gordon commented in *Woman's Body, Woman's Right:*

> The closer we look, the harder it is to distinguish social-purity groups from feminist ones. Feminists from very disparate groups were advocates of most major social purity issues . . .[31]

Although social purity that stemmed from the purity of the individual conscience was a goal of abolitionist feminists, the crucial difference of the post-Civil War feminists seemed to be their willingness to enforce morality through law. While the abolitionist feminists, who were largely Quaker, believed that the individual must be free to find salvation and

[29]As with most suffrage policies this evolved; later suffragists appealed to immigrant women for support. For an excellent presentation of the movement's xenophobia, see Alan P. Grimes, *The Puritan Ethic and Woman Suffrage* (New York: Oxford University Press, 1967).

[30]Grimes, *The Puritan Ethic and Woman Suffrage*, p. 94.

[31]Linda Gordon, *Woman's Body, Woman's Right* (New York: Penguin Books, Inc., 1976), pp. 117–118.

perfect the soul, later feminists wished to take choice out of morality issues. Among the many implications of this key difference was the post-war feminist tendency to look toward the state for purity rather than toward the individual.

The relatively pacifist nature of abolitionist feminism had been so compromised by the Civil War that by the 20th century feminists supported World War I even though the movement had strong ties with woman's groups in Germany and many of the American leaders were staunch pacifists. It was feared that opposition to the war would hurt the suffrage cause.[32] When the Nineteenth Amendment was ratified (1920), some considered it a pyrrhic victory. For one thing, by 1920, 28 of the 48 states already had full or presidential suffrage for women, and the overwhelming majority of women outside of New England and parts of the South could vote if they chose to. More importantly, the mainstream movement had abandoned its ideological framework from which it could have proceeded systematically beyond suffrage.

Although suffrage undoubtedly contributed to "purity" legislation, which most feminists approved, it is not clear that such legislation would not have been ushered in with the Progressive era apart from women's suffrage. To those women who believed that the Nineteenth Amendment would provide virtually a utopian society, the reality of their only slightly changed status must have been a crushing blow.[33]

Individualist Feminism

While mainstream feminism concentrated on suffrage, more radical feminists looked elsewhere for progress. Individualist feminists became especially involved in the reform of birth control and marriage laws. Their goal was not purity but freedom.

In 1889, a woman who had just risked her life in a dangerous self-induced abortion wrote to the libertarian periodical, *Lucifer the Light Bearer* (1883–1907), pleading:

> I know I am dreadful wicked, but I am sure to be in the condition from which I risked my life to be free, and I cannot stand it . . . Would

[32]Stanton's *The Woman's Bible* (1895), a series of commentaries on those parts of the Bible referring to women, was generally condemned by the suffragist movement whose members consisted more and more of conservative women. For additional information on this general trend within suffrage, see Aileen Kraditor's *The Ideas of the Woman Suffrage Movement 1890–1920* (New York: W. W. Norton & Co., 1981).

[33]Social feminists, as opposed to political feminists, who refused to view suffrage as a panacea and worked instead within the labor movement, must have felt vindicated.

> you know of any appliance that will prevent conception? If there is anything reliable, you will save my life by telling me of it.[34]

The woman wrote to *Lucifer* because, in the late 1800s, it was one of the few forums openly promoting birth control. Its main ally was *The Word* (1872–1893), a libertarian periodical edited by Ezra Heywood.

Lucifer, published and edited by Moses Harman (1830–1910), was a free-love paper; free love being the movement which sought to separate the state from sexual matters such as marriage, adultery, divorce, age of consent, and birth control. These issues were to be decided by the individuals involved. The libertarian Josiah Warren, to whom the origins of free love are often traced, expressed its theme:

> Everyone is at liberty to dispose of his or her person, and time, and property in any manner in which his or her feelings, or judgment may dictate, without involving the persons or interests of others.[35]

(This quotation is an early instance of using both "his" and "her" to explicitly include women within a statement of rights.)

Moses Harman insisted that woman's self-ownership be fully acknowledged in marriage and other sexual arrangements. In doing so, he amended Robert Ingersoll's famous statement that women merited all the rights claimed by men, plus the additional right to be protected, by observing that women should be protected against their protectors.

Unfortunately, in living his principles, Harman ran counter to the Comstock laws (1873), which prohibited the mailing of obscene matter but did not define what constituted obscenity. Whatever it was, however, it specifically included contraceptives and birth control information. A veritable witchhunt ensued, with Anthony Comstock personally persecuting those who advocated sexual nonconformity. When Ann Lohman, an abortionist and dispensor of contraceptives, committed suicide to escape Comstock's incessant harassment, he proudly pointed to her as the 15th person he had driven to such an end.

Against this backdrop, Harman began his "free word" policy (1886) by which he refused to edit correspondence submitted to *Lucifer* that contained explicit language. Although Harman was somewhat puritanical, he maintained, "Words are not deeds, and it is not the province

[34]Hal D. Sears, *The Sex Radicals: Free Love in High Victorian America* (Lawrence, Kans.: Regents Press, 1977), p. 129.

[35]Josiah Warren, *Practical Details* (New York: 1852), p. 13.

of civil law to take preventative measures against remote or possible consequences of words, no matter how violent or incendiary."[36] Harman looked forward to a generation which would not be overwhelmed by the word "penis" in print. He pursued an open policy of providing discussion and information concerning birth control.

On February 23, 1887, the staff of *Lucifer* was arrested for the publication of three letters. One, infamously known as the Markland letter, described the plight of a woman whose husband forced sex upon her even though it tore the stitches from a recent operation. It is an early analysis of rape within marriage. The letter read:

> About a year ago F______ gave birth to a baby, and was severely torn by the instruments in incompetent hands. She has gone through three operations and all failed. I brought her home and had Drs. ______ and ______operate on her and she was getting along nicely until last night when her husband came down, forced himself into her bed, and the stitches were torn from her healing flesh, leaving her in worse condition than ever. . . .[37]

The letter rhetorically asked what legal redress was available for such an attack. Of course, there was none.

As a result of these letters, the federal grand jury in Topeka indicted the staff on 270 counts of obscenity. The charges were eventually dropped against all but Moses Harman, who was sentenced to five years imprisonment and a $300 fine. After serving 17 weeks, he was released on a technicality, retried without a jury on a slightly different charge, and sentenced to one year. After eight months, he was again released on a technicality. In 1895, he was sentenced to one-year imprisonment, which he served in its entirety. Until his death, Harman battled the Comstock laws. His last imprisonment was in 1906 when he spent a year at hard labor, often breaking rocks for eight hours a day in the Illinois snow. Harman was 75 at the time.[38]

During Harman's first trial, the libertarian Ezra Heywood showed

[36]Sears, *The Sex Radicals*, p. 79. For information regarding the overlap between feminists and social reformers, both of whom called for censorship, see Gordon, *Woman's Body, Woman's Right*, chap. 6.

[37]Ibid., p. 75.

[38]*Lucifer the Light Bearer*, May 24, 1906, provides an excellent account of Harman's last imprisonment. *Lucifer* ran appeals for support throughout Harman's incarceration, emphasizing his age. In the May 24th issue he was reported to be "75 years, 7 months and 12 days old."

support for him by republishing the Markland letter in *The Word;* for this he too was arrested. Heywood had been previously arrested by Comstock for mailing his pamphlet *Cupid's Yokes* (which attacked the institution of marriage) and for advertising a contraceptive called the "Comstock syringe." The consequences of this became apparent in November 1877, when, in Heywood's words: "A stranger sprang upon me and, refusing to read a warrant or even to give his name, hurried me into a hack, drove swiftly through the streets on a dark, rainy night and lodged me in jail as a United States prisoner."[39] The stranger was Anthony Comstock; Heywood was sentenced to two years in prison.

When the U.S. Deputy Marshall arrived in the small town of Valley Falls, Kansas, to arrest the staff of *Lucifer,* the co-editor, E. C. Walker, was nowhere to be found. He was already lodged in the Oskaloosa County Jail in the cell next to Lillian Harman, Moses Harman's 16-year-old daughter. The couple had been imprisoned for their non-state, non-church marriage of September 1886.

Through this widely publicized marriage, the couple had hoped to gain government tolerance of their union and so deal a severe blow to the institution of marriage. In their ceremony, E. C. Walker pledged, "Lillian is and will continue to be as free to repulse any and all advances of mine as she had been heretofore. In joining with me in this love and labor union, she has not alienated a single natural right." Lillian pledged, "I make no promises that it may become impossible or immoral for me to fulfill, but retain the right to act always as my conscience and best judgment shall dictate." The ceremony concluded with Moses Harman declaring, "I do not 'give away the bride', as I wish her to be always the owner of her own person . . ."[40]

News of the marriage had brought threats of mob violence to Valley Falls, and the officials—seeking to soothe the situation—arrested the couple on the morning after their wedding night. The charge was unlawfully and feloniously living together as man and wife without being married according to statute. Walker was sentenced to 75 days imprisonment; Lillian Harman to 45 days. When asked if there was any reason why sentence should not be passed, Lillian answered: "Nothing except that we have committed no crime. But we are in your power, and you can, of course, do as you please."[41]

[39]Sears, *Sex Radicals,* p. 165.

[40]Ibid., p. 85.

[41]Ibid., p. 92.

In March 1887, the Kansas Supreme Court upheld this decision. In a contradictory ruling, the court held that the common-law marriage was legal but nevertheless punishable for violation of the marriage license statute. In other words, the couple had violated regulations designed to secure a record of their marriage. As Chief Justice Horton said, disregarding the issue of the validity of their marriage: "The question, in my opinion, . . . is not whether Edwin Walker and Lillian Harman are married, but whether, in marrying, or rather living together as man and wife, they have observed the statutory requirements."[42]

Although the couple served their term, they refused to pay the court costs; they remained in jail for six months until the costs were paid.

Lillian Harman gave her reason for breaking the law:

> I consider uniformity in mode of sexual relations as undesirable and impractical as enforced uniformity in anything else. For myself, I want the right to profit by my mistakes . . . and why should I be unwilling for others to enjoy the same liberty? If I should be able to bring the entire world to live exactly as I live at present, what would that avail me in ten years, when as I hope, I shall have a broader knowledge of life, and my life therefore probably changed?[43]

The Comstock laws were a litmus test for individualist feminism. The more respectable feminists often supported the statutes that banned birth control information from the mail on the grounds that it was obscene. One of the pledges of the women candidates in the Kansas election of 1889 was that they would shut down *Lucifer the Light Bearer*. Hal Sears observed:

> Conventional feminists bowed before the statute. The sex radicals, on libertarian principles, broke this law in order to raise the questions of government censorship and individual self-ownership.[44]

Although Harman and Walker were one of the first couples in America imprisoned for violating marriage statutes, and Moses Harman was an early champion of birth control, they have been ignored by feminists and feminist histories. While minor socialist figures have been examined in depth, the *Lucifer* staff has barely received a mention. This

[42]Ibid., p. 93.

[43]Ibid., p. 258.

[44]Ibid., p. 24. Alice Blackwell was something of an exception. She denounced censorship attempts aimed at the reprint of an editorial from her periodical, *Woman's Journal*. The Socialist Party's woman's journal, *The Socialist Woman*, did not begin to discuss the birth control issue before 1914. Socialist women had to publish articles on this subject elsewhere.

marked tendency to exclude individualists from feminist history indicates its bias.[45]

Socialist Feminism

According to many feminist histories, the socialist movement was the early, radical champion of women's rights. There is reason to be skeptical of this claim.

A pioneering work, *The Radical Persuasion,* by Aileen S. Kraditor, investigates the relationship between early socialism and woman's rights, not by relying on secondary sources (a large percentage of which have been written by socialist historians), but by consulting the original sources for herself. The book relies on representative excerpts from such prominent early socialist periodicals as *Solidarity, The Industrial Worker,* and *People.* These extracts speak for themselves.

> The impulse below intellect is intuition, which is developed further in many animals than in man . . . And because woman is nearer to the lower forms than man, intuition is more deeply seated in the female of the race . . .[46]
>
> The workers will never be satisfied until all the rights they suffered under are righted, until the mother returns from factory life to a home restored for her and the children.[47]
>
> (Addressed to fellow-socialists) You say you want us girls to keep out of the factory and mill so you can get more pay, then you can marry some of us and give us a decent home. Now that is just what we are trying to escape; being obligated to marry you for a home. And aren't you a little inconsistent. You tell us to get into the I.W.W. If we got out of the shop, the mill and the factory how are we to get into the I.W.W., an organization for wage workers only?[48]
>
> . . . if the test time came to cast a vote at the polls for woman's suffrage many Socialist men would vote against the measure.[49]
>
> Modern Socialists have never claimed that *all* women will be in the service of the collectivity. In fact I do not believe that the majority of

[45]Gordon's *Woman's Body, Woman's Right* is a notable exception. Although the slant of the book is conspicuously socialist, Gordon deals fairly with Moses Harman and Ezra Heywood. Unfortunately, she does not identify them as individualists.

[46]Quoted in Kraditor, *The Radical Persuasion, 1890–1917* (Baton Rouge: Louisiana State University Press, 1981), p. 192.

[47]Ibid., p. 189.

[48]Ibid., p. 189.

[49]Ibid., p. 194.

them ever will be, except in the sense then that they will be mothers and wives.[50]

The April 1891 woman's page of the *People* had a column entitled "How to Make Some Pretty Things for the House." A later column was entitled "Upon Wife and Mother Rests Man's Respect for Women." The August 1908 issue of the New York *Call* ran a cartoon of a matronly muscular woman peeling potatoes. The *Call* also gave advice to the lovelorn through a column by Betty Beeswax.

Needless to say, such data do great damage to the popular image of socialism as the early advocate of woman's rights. A more accurate rendering of how socialists viewed women comes from Daniel de Leon, editor of the *People* and the most prominent socialist of his time. He wrote: "There is no woman question . . . To take up sex, color, creed or race is to fritter away energy at the twigs of the tree whose trunk should be attended to . . . that tree is capitalism."[51]

Women ran up against the argument that they were, theoretically speaking, not a class. They were part of the working class, not in a category defined by their sex. When they tried to join unions and other organizations, however, they found themselves in practical terms defined by their sex and treated as a class apart. As women, they were often told to refrain from wage earning because such competition drove down the wages of men. "Many socialists," observes Linda Gordon, "found any concentration of woman's problems dangerous because it deflected attention from the main issue of the class struggle: wage slavery."[52]

This does not dispute the fact that there were prominent and influential socialist feminists in the late 19th and early 20th centuries. Florence Kelley (1859–1932) was a significant force behind child labor laws in this country; Charlotte Perkins Gilman authored *Women and Economics,* perhaps the most influential book by an American feminist; Mary White Ovington was a founder of the NAACP. There is much reason, however, to assume that most of these women were socialist feminists despite the socialist movement rather than because of it or with its support. As Kraditor points out: "When Kelley, Ovington and other socialists devoted most of their efforts to those other causes, they did not do so as missionaries from the Socialist Party, as Communist Party members later would go into 'mass organizations' so as to enlarge their party's influence. These socialists formulated their own 'lines' on their

[50]Ibid., p. 193.

[51]Ibid., p. 189.

[52]Gordon, *Woman's Body, Woman's Right,* p. 240.

special reforms and acted independently of the party."[53] The socialist feminists seemed to find more common cause with non-socialist allies and tended to work toward their particular goals through non-socialist organizations.

A reasonable question at this point is: Is this also true of individualist feminism? Did Moses and Lillian Harman fight against birth control and marriage laws despite the general libertarian milieu of their time? The answer is clearly "no." Prior to the 1880s, the most prominent libertarian periodical was *The Word,* subtitled *A Monthly Journal of Reform. The Word* put heavy emphasis on birth control and women's rights. In 1881, *Liberty,* the most influential organ of libertarianism, began publication. Although *Liberty* did not emphasize women's rights, as did *Lucifer* and *The Word,* it firmly and consistently declared all human beings to be equal and protested all violation of women's natural rights.[54]

The contemporary feminist movement is not an expression of individualism. The dominant viewpoint of mainstream feminism is political liberalism (in the modern sense of that term) with a strong socialist influence. The stress upon positive rights (the "right" to equal pay, the "right" to day care centers) demonstrates the link between feminism and liberalism, while much of the rhetoric ("exploitation," "consciousness raising") indicates its debt to socialism. It is not surprising, therefore, that women who uphold radical individualism are uncomfortable with the label of "feminist." The situation becomes puzzling, however, when one considers that the roots of American feminism were basically individualistic and that much of the non-political feminist literature is highly individualistic in its call for the independent, liberated woman. This literature often stands in striking contrast to the political material that demands collective, government solutions to women's problems.

Tracing the decline of individualism in America is a fascinating, albeit discouraging, process. The primary cause of its decline in the 19th century was the Civil War, which dealt a stunning blow to a young libertarian movement embodied in such figures as Josiah Warren, Lysander Spooner, William Lloyd Garrison, and Ezra Heywood. Feminism was among various social causes which responded to this shift toward

[53]*The Radical Persuasion,* p. 346n3. For further discussion, see Lydia Sargent, ed., *Women and Revolution. A Discussion of the Unhappy Marriage of Marxism and Feminism* (Boston: South End Press, 1981), pp. 27–28. See also Zillah R. Eisenstein, *The Radical Future of Liberal Feminism* (New York: Longman Inc., 1981).

[54]All three papers actively encouraged women to contribute. *The Word* was co-edited by Angela Heywood. During Harman's imprisonment, *Lucifer* was edited by three women: Lois Waisbrooker, Lillie D. White, and Lillian Harman.

statism by gradually altering its goals and strategies to accommodate, rather than retard, the process. Although the bond between feminism and libertarianism was not broken, it was severely weakened. Today the activities of 19th-century libertarian feminists are virtually ignored by the current movement or at least their ideology is not mentioned; but even the most minor socialists are identified as socialists. This Orwellian memory hole in the fabric of feminism exists despite the fact that the libertarians Moses Harman and Ezra Heywood were among the first to be arrested under the Comstock laws for distributing birth control information; Angela Heywood was virtually the only voice calling for legalized abortion in America in the 1890s; and Lillian Harman and E. C. Walker were perhaps the first couple to be imprisoned for violation of marriage statutes in America.

The prominence of socialism undoubtedly accounts for the bias with which histories of the feminist movement have been written. As libertarian ideas are aired and applied to a widening range of social problems, a confrontation between socialist and individualist ideologies is bound to occur.

Feminism is based on the idea of women as a "class"—defined as a group of individuals classified according to common characteristics. The common characteristic is subjective, dictated by the purpose of the grouping. It could be blue eyes, income bracket, race, geography, or religion. For a political theory, as feminism purports to be, the crucial question is: What characteristic explains something politically significant about the group? Is there something over and above the sexual characteristics of women which best explains the political problems confronting them?

This is the first point at which individualist feminism diverges from both mainstream and Marxist feminism. The notion of women as a distinct class presents a difficult problem for Marxists. Orthodox Marxism distinguishes classes solely according to economic criteria (the ownership of the means of production), not according to sexual characteristics. By this theory, women belong either to the exploited working class or to the exploiting ruling class; individual women can be laborers or capitalists. There is no unity provided by sharing a common sex. It is therefore difficult for Marxists to define women as a class.

Marxist feminists have offered different solutions to this dilemma. The most popular of these seems to be the postulating of a dual system; capitalism and patriarchy are viewed as separate systems which coexist and support each other. Thus, women can be categorized not only according to their economic status as workers, but also according to sex.

Mainstream feminism faces an equally perplexing situation. By demanding equal representation of women in politics, they point to sex as the essential characteristic. But many women who have entered politics are notably conservative in their views and oppose such popular feminist measures as abortion and the ERA. Is having these women in a position of power a victory or setback for mainstream feminism? Is there a sense in which having a man in power who advocates abortion and the ERA would be preferable to having a woman who opposes them? If the stress is on women as a sex, then the election of the most reactionary of women must be regarded as a triumph. If, however, liberal feminists condemn women with conservative positions, then ideas—principles rather than sexual characteristics—are the defining common characteristic. A key question is: If the government were executing male dissidents, would feminists—in the name of equality—demand that an equal number of females be executed? In most cases, they would not. Thus, no matter what is said, it is not merely a matter of equal treatment under the law. Underlying this or any theory of equality is a theory of rights and of what can properly be enforced by government. Otherwise, equality under reprehensible laws would be an acceptable goal. There is an implicit concept of "justice" which is the crux of the difference between individualist feminism and liberal or Marxist feminism.

The libertarian theory of justice applies to all human beings regardless of secondary characteristics such as sex or color. Every human being has moral jurisdiction over his or her own body. To the extent that laws infringe upon self-ownership, they are unjust. To the extent that such violation is based upon sex, there is room for a libertarian feminist movement. Women become a political class not due to their sexual characteristics but because the government directs laws against them as a group. As a political class, feminism is a response to the legal discrimination women have suffered from the state.

Although most women have experienced the uncomfortable and often painful discrimination that is a part of our culture, this is not a political matter. Peaceful discrimination is not a violation of rights. One of the risks of claiming autonomy is that you must extend this right to all other individuals, some of whom may refuse to deal with you or may deal with you in an offensive manner. The freedom of association requires the right to refuse association. Freedom of speech requires the right to be rude, biased, and wrong. As offensive as this behavior might be, it is not a violation of rights and not a subject that libertarianism as a political philosophy addresses except to state that all remedies for it must be peaceful.

While Marxist class analysis uses the relationship to the mode of production as its point of reference, libertarian class analysis uses the relationship to the political means as its standard. Society is divided into two classes: those who use the political means, which is force, to acquire wealth or power and those who use the economic means, which requires voluntary interaction. The former is the ruling class which lives off the labor and wealth of the latter.

This form of class analysis leads to another major difference between individualist feminism and the liberal or Marxist variety. By rejecting the political ruling class, libertarian feminists are logically led to reject the political means of solving social problems, in particular, legal discrimination against women. Libertarian feminists cannot consistently condemn the ruling class as parasitical while trying to swell its ranks by attaining political power. Although discrimination may always occur on an individual level, it is only through the political means that such discrimination can be institutionalized and maintained by force. Given this context, individualist feminists must view the state with great suspicion if not outright condemnation.

This is a moral, not a strategic point. The individualist feminist Voltairine de Cleyre expressed her view of government as force:

> A body of voters cannot give into your charge any rights but their own. By no possible jugglery of logic can they delegate the exercise of any function which they themselves do not control. If any individual on earth has a right to delegate his powers to whomsoever he chooses, then every other individual has an equal right: and if each has an equal right, then none can choose an agent for another, without that other's consent. Therefore, if the power of government resides in the whole people and out of that whole all but one elected you as their agent, you would still have no authority whatever to act for that one.[55]

Lysander Spooner, perhaps the foremost American libertarian theorist,

[55] *Liberty* VI, February 15, 1890, p. 7. This quote should not be construed to represent a consensus opinion on suffrage within individualist feminism. Although de Cleyre and the contributors to *Liberty* were against voting and political action on principle, other libertarian periodicals, such as *The Word*, did not have similar objections. The reservations toward woman's suffrage voiced by *The Word* were of a strategic nature. Specifically, Ezra Heywood believed that the women's suffrage movement was compromising its integrity by aligning with corrupt politicians. See *The Word* I, no. 9, p. 3.

echoed this sentiment in an article criticizing women's suffrage. It is extracted from Benjamin Tucker's *Liberty:*

> Women are human beings, and consequently have all the natural rights that any human being can have. They have just as good a right to *make laws* as men have, and no better; AND THAT IS JUST NO RIGHT AT ALL. No human being, nor any number of human beings, have any right to *make laws,* and compell other human beings to obey them. To say that they have is to say that they are the masters and owners of those of whom they require such obedience. . . . (Emphasis his)

Spooner concluded:

> If the women, instead of petitioning to be admitted to a participation in the power of making more laws, will give notice to the present lawmakers that they are going up to the State House, and are going to throw all the existing statute books in the fire, they will do a very sensible thing.[56]

The libertarian view of class, justice, and government is in direct opposition to contemporary feminism. In particular, the concept of justice conflicts with the liberal and Marxist demand for enforced socio-economic equality. Libertarians insist that the freely chosen actions of individuals be respected. This concept of justice is "means oriented." As long as a given social state results from the voluntary interactions of everyone involved, it is just. Justice, therefore, refers not to a specific end state, such as equality, but to the process by which the end state is achieved. If no rights are violated, justice is achieved. This is not to say that an ideal, humanitarian society will be the result. It is to say that the best we can do is respect people's freedom. In contrast, the Marxist and liberal feminists' conception of justice is "ends oriented." The end is equality or a classless state. Within this context, the demand for socio-economic egalitarianism may be instituted by force.

The mainstream and Marxist feminists call upon the state to protect women from the consequences of autonomy, from the peaceful actions of others. Although the relationship between an employer and employee is voluntary, the state is pressured to enforce equal-pay legislation to protect the interests of exploited women. Any coercive interference in a voluntary exchange which is undertaken for the benefit of one or both of the contracting parties, as opposed to the benefit of the aggressor, is paternalism. When the government discriminates in favor of any

[56]*Liberty* I, June 10, 1882, p. 4.

group on the grounds that the group is unable to take care of itself, the government is assuming the role of parent. Although paternalism is a doctrine most often applied to children and mental incompetents, it is now applied to women. Women are granted a legal overseer to monitor their interactions in order to prevent "exploitation." Feminism is the paternalism of our time.

For some feminists, it is also the new puritanism. Coupling a demand for sexual freedom with a horror of publications such as *Playboy* or *Hustler*, many feminists attempt to stretch theories of exploitation and the demand for paternalism into sexual areas. Although it would be denied by the women who become *Playboy* centerfolds and who flock to interview for that well-paying position, these feminists say that men's magazines exploit women. It does not exploit the women who read *Playboy* since they have expressed a desire for such treatment by paying for the magazine. It exploits womanhood in general because it contributes to the tendency to view women as sexual objects. Such a tendency is wrong and should be discouraged by laws restricting how women may be presented. In basic terms, pornography is sin, and laws should promote virtue.

Paternalism often results in a form of puritanism since in order to protect the interests of a particular group, the government must assess what is "good" and "bad" for that group. The good is institutionalized into society while the bad is prohibited. In libertarian theory, however, laws protect rights instead of virtue, and the individual is free to be wrong. To deny this freedom is to take from women, as well as all others, the power of choice in yet another area of their lives.

Abolitionist feminists struggled to increase choice by breaking social taboos and repealing discriminatory laws. It is sad that contemporary feminism has reversed the process and now calls for censorship and protective legislation. With time and scholarship perhaps a fine tradition can be redeemed.

The following essays are in the individualist-feminist tradition. Many appeared in 19th-century libertarian periodicals such as Benjamin Tucker's *Liberty*. Not all of the women represented in the "issues" section of the anthology would identify themselves as individualist feminists. Rather, the essays have been selected because they exemplify the individualist approach to a specific issue regardless of whether the author consistently applied this approach in other areas. Also, many of the most prominent women in this tradition are not represented. The focus of this book is American feminism, thus excluding such major figures as Mary Wollstonecraft and Harriet Mill of England. Priority has been given to lesser-known figures whose work has been undeservedly neglected.

This anthology is no more than a sampling of the individualist-feminist tradition. I hope it is one of the first steps toward a more general appreciation of the contribution individualism has made to the freedom of women.

THEORY

I. Human Rights Not Founded on Sex

Angelina Grimké

Although Angelina Grimké (1805–1879) was the genteel daughter of a prominent plantation owner, she became one of the foremost crusaders against slavery and the first woman in America to lecture before mixed audiences—audiences composed of both men and women. Angelina exemplified many of the characteristics common among abolitionist women: a Quaker background and pietistic spirit; the dramatic influence of William Lloyd Garrison; the determination to wed women's rights to the anti-slavery cause. She insisted that the struggle against slavery was a battle for the dignity of human beings, not just men. Even though many of the abolitionists were sympathetic to feminism, they objected to linking the two issues for fear that the more popular anti-slavery cause would be damaged by the less popular women's rights. It is in this context that the following essay must be understood. Angelina Grimké was writing not only for the general public, but for her fellow abolitionists who wished to separate the issues of slavery and sex.

Her views of feminism were best expressed in a line from the following essay drawn from a letter written in 1837: "My doctrine then is, that whatever it is morally right for man to do, it is morally right for woman to do."

The investigation of the rights of the slave has led me to a better understanding of my own. I have found the Anti-Slavery cause to be the high school of morals in our land—the school in which *human rights* are more fully investigated, and better understood and taught, than in any other. Here a great fundamental principle is uplifted and illuminated, and from this central light, rays innumerable stream all around. Human beings have *rights*, because they are *moral* beings: the rights of *all* men grow out of their moral nature; and as all men have the same moral nature, they have essentially the same rights. These rights may be wrested from the slave, but they cannot be alienated: his title to himself is as perfect *now*, as is that of Lyman Beecher: it is stamped on his moral being, and is, like it, imperishable. Now if rights are founded in the nature of our moral being, then the *mere circumstance of sex* does not give to man higher rights and responsibilities, than to woman. To suppose that it does, would be to deny the self-evident truth, that the "physical constitution is the mere instrument of the moral nature." To suppose that it does, would be to break up utterly the relations, of the two natures, and to reverse their functions, exalting the animal nature into a monarch, and humbling the moral into a slave; making the former a proprietor, and the latter its property. When human beings are regarded as *moral* beings, *sex,* instead of being enthroned upon the summit, administering upon rights and responsibilities, sinks into insignificance and nothingness. My doctrine then is, that whatever it is morally right for man to do, it is morally right for woman to do. Our duties originate, not from difference of sex, but from the diversity of our relations in life, the various gifts and talents committed to our care, and the different eras in which we live.

This regulation of duty by the mere circumstance of sex, rather than by the fundamental principle of moral being, has led to all that multifarious train of evils flowing out of the anti-christian doctrine of masculine and feminine virtues. By this doctrine, man has been converted into the warrior, and clothed with sternness, and those other kindred qualities, which in common estimation belong to his character as a *man;* whilst woman has been taught to lean upon an arm of flesh, to sit as a doll arrayed in "gold, and pearls, and costly array," to be admired for her personal charms, and caressed and humored like a spoiled child, or converted into a mere drudge to suit the convenience of her lord and master. . . . This principle has given to man a charter for the exercise of tyranny and selfishness, pride and arrogance, lust and brutal violence. It has robbed woman of essential rights, the right to think and speak and act; the right to share their responsibilities, perils, and toils; the right to fulfil the great end of her being, as a moral, intellectual and immortal creature, and of glorifying God in her body and her spirit which are His. Hitherto, instead of being a helpmeet to man, as a companion, a co-worker, an equal; she has been a mere appendage of his being, an instrument of his convenience and pleasure, the pretty toy with which he w[h]iled away his leisure moments, or the pet animal whom he humored into playfulness and submission. Woman, instead of being regarded as the equal of man, has uniformly been looked down upon as his inferior, a mere gift to fill up the measure of his happiness. In "the poetry of romantic gallantry," it is true, she has been called "the last *best* gift of God to man;" but I believe I speak forth the words of truth and soberness when I affirm, that woman never was given to man. She was created, like him, in the image of God, and crowned with glory and honor; created only a little lower than the angels,—not, as is almost universally assumed, a little lower than man; on her brow, as well as on his, was placed the "diadem of beauty," and in her hand the sceptre of universal dominion. Gen: i. 27, 28. "The last *best gift* of God to Man!" Where is the scripture warrant for this "rhetorical flourish, this splendid absurdity?" Let us examine the account of her creation. "And the rib which the Lord God had taken from man, made he a woman, and brought her unto the man." Not as a gift—for Adam immediately recognized her *as a part of himself*—("this is now bone of my bone, and flesh of my flesh")—a companion and equal, not one hair's breadth beneath him in the majesty and glory of her moral being; not placed under his authority as a *subject*, but by his side, on the same platform of human rights, under the government of God only. This idea of woman's being "the last best gift of God to man," however pretty it may sound to the ears of those who love to discourse upon "the poetry of romantic chivalry," has nevertheless been the means of sinking her from an *end* into a mere *means*—of turning her into an *appendage* to man, instead of recognizing her as *a part of man*—of destroying her individuality, and rights, and responsibilities, and merging her moral being in that of man. Instead of *Jehovah* being *her* king, *her* lawgiver, and *her* judge, she has been taken out of the exalted scale of existence in which He placed her, and subjected to the despotic control of man.

I have often been amused at the vain efforts made to define the rights and responsibilities of immortal beings as *men* and *women*. No one has yet found out just where the line of separation between them should be drawn, and for this simple reason, that no one knows just how far below man woman is, whether she be a head shorter in her moral responsibilities, or head and shoulders, or the full length of his noble stature, below him, i.e. under his feet. Confusion, uncertainty, and great inconsistencies, must exist on this point, so long as woman is regarded in the least degree inferior to man; but place her where her Maker placed her, on the same high level of human rights with man, side by side with him, and difficulties vanish, the mountains of perplexity flow down at the presence of this grand equalizing principle. Measure her rights and duties by the unerring standard of *moral being*, not by the false weights and measures of a mere circumstance of her human existence, and then the truth will be self-evident, that whatever it is *morally* right for a man to do, it is *morally* right for a woman to do. I recognize no rights but *human* rights—I know nothing of men's rights and women's rights; for in Christ Jesus, there is neither male nor female. It is my solemn conviction, that, until this principle of equality is recognised and embodied in practice, the Church can do nothing effectual for the permanent reformation of the world. Woman was the first transgressor, and the first victim of power. In all heathen nations, she has been the slave of man, and Christian nations have never acknowledged her rights. Nay more, no Christian denomination or Society has ever acknowledged them on the broad basis of humanity. I know that in some denominations, she is permitted to preach the gospel; not from the conviction of her rights, nor upon the ground of her equality as a *human being,* but of her equality in spiritual gifts—for we find that woman, even in these Societies, is allowed no voice in framing the Discipline by which she is to be governed. Now, I believe it is woman's right to have a voice in all the laws and regulations by which she is to be *governed,* whether in Church or State; and that the present arrangements of society, on these points, are a *violation of human rights, a rank usurpation of power,* a violent seizure and confiscation of what is sacredly and inalienably hers—thus inflicting upon woman outrageous wrongs, working mischief incalculable in the social circle, and in its influence on the world producing only evil, and that continually. *If* Ecclesiastical and Civil governments are ordained of God, *then* I contend that woman has just as much right to sit in solemn counsel in Conventions, Conferences, Associations and General Assemblies, as man—just as much right to sit upon the throne of England, or in the Presidential Chair of the United States.

Dost thou ask me, if I would wish to see woman engaged in the contention and strife of sectarian controversy, or in the intrigues of political partizans? I say no! never—never. I rejoice that she does not stand on the same platform which man now occupies in these respects; but I mourn, also, that he should thus prostitute his higher nature, and vilely cast away his birthright. I prize the rarity of *his* character as highly as I do that of hers. As a moral being, *whatever it is morally wrong for her to do, it is morally wrong for him to do.* The fallacious doctrine of male and female virtues has well nigh ruined all that is morally great and lovely in his character: he has been quite as deep a sufferer by it as woman, though mostly in different respects and by other processes. . . .

Thou sayest, "an ignorant, a narrow-minded, or a stupid woman, cannot feel nor understand the rationality, the propriety, or the beauty of this relation"—i.e. subordination to man. Now, verily, it does appear to me, that nothing but a narrow-minded view of the subject of human rights and responsibilities can induce any one to believe in *this subordination to a fallible* being. Sure I am, that the signs of the times clearly indicate a vast and rapid change in public sentiment, on this subject. Sure I am that she is not to be, as she has been, *"a mere second-hand agent"* in the regeneration of a fallen world. Not that "she will carry her measures by tormenting when she cannot please, or by petulant complaints or obtrusive interference, in matters which are out of her sphere, and which she cannot comprehend." But just in proportion as her moral and intellectual capacities become enlarged, she will rise higher and higher in the scale of creation, until she reaches that elevation prepared for her by her Maker, and upon whose summit she was originally stationed, only "a little lower than the angels." Then will it be seen that nothing which concerns the well-being of mankind is either beyond her sphere, or above her comprehension: *Then* will it be seen "that America will be distinguished above all other nations for well educated women, and for the influence they will exert on the general interests of society. . . ."

II. Anarchism and American Traditions

Voltairine de Cleyre

In his biography of Voltairine de Cleyre (1866–1912), Paul Avrich describes her as "A brief comet in the anarchist firmament." At the age of 20, the already unconventional de Cleyre turned her attention toward anarchism, which became the organizing principle of her life. The following essay, "Anarchism and American Traditions," is de Cleyre's best-known work and argues that anarchism is the logical consequence of the principles of the American Revolution. Unfortunately, most of her work is buried in the pages of obscure radical papers, and her reputation is based on a small fraction of her writing.

De Cleyre's anarchism is intimately related to her battle for women's rights, for they have the same root—the hatred of tyranny. Her condemnation of man's dominance over woman led her to condemn marriage and question the wisdom of living with the men who were her lovers. Such an arrangement too easily stifled independence. "To me," wrote Voltairine de Cleyre, "any dependence, any thing which destroys the complete selfhood of the individual, is in the line of slavery." To her, equality and dignity for both sexes led to anarchism.

American traditions, begotten of religious rebellion, small self-sustaining communities, isolated conditions, and hard pioneer life, grew during the colonization period of one hundred and seventy years from the settling of Jamestown to the outburst of the Revolution. This was in fact the great constitution-making epoch, the period of charters guaranteeing more or less of liberty, the general tendency of which is well described by Wm. Penn in speaking of the charter for Pennsylvania: "I want to put it out of my power, or that of my successors, to do mischief."

The revolution is the sudden and unified consciousness of these traditions, their loud assertion, the blow dealt by their indomitable will against the counter force of tyranny, which has never entirely recovered from the blow, but which from then till now has gone on remolding and regrappling the instruments of governmental power, that the Revolution sought to shape and hold as defenses of liberty.

To the average American of today, the Revolution means the series of battles fought by the patriot army with the armies of England. The millions of school children who attend our public schools are taught to draw maps of the siege of Boston and the siege of Yorktown, to know the general plan of the several campaigns, to quote the number of prisoners of war surrendered with Burgoyne; they are required to remember the date when Washington crossed the Delaware on the ice; they are told to "Remember Paoli," to repeat "Molly Stark's a widow," to call General Wayne "Mad Anthony Wayne," and to execrate Benedict Arnold; they know that the Declaration of Independence was signed on the Fourth of July, 1776, and the Treaty of Paris in 1783; and then they think they have learned the Revolution—blessed be George Washington! They have no idea why it should have been called a "revolution" instead of the "English war," or any similar title: it's the name of it, that's all. And name-worship, both in child and man, has acquired such mastery of them, that the name "American Revolution" is held sacred, though it means to them nothing more than successful force, while the name "Revolution" applied to a further possibility, is a spectre detested and abhorred. In neither case have they any idea of the content of the word, save that of armed force. That has already happened, and long happened, which Jefferson foresaw when he wrote:

"The spirit of the times may alter, will alter. Our rulers will become corrupt, our people careless. A single zealot may become persecutor, and better men be his victims. It can never be too often repeated that the time for fixing every essential right, on a legal basis, is while our rulers are honest, ourselves united. *From the conclusion of this war we shall be going down hill.* It will not then be necessary to resort every moment to the people for support. They will be forgotten, therefore, and their rights disregarded. They will forget themselves in the sole faculty of making money, and will never think of uniting to effect a due respect for their rights. The shackles, therefore, which shall not be knocked off at the conclusion of this war, will be heavier and heavier, till our rights shall revive or expire in a convulsion."

To the men of that time, who voiced the spirit of that time, the battles that they fought were the least of the Revolution; they were the incidents of the hour, the things they met and faced as part of the game they were playing; but the stake they had in view, before, during, and after the war, the real Revolution, was a change in political institutions which should make of government not a thing apart, a superior power to stand over the people with a whip, but a serviceable agent, responsible, economical, and trustworthy (but never so much trusted as not to be continually watched), for the transaction of such business as was the common concern, and to set the limits of the common concern at the line where one man's liberty would encroach upon another's.

They thus took their starting point for deriving a minimum of government upon the same sociological ground that the modern Anarchist derives the no-government theory; viz., that equal liberty is the political ideal. The difference lies in the belief, on the one hand, that the closest approximation to equal liberty might be best secured by the rule of the majority in those matters involving united action of any kind (which rule of the majority they thought it possible to secure by a few simple arrangements for election), and, on the other hand, the belief that majority rule is both impossible and undesirable; that any government, no matter what its forms, will be manipulated by a very small minority, as the development of the State and United States governments has strikingly proved; that candidates will loudly profess allegiance to platforms before elections, which as officials in power they will openly disregard, to do as they please; and that even if the majority will could be imposed, it would also be subversive of equal liberty, which may be best secured by leaving to the voluntary association of those interested in the management of matters of common concern, without coercion of the uninterested or the opposed.

Among the fundamental likenesses between the Revolutionary Republicans and the Anarchists is the recognition that the little must precede the great; that the local must be the basis of the general; that there can be a free federation only when there are free communities to federate; that the spirit of the latter is carried into the councils of the former, and a local tyranny may thus become an instrument for general enslavement. Convinced of the supreme importance of ridding the municipalities of the institutions of tyranny, the most strenuous advocates of independence, instead of spending their efforts mainly in the general Congress, devoted themselves to their home localities, endeavoring to work out of the minds of their neighbors and fellow-colonists the institutions of entailed property, of a State-Church, of a class-divided people, even the institution of African slavery itself. Though largely unsuccessful, it is to the measure of success they did achieve that we are indebted for such liberties as we do retain, and not to the general government. They tried to inculcate local initiative and independent action. The author of the Declaration of Independence, who in the fall of '76 declined a re-election to Congress in order to return to Virginia and do his work in his own local assembly, in arranging there for public education which he justly considered a matter of "common concern," said his advocacy of public schools was not with any "view to take its ordinary branches out of the hands of private enterprise, which manages *so much better* the concerns to which it is equal"; and in endeavoring to make clear the restrictions of the Constitution upon the functions of the general government, he likewise said: "Let the general government be reduced to foreign concerns only, and let our affairs be disentangled from those of all other nations, except as to commerce, *which the merchants will manage the better the more they are left free to manage for themselves,* and the general government may be reduced to a very simple organization, and a very inexpensive one; a few plain duties to be performed by a few servants." This then was the American tradition, that private enterprise manages better all that to which it is equal. Anarchism declares that private enterprise, whether individual or co-operative, is equal to all the undertakings of society. And it quotes the particular two instances, Education and Commerce, which the governments of the States and of the United States have undertaken to manage and regulate, as the very two which in operation have done more to destroy American freedom and equality, to warp and distort American tradition, to make of government a mighty engine of tyranny, than any other cause save the unforeseen developments of Manufacture.

It was the intention of the Revolutionists to establish a system of common education, which should make the teaching of history one of its principal branches; not with the intent of burdening the memories of our youth with the dates of battles or the speeches of generals, nor to make of the Boston Tea Party Indians the one sacrosanct mob in all history, to be revered but never on any account to be imitated, but with the intent that every American should know to what conditions the masses of people had been brought by the operation of certain institutions, by what means they had wrung out their liberties, and how those liberties had again and again been filched from them by the use of governmental force, fraud, and privilege. Not to breed security, laudation, complacent indolence, passive acquiescence in the acts of a government protected by the label "home-made," but to beget a wakeful jealousy, a never-ending watchfulness of rulers, a determination to squelch every attempt of those entrusted with power to encroach upon the sphere of individual action—this was the prime motive of the revolutionists in endeavoring to provide for common education.

"Confidence," said the revolutionists who adopted the Kentucky Resolutions, "is everywhere the parent of despotism; free government is founded in jealousy, not in confidence; it is jealousy, not confidence, which prescribes limited constitutions to bind down those whom we are obliged to trust with power; our Constitution has accordingly fixed the limits to which, and no further, our confidence may go. * * * In questions of power, let no more be heard of confidence in man, but bind him down from mischief by the chains of the Constitution."

These resolutions were especially applied to the passage of the Alien laws by the monarchist party during John Adams' administration, and were an indignant call from the State of Kentucky to repudiate the right of the general government to assume undelegated powers, for, said they, to accept these laws would be "to be bound by laws made, not with our consent, but by others against our consent—that is, to surrender the form of government we have chosen, and to live under one deriving its powers from its own will, and not from our authority." Resolutions identical in spirit were also passed by Virginia, the following month; in those days the States still considered themselves supreme, the general government subordinate.

To inculcate this proud spirit of the supremacy of the people over their governors was to be the purpose of public education! Pick up today any common school history, and see how much of this spirit you will find therein. On the contrary, from cover to cover you will find nothing but the cheapest sort of patriotism, the inculcation of the most unquestioning acquiescence in the deeds of government, a lullaby of rest, security, confidence,—the doctrine that the Law can do no wrong, a Te Deum in praise of the continuous encroachments of the powers of the general government upon the reserved rights of the States, shameless falsification of all acts of rebellion, to put the government in the right and the rebels in the wrong, pyrotechnic glorifications of union, power, and force, and a complete ignoring of the essential liberties to maintain which was the purpose of the revolutionists. The anti-Anarchist law of post-McKinley passage, a much worse law than the Alien and Sedition acts which roused the wrath of Kentucky and Virginia to the point of threatened rebellion, is exalted as a wise provision of our All-Seeing Father in Washington.

Such is the spirit of government-provided schools. Ask any child what he knows about Shays's rebellion, and he will answer, "Oh, some of the farmers couldn't pay their taxes, and Shays led a rebellion against the court-house at Worcester, so they could burn up the deeds; and when Washington heard of it he sent over an army quick and taught 'em a good lesson"—"And what was the result of it?" "The result? Why—why—the result was—Oh yes, I remember—the result was they saw the need of a strong federal government to collect the taxes and pay the debts." Ask if he knows what was said on the other side of the story, ask if he knows that the men who had given their goods and their health and their strength for the freeing of the country now found themselves cast into prison for debt, sick, disabled, and poor, facing a new tyranny for the old; that their demand was that the land should become the free communal possession of those who wished to work it, not subject to tribute, and the child will answer "No." Ask him if he ever read Jefferson's letter to Madison about it, in which he says:

"Societies exist under three forms, sufficiently distinguishable. 1. Without government, as among our Indians. 2. Under government wherein the will of every one has a just influence; as is the case in England in a slight degree, and in our States in a great one. 3. Under government of force, as is the case in all other monarchies, and in most of the other republics. To have an idea of the curse of existence in these last, they must be seen. It is a government of wolves over sheep. It is a problem not clear in my mind that the first condition is not the best. But I believe it to be inconsistent with any great degree of population. The second state has a great deal of good in it. . . . It has its evils, too, the principal of which is the turbulence to which it is subject. . . . But even this evil is productive of good. It prevents the degeneracy of government, and nourishes a general attention to public affairs. I hold that a little rebellion now and then is a good thing."

Or to another correspondent: "God forbid that we should ever be twenty years without such a rebellion! . . . What country can preserve its liberties if its rulers are not warned from time to time that the people preserve the spirit of resistance? Let them take up arms. . . . The tree of liberty must be refreshed from time to time with the blood of patriots and tyrants. It is its natural manure." Ask any school child if he was ever taught that the author of the Declaration of Independence, one of the great founders of the common school, said these things, and he will look at you with open mouth and unbelieving eyes. Ask him if he ever heard that the man who sounded the bugle note in the darkest hour of the Crisis, who roused the courage of the soldiers when Washington saw only mutiny and despair ahead, ask him if he knows that this man also wrote, "Government at best is a necessary evil, at worst an intolerable one," and if he is a little better informed than the average he will answer, "Oh well, *he* was an infidel!" Catechize him about the merits of the Constitution which he has learned to repeat like a poll-parrot, and you will find his chief conception is not of the powers withheld from Congress, but of the powers granted.

Such are the fruits of government schools. We, the Anarchists, point to them and say: If the believers in liberty wish the principles of liberty taught, let them never intrust that instruction to any government; for the nature of government is to become a thing apart, an institution existing for its own sake, preying upon the people, and teaching whatever will tend to keep it secure in its seat. As the fathers said of the governments of Europe, so say we of this government also after a century and a quarter of independence: "The blood of the people has become its inheritance, and those who fatten on it will not relinquish it easily."

Public education, having to do with the intellect and spirit of a people, is probably the most subtle and far-reaching engine for molding the course of a nation; but commerce, dealing as it does with material things and producing immediate effects, was the force that bore down soonest upon the paper barriers of constitutional restriction, and shaped the government to its requirements. Here, indeed, we arrive at the point where we, looking over the hundred and twenty-five years of independence can see that the simple government conceived by the revolutionary republicans was a foredoomed failure. It was so because of (1) the essence of government itself; (2) the essence of human nature; (3) the essence of Commerce and Manufacture.

Of the essence of government, I have already said, it is a thing apart, developing its own interests at the expense of what opposes it; all attempts to make it anything else fail. In this Anarchists agree with the traditional enemies of the Revolution, the monarchists, federalists, strong government believers, the Roosevelts of to-day, the Jays, Marshalls, and Hamiltons of then,—that Hamilton, who, as Secretary of the Treasury, devised a financial system of which we are the unlucky heritors, and whose objects were twofold: To puzzle the people and make public finance obscure to those that paid for it; to serve as a machine for corrupting the legislatures; "for he avowed the opinion that man could be governed by two motives only, force or interest;" force being then out of the question, he laid hold of interest, the greed of the legislators, to set going an association of persons having an entirely separate welfare from the welfare of their electors, bound together by mutual corruption and mutual desire for plunder. The Anarchist agrees that Hamilton was logical, and understood the core of government; the difference is, that while strong governmentalists believe this is necessary and desirable, we choose the opposite conclusion, NO GOVERNMENT WHATEVER.

As to the essence of human nature, what our national experience has made plain is this, that to remain in a continually exalted moral condition is not human nature. That has happened which was prophesied: we have gone down hill from the Revolution until now; we are absorbed in "mere money-getting." The desire for material ease long ago vanquished the spirit of '76. What was that spirit? The spirit that animated the people of Virginia, of the Carolinas, of Massachusetts, of New York, when they refused to import goods from England; when they preferred (and stood by it) to wear coarse homespun cloth, to drink the brew of their own growths, to fit their appetites to the home supply, rather than submit to the taxation of the imperial ministry. Even within the lifetime of the revolutionists the spirit decayed. The love of material ease has been, in the mass of men and permanently speaking, always greater than the love of liberty. Nine hundred and ninety-nine women out of a thousand are more interested in the cut of a dress than in the independence of their sex; nine hundred and ninety-nine men out of a thousand are more interested in drinking a glass of beer than in questioning the tax that is laid on it; how many children are not willing to trade the liberty to play for the promise of a new cap or a new dress? This it is which begets the complicated mechanism of society; this it is which, by multiplying the concerns of government, multiplies the strength of government and the corresponding weakness of the people; this it is which begets indifference to public concern, thus making the corruption of government easy.

As to the essence of Commerce and Manufacture, it is this: to establish bonds between every corner of the earth's surface and every other corner, to multiply the needs of mankind, and the desire for material possession and enjoyment.

The American tradition was the isolation of the States as far as possible. Said they: We have won our liberties by hard sacrifice and struggle unto death. We wish now to be let alone and to let others alone, that our principles may have time for trial; that we may become accustomed to the exercise of our rights; that we may be kept free from the contaminating influence of European gauds, pagents, distinctions. So richly did they esteem the absence of these that they could in all fervor write: "We shall see multiplied instances of Europeans coming to America, but no man living will ever see an instance of an American removing to settle in Europe, and continuing there." Alas! In less than a hundred years the highest aim of a "Daughter of the Revolution" was, and is, to buy a castle, a title, and a rotten lord, with the money wrung from American servitude! And the commercial interests of America are seeking a world-empire!

In the earlier days of the revolt and subsequent independence, it appeared that the "manifest destiny" of America was to be an agricultural people, exchanging food stuffs and raw materials for manufactured articles. And in those days it was written: "We shall be virtuous as long as agriculture is our principal object, which will be the case as long as there remain vacant lands in any part of America. When we get piled upon one another in large cities, as in Europe, we shall become corrupt as in Europe, and go to eating one another as they do there." Which we are doing, because of the inevitable development of Commerce and Manufacture, and the concomitant development of strong government. And the parallel prophecy is likewise fulfilled: "If ever this vast country is brought under a single government, it will be one of the most extensive corruption, indifferent and incapable of a wholesome care over so wide a spread of surface." There is not upon the face of the earth to-day a government so utterly and shamelessly corrupt as that of the United States of America. There are others more cruel, more tyrannical, more devastating; there is none so utterly venal.

And yet even in the very days of the prophets, even with their own consent, the first concession to this later tyranny was made. It was made when the Constitution was made; and the Constitution was made chiefly because of the demands of Commerce. Thus it was at the outset a merchant's machine, which the other interests of the country, the land and labor interests, even then foreboded would destroy their liberties. In vain their jealousy of its central power made them enact the first twelve amendments. In vain they endeavored to set bounds over which the federal power dare not trench. In vain they enacted into general law the freedom of speech, of the press, of assemblage and petition. All of these things we see ridden rough-shod upon every day, and have so seen with more or less intermission since the beginning of the nineteenth century. At this day, every police lieutenant considers himself, and rightly so, as more powerful than the General Law of the Union; and that one who told Robert Hunter that he held in his fist something stronger than the Constitution, was perfectly correct. The right of assemblage is an American tradition which has gone out of fashion; the police club is now the mode. And it is so in virtue of the people's indifference to liberty, and the steady progress of constitutional interpretation towards the substance of imperial government.

It is an American tradition that a standing army is a standing menace to liberty; in Jefferson's presidency the army was reduced to 3,000 men. It is American tradition that we keep out of the affairs of other nations. It is American practice that we meddle with the affairs of everybody else from the West to the East Indies, from Russia to Japan; and to do it we have a standing army of 83,251 men.

It is American tradition that the financial affairs of a nation should be transacted on the same principles of simple honesty that an individual conducts his own business; viz., that debt is a bad thing, and a man's first surplus earnings should be applied to his debts; that offices and office-holders should be few. It is American practice that the general government should always have millions of debt, even if a panic or a war has to be forced to prevent its being paid off; and as to the application of its income, office-holders come first. And within the last administration it is reported that 99,000 offices have been created at an annual expense of $63,000,000. Shades of Jefferson! "How are vacancies to be obtained? Those by deaths are few; by resignation none." Roosevelt cuts the knot by making 99,000 new ones! And few will die,—and none resign. They will beget sons and daughters, and Taft will have to create 99,000 more! Verily, a simple and a serviceable thing is our general government.

It is American tradition that the judiciary shall act as a check upon the impetuosity of Legislatures, should these attempt to pass the bounds of constitutional limitation. It is American practice that the Judiciary justifies every law which trenches on the liberties of the people and nullifies every act of the Legislature by which the people seek to regain some measure of their freedom. Again, in the words of Jefferson: "The Constitution is a mere thing of wax in the hands of the Judiciary, which they may twist and shape in any form they please." Truly, if the men who fought the good fight for the triumph of simple, honest, free life in that day, were now to look upon the scene of their labors, they would cry out together with him who said: "I regret that I am now to die in the belief that the useless sacrifice of themselves by the generation of '76 to acquire self-government and happiness to their country, is to be thrown away by the unwise and unworthy passions of their sons, and that my only consolation is to be that I shall not live to see it."

And now, what has Anarchism to say to all this, this bankruptcy of republicanism, this modern empire that has grown up on the ruins of our early freedom? We say this, that the sin our fathers sinned was that they did not trust liberty wholly. They thought it possible to compromise between liberty and government, believing the latter to be "a necessary evil," and the moment the compromise was made, the whole misbegotten monster of our present tyranny began to grow. Instruments which are set up to safeguard rights become the very whip with which the free are struck.

Anarchism says, Make no laws whatever concerning speech, and speech will be free; so soon as you make a declaration on paper that speech shall be free, you will have a hundred lawyers proving that "freedom does not mean abuse, nor liberty license"; and they will define and define freedom out of existence. Let the guarantee of free speech be in every man's determination to use it, and we shall have no need of paper declarations. On the other hand, so long as the people do not care to exercise their freedom, those who wish to tyrannize will do so; for tyrants are active and ardent, and will devote themselves in the name of any number of gods, religious and otherwise, to put shackles upon sleeping men.

The problem then becomes, Is it possible to stir men from their indifference? We have said that the spirit of liberty was nurtured by colonial life; that the elements of colonial life were the desire for sectarian independence, and the jealous watchfulness incident thereto; the isolation of pioneer communities which threw each individual strongly on his own resources, and thus developed all-around men, yet at the same time made very strong such social bonds as did exist; and, lastly, the comparative simplicity of small communities.

All this has mostly disappeared. As to sectarianism, it is only by dint of an occasional idiotic persecution that a sect becomes interesting; in the absence of this, outlandish sects play the fool's role, are anything but heroic, and have little to do with either the name or the substance of liberty. The old colonial religious parties have gradually become the "pillars of society," their animosities have died out, their offensive peculiarities have been effaced, they are as like one another as beans in a pod, they build churches and—sleep in them.

As to our communities, they are hopelessly and helplessly interdependent, as we ourselves are, save that continuously diminishing proportion engaged in all around farming; and even these are slaves to mortgages. For our cities, probably there is not one that is provisioned to last a week, and certainly there is none which would not be bankrupt with despair at the proposition that it produce its own food. In response to this condition and its correlative political tyranny, Anarchism affirms the economy of self-sustenance, the disintegration of the great communities, the use of the earth.

I am not ready to say that I see clearly that this *will* take place; but I see clearly that this *must* take place if ever again men are to be free. I am so well satisfied that the mass of mankind prefer material possessions to liberty, that I have no hope that they will ever, by means of intellectual or moral stirrings merely, throw off the yoke of oppression fastened on them by the present economic system, to institute free societies. My only hope is in the blind development of the economic system and political oppression itself. The great characteristic looming factor in this gigantic power is Manufacture. The tendency of each nation is to become more and more a manufacturing one, an exporter of fabrics, not an importer. If this tendency follows its own logic, it must eventually circle round to each community producing for itself. What then will become of the surplus product when the manufacturer shall have no foreign market? Why, then mankind must face the dilemma of sitting down and dying in the midst of it, or confiscating the goods.

Indeed, we are partially facing this problem even now; and so far we are sitting down and dying. I opine, however, that men will not do it forever; and when once by an act of general expropriation they have overcome the reverence and fear of property, and their awe of government, they may waken to the consciousness that things are to be used, and therefore men are greater than things. This may rouse the spirit of liberty.

If, on the other hand, the tendency of invention to simplify, enabling the advantages of machinery to be combined with smaller aggregations of workers, shall also follow its own logic, the great manufacturing plants will break up, population will go after the fragments, and there will be seen not indeed the hard, self-sustaining, isolated pioneer communities of early America, but thousands of small communities stretching along the lines of transportation, each producing very largely for its own needs, able to rely upon itself, and therefore able to be independent. For the same rule holds good for societies as for individuals,—those may be free who are able to make their own living.

In regard to the breaking up of that vilest creation of tyranny, the standing army and navy, it is clear that so long as men desire to fight, they will have armed force in one form or another. Our fathers thought they had guarded against a standing army by providing for the voluntary militia. In our day we have lived to see this militia declared part of the regular military force of the United States, and subject to the same demands as the regulars. Within another generation we shall probably see its members in the regular pay of the general government. Since any embodiment of the fighting spirit, any military organization, inevitably follows the same line of centralization, the logic of Anarchism is that the least objectionable form of armed force is that which springs up voluntarily, like the minute-men of Massachusetts, and disbands as soon as the occasion which called it into existence is past: that the really desirable thing is that all men—not Americans only—should be at peace; and that to reach this, all peaceful persons should withdraw their support from the army, and require that all who make war shall do so at their own cost and risk; that neither pay nor pensions are to be provided for those who choose to make man-killing a trade.

As to the American tradition of non-meddling, Anarchism asks that it be carried down to the individual himself. It demands no jealous barrier of isolation; it knows that such isolation is undesirable and impossible; but it teaches that by all men's strictly minding their own business, a fluid society, freely adapting itself to mutual needs, wherein all the world shall belong to all men, as much as each has need or desire, will result.

And when Modern Revolution has thus been carried to the heart of the whole world—if it ever shall be, as I hope it will,—then may we hope to see a resurrection of that proud spirit of our fathers which put the simple dignity of Man above the gauds of wealth and class, and held that to be an American was greater than to be a king.

In that day there shall be neither kings nor Americans,—only Men; over the whole earth, MEN.

III. Give Me Liberty

Rose Wilder Lane

At the age of 79, Rose Wilder Lane (1886–1968) was a correspondent from Vietnam for Woman's Day. *This was simply one phase of a life dedicated to the individualism and liberty expressed in Lane's two major works,* The Discovery of Freedom *(1943) and* Give Me Liberty *(1936) which revolve around the American ideal of personal freedom.* Give Me Liberty, *from which the following essay is extracted, charts Lane's progress from socialism to libertarianism as a result of directly experiencing life under socialist regimes. First published during the Great Depression by the* Saturday Evening Post, *it served as a warning against the state socialism inherent in Roosevelt's New Deal.*

An early and consistent critic of Roosevelt, Lane withdrew to her farm in Danbury, Connecticut (1938), where she refused to participate in Social Security or to publish writing which would be a source of revenue, through taxes, for government. "Taxation is armed robbery," she declared. "Tax collectors are armed robbers." In regard to the state, she maintained: "I am law-abiding purely for expediency, for self-defense, in the main against my conscientious principles, so at bottom I am ashamed of not being a conscientious objector practicing Gandhi's or Thoreau's civil disobedience."

I came out of the Soviet Union no longer a communist, because I believed in personal freedom. Like all Americans, I took for granted the individual liberty to which I had been born. It seemed as necessary and as inevitable as the air I breathed; it seemed the natural element in which human beings lived.

The thought that I might lose it had never remotely occurred to me. And I could not conceive that multitudes of human beings would ever willingly live without it.

It happened that I spent many years in the countries of Europe and Western Asia, so that at last I learned something, not only of the words that various peoples speak, but of the real meanings of those words. No word, of course, is ever exactly translatable into another language; the words we use are the most clumsy symbols for meanings, and to suppose that such words as "war," "glory," "justice," "liberty," "home," mean the same in two languages, is an error.

Everywhere in Europe I encountered the living facts of medieval caste and of the static medieval social order. I saw them resisting, and vitally resisting, individual freedom and the industrial revolution.

It was impossible to know France without knowing that the French demand order, discipline, the restraint of traditional forms, the bureaucratic regulation of human lives by centralized police power, and that the fierce French democracy is not a cry for individual liberty but an insistence that the upper classes shall not too harshly exploit the lower classes.

I saw in Germany and in Austria scattered and leaderless sheep running this way and that, longing for the lost security of the flock and the shepherd.

Resisting step by step, I was finally compelled to admit to my Italian friends that I had seen the spirit of Italy revive under Mussolini. And it seemed to me that this revival was based on a separation of individual liberty from the industrial revolution whose cause and source is individual liberty. I said that in Italy, as in Russia, an essentially medieval, planned and controlled economic order was taking over the fruits of the industrial revolution while destroying its root, the freedom of the individual.

"Why *will* you talk about the rights of individuals!" Italians exclaimed, at last impatient. "An individual is nothing. As individuals we have no importance whatever. I will die, you will die, millions will live and die, but Italy does not die. Italy is important. Nothing matters but Italy."

This rejection of one's self as an individual was, I knew, the spirit animating the members of the Communist Party. I heard that it was the spirit beginning to animate Russia. It was the spirit of Fascism, the spirit that indubitably did revive Italy. Scores, hundreds of the smallest incidents revealed it.

In 1920, Italy was a fleas' nest of beggars and thieves. They fell on the stranger and devoured him. There was no instant in which baggage could be left unguarded; every bill was an over-charge and no service however small was unaccompanied by a bill; taxis dodged into vacant streets and boats stopped midway to ships, that drivers and boatmen might terrorize timid passengers into paying twice. Every step in Italy was a wrangle and a fight.

In 1927, my car broke down after nightfall in the edge of a small Italian village. Three men, a waiter, a charcoal burner, and the uniformed chauffeur of wealthy travelers sleeping in the inn, worked all night on the engine. When it was running smoothly in the bleak dawn, all three refused to take any payment. Americans in a similar situation would have refused from human friendliness and personal pride. The Italians said firmly, "No, signora. We did it for Italy." This was typical.

Italians were no longer centered in themselves, but in that mythical creation of their imaginations unto which they poured their lives, Italy, immortal Italy.

I began at last to question the value of this personal freedom which had seemed so inherently right. I saw how rare, how new in history, is a recognition of human rights. From Brittany to Basra I considered the ruins of brilliant civilizations whose peoples had never glimpsed the idea that men are born free. In sixty centuries of human history that idea was an element of Jewish-Christian-Moslem religious faith, never used as a political principle.

It has been a political principle to only a few men on earth, for little more than two centuries. Asia did not know it. Africa did not know it. Europe had never wholly accepted it, and was now rejecting it.

I began to question, What is individual liberty? When I asked myself, "Am I truly free?" I began slowly to understand the nature of man and man's situation on this planet. I understood at last that every human being is free; that I am endowed by the Creator with inalienable liberty as I am endowed with life; that my freedom is inseparable from my life, since freedom is the individual's self-controlling nature. My freedom is my control of my own life-energy, for the uses of which I, alone, am therefore responsible.

But the exercise of this freedom is another thing, since in every use of my life-energy I encounter obstacles. Some of these obstacles, such as time, space, weather, are eternal in the human situation on this planet. Some are self-imposed and come from my own ignorance of realities. And for all the years of my residence in Europe, a great many obstacles were enforced upon me by the police-power of the men ruling the European States.

I hold the truth to be self-evident, that all men are endowed by the Creator with inalienable liberty, with individual self-control and responsibility for thoughts, speech and acts, in every situation. The extent to which this natural liberty can be exercised depends upon the amount of external coercion imposed upon the individual. No jailer can compel any prisoner to speak or act against that prisoner's will, but chains can prevent his acting, and a gag can prevent his speaking.

Americans have had more freedom of thought, of choice, and of movement than other peoples have ever had. We inherited no limitations of caste to restrict our range of desires and of ambition to the class in which we were born.

We had no governmental bureaucracy to watch our every move, to make a record of friends who called at our homes and the hours at which they arrived and left, in order that the police might be fully informed in case we were murdered. We had no officials who, in the interests of a just and equitable collection of gasoline taxes, stopped our cars and measured the gasoline in the tanks whenever we entered or left an American city.

We were not obliged, as Continental Europeans have been, to carry at all times a police card, renewed and paid for at intervals, bearing our pictures properly stamped and stating our names, ages, addresses, parentage, religion and occupation.

American workers were not classified; they did not carry police cards on which employers recorded each day they work; they have no places of amusement separate from those of higher classes, and their amusements are not subject to interruption by raiding policemen inspecting their workingmen's cards and acting on the assumption that any workingman is a thief whose card shows he has not worked during the past week.

In 1922, as a foreign correspondent in Budapest, I accompanied such a police raid. The Chief of Police was showing the mechanisms of his work to a visiting operative from Scotland Yard. We set out at ten o'clock at night, leading sixty policemen who moved with the beautiful precision of soldiers.

They surrounded a section of the workingmen's quarter of the city and closed in, while the Chief explained that this was ordinary routine; the whole quarter was combed in this way every week.

We appeared suddenly in the doorways of workingmen's cafes, dingy places with sawdust on earthen floors where one musician forlornly tried to make music on a cheap fiddle and men and women in the gray rags of poverty sat at bare tables and economically sipped beer or coffee. Their terror at the sight of uniforms was abject. All rose and meekly raised their hands. The policemen grinned with that peculiar enjoyment of human beings in possessing such power.

They went through the men's pockets, making some little jest at this object and that. They found the Labor cards, inspected them, thrust them back in the pockets. At their curt word of release, the men dropped into chairs and wiped their foreheads.

In every place, a few cards failed to pass the examination. No employer had stamped them during the past three days. Men and women were loaded into the patrol wagon.

Now and then, at our entrance, someone tried to escape from back door or window and ran, of course, into the clutch of policemen. We could hear the policemen laughing. The Chief accepted the compliments of the British detective. Everything was perfectly done; no one escaped.

Several women frantically protested, crying, pleading on their knees, so that they had almost to be carried to the wagon. One young girl fought, screaming horribly. It took two policemen to handle her; they were not rough, but when she bit at their hands on her arms, a third slapped her face. In the wagon she went on screaming insanely. I could not understand Hungarian. The Chief explained that some women objected to being given prostitutes' cards.

When a domestic servant had been several days without work, the police took away the card that identified her as a working girl and permitted her to work; they gave her instead a prostitute's card. Men who had not worked recently were sentenced to a brief imprisonment for theft. Obviously, the Chief said, if they were not working, they were prostitutes and thieves; how else were they living?

Perhaps on their savings? I suggested.

Working people make only enough to live on from day to day, they can not save, the Chief said. Of course, if by any remarkable chance one of them had got some money honestly and could prove it, the judge would release him.

Having gone through all the cafes, we began on the tenements. I have lived in the slums of New York and of San Francisco. Americans who have not seen European slums have not the slightest idea of what slums are.

Until dawn, the police were clambering through those filthy tenements and down into their basements, stirring up masses of rags and demanding from staring faces their police cards. We did not capture so many unemployed there, because it costs more to sleep under a roof than to sit in a cafe; the very fact that these people had any shelter argued that they were working. But the police were thorough and awakened everyone. They were quiet and good-humored; this raid had none of the violence of an American police raid. When a locked door was not opened, the police tried all their master keys before they set their shoulders to the door and went in.

The Scotland Yard man said, "Admirable, sir, admirable. Continental police systems are marvelous, really. You have absolute control over here." Then his British pride spoke, deprecatingly, as it always speaks. "We could never do anything like this in London, don't you know. An Englishman's home is his castle, and all that. We have to have a warrant before we can search the premises or touch a man's person. Beastly handicap, you know. We have nothing like your control over here on the Continent."

This is the only police search of workingmen's quarters that I saw in Europe. I do not believe that regimentation elsewhere went so far then as to force women into prostitution, and it may be that it no longer does so in Hungary. But that the systematic surrounding and searching of workingmen's quarters went on normally everywhere in Europe, and that unemployment was assumed to push them over the edge of destitution into crime, I do know.

Like everyone else domiciled in Europe, I was many times stopped on my way home by two courteous policemen who asked to see my identification card. This became too commonplace to need explanation. I knew that my thoroughly respectable, middle-class quarter was surrounded, simply as a matter of police routine, and that everyone in it was being required to show police cards.

Nevertheless, I question whether there was less crime in police-controlled Europe than in America. Plenty of crimes were reported in brief paragraphs of small type in every paper. There is no section of an American city which I would fear to go into alone at night. There were always many quarters of European cities that were definitely dangerous after nightfall, and whole classes of criminals who would kill any moderately well-dressed man, woman or child for the clothes alone.

The terrible thing is that the motive behind all this supervision of the individual is a good motive, and a rational one. How is any ruler to maintain a social order without it?

There is a certain instinct of orderliness and of self-preservation which enables multitudes of free human beings to get along after a fashion. No crowd leaves a theatre with any efficiency, nor without discomfort, impatience and wasted time, yet we usually reach the sidewalk without a fight. Order is another thing. Any teacher knows that order cannot be maintained without regulation, supervision and discipline. It is a question of degree; the more rigid and autocratic the discipline, the greater the order. Any genuine social order requires, as its first fundamental, the classification, regulation and obedience of individuals. Individuals being what they are, infinitely various and willful, their obedience must be enforced.

The serious loss in a social order is in time and energy. Sitting around in waiting rooms until one can stand in line before a bureaucrat's desk seems to any American a dead loss, and living in a social order thus shortens every person's life. Outside the bureaucrat's office, too, these regulations for the public good constantly hamper every action. It is as impossible to move freely in one's daily life as it is to saunter or hasten while keeping step in a procession.

In America, commercial decrees did not hamper every clerk and customer, as they did in France, so that an extra half-hour was consumed in every department-store purchase. French merchants are as intelligent as American, but they could not install vacuum tubes and a swift accounting system in a central cashier's department. What is the use? they asked you. They would still be obliged to have every purchase recorded in writing in a ledger, in the presence of both buyer and seller, as Napoleon decreed.

It was an intelligent decree, too, when Napoleon issued it. Could French merchants change it now? It is to laugh, as they say; a phrase with no mirth in it. The decree was entangled with a hundred years of bureaucratic complications, and besides, think how much unemployment its repeal would have caused among those weary cashiers, dipping their pens in the prescribed ink, setting down the date and hour on a new line and asking, "Your name, madame?" writing. "Your address?" writing. "You pay cash?" writing. "You will take the purchase with you? Ah, good," writing. "Ah, I see. One reel of thread, cotton, black, what size?" writing. "You pay for it how much?" writing. "And you offer in payment—Good; one franc," writing. "From one franc, perceive, madame, I give you fifty centimes change. Good. And you are satisfied, madame?"

No one considered how much unemployment this caused to the daily multitudes of patiently waiting customers, nor that if these clerks had never been thus employed they might have been doing something useful, something creative of wealth. Napoleon wished to stop the waste of disorganization, of cheating and quarreling, in the markets of his time. And he did so. The result is that so much of France was permanently fixed firmly in Napoleon's time. If he had let Frenchmen waste and quarrel, and cheat and lose, as Americans were then doing in equally primitive markets, French department stores certainly would have been made as briskly efficient and time-saving as America's.

No one who dreams of the ideal social order, the economy planned to eliminate waste and injustice, considers how much energy, how much human life, is wasted in administering and in obeying the best of regulations. No one considers how rigid such regulations become, nor that they must become rigid and resist change because their underlying purpose is to preserve men from the risks of chance and change in flowing time.

Americans have had in our country no experience of the discipline of a social order. We speak of a better social order when in fact we do not know what any social order is. We say that something is wrong with this system, when in fact we have no system. We use phrases learned from Europe, with no conception of the meaning of those phrases in actual living experience.

In America we do not have even universal military training, that basis of a social order which teaches every male citizen his subservience to The State and subtracts some years from every young man's life, and has thereby weakened the military power of every nation that has adopted it.

An apartment lease in America is legal when it is signed; it is not necessary to take it to the police to be stamped, nor to file triplicate copies of it with the collector of internal revenue, so that for taxation purposes our incomes may be set down as ten times what we pay for rent. In economic theory, no doubt it is not proper to pay for rent more than 10 per cent of income, and perhaps it is economic justice that anyone so extravagant as to pay more should be fined by taxation. It was never possible to quarrel with the motives behind these bureaucracies of Europe; they were invariably excellent motives.

An American could look at the whole world around him and take what he wanted from it, if he were able. Only criminal law and his own character, abilities and luck restrained him.

That is what Europeans meant when, after a few days in this country, they exclaimed, "You are so free here!" And it was the most infinite relief to an American returning after long living abroad, to be able to move from hotel to hotel, from city to city, to be able to rush into a store and buy a spool of thread, to decide at half past three to take a four o'clock train, to buy an automobile if one had the money or the credit and to drive it wherever one liked, all without making any reports whatever to the government.

But anyone whose freedom has been, as mine has always been, freedom to earn a living if possible, knows that this independence is another name for responsibility.

The American pioneers phrased this clearly and bluntly. They said, "Root, hog, or die."

There can be no third alternative for the shoat let out of the pen, to go where he pleases and do what he likes. Individual liberty is individual responsibility. Whoever makes decisions is responsible for results. When common men were slaves and serfs, they obeyed and they were fed, but they died by thousands in plagues and famines. Free men paid for their freedom by leaving that false and illusory security.

The question is whether personal freedom is worth the terrible effort, the never-lifted burden, and the risks, the unavoidable risks, of self-reliance.

For each of us, the answer to that question is a personal one. But the final answer cannot be personal, for individual freedom of choice and of action cannot long exist except among multitudes of individuals who choose it and who are willing to pay for it.

Multitudes of human beings will not do this unless their freedom is worth more than it costs, not only in value to their own souls but also in terms of the general welfare and the future of their country, which means the welfare and the future of their children.

The test of the worth of personal freedom, then, can only be its practical results in a country whose institutions and ways of life and of thought have grown from individualism. The only such country is the United States of America.

Here, on a new continent, peoples with no common tradition founded this republic on the rights of the individual. This country was the only country in the western world whose territory was largely settled and whose culture is dominated by those northwestern Europeans from whom the idea of individual liberty came into the world's history as a political principle.

When one thinks of it, that's an odd fact. Why did this territory become American? How did it happen that those British colonists released from England spread across half this continent?

Spaniards were in Missouri before Englishmen were in Virginia or Massachusetts. French settlements were old in Illinois, French mines in Missouri were furnishing the western world with bullets, French trading posts were in Arkansas, half a century before farmers fired on British soldiers at Lexington.

Why did Americans, spreading westward, not find a populated country, a vigorous colony to protest in France against the sale of Louisiana?

This is an important fact: Americans were the only settlers who built their houses far apart, each on his own land. America is the only country I have seen where farmers do not live today in close, safe village-groups. It is the only country I know where each person does not feel an essential, permanent solidarity with a certain class, and with a certain group within that class. The first Americans came from such groups in Europe, but they came because they were individuals rebelling against groups. Each in his own way built his own house at a distance from others in the American wilderness. This is individualism.

The natural diversity of human beings, the natural tendency of man to go into the future like an explorer finding his own way, was released in those English colonies on the Atlantic coast. Men from the British islands rushed so eagerly toward that freedom that Parliament and the King refused to open any more land for settlement; the statistics of the time proved clearly that a western expansion of the American colonies would depopulate England.

Nevertheless, before tea went overboard in Boston harbor the lawless settlers had penetrated to the crests and valleys of the Appalachians and were scouting into forbidden lands beyond.

There was no plan that these young United States should ever cover half this continent. The thought of New York and Washington lagged far behind that surge. It was the released energies of individuals that poured westward at a speed never imagined, sweeping away and overwhelming settlements of more cohesive peoples and reaching the Pacific in the time that Jefferson thought it would take to settle Ohio.

I have no illusions about the pioneers. My own people for eight generations were American pioneers, and when as a child I remembered too proudly an ancestry older than Plymouth, my mother would remind me of a great-great-uncle, jailed for stealing a cow.

The pioneers were by no means the best of Europe. In general they were trouble-makers of the lower classes, and Europe was glad to be rid of them. They brought no great amount of intelligence or culture. Their principal desire was to do as they pleased, and they were no idealists. When they could not pay their debts, they skipped out between two days. When their manners, their personal habits or their loudly expressed and usually ignorant opinions offended the gently bred, they remarked, "It's a free country, ain't it?" A frequent phrase of theirs was "free and independent." They also said, "I'll try anything once," and "Sure, I'll take a chance!"

They were riotous speculators; they gambled in land, in furs, in lumber and canals and settlements. They were town-lot salesmen for towns that did not yet exist and, more often than not, never did materialize. They were ignorant peasants, prospectors, self-educated teachers and lawyers, ranting politicians, printers, lumberjacks, horse thieves and cattle rustlers.

Each was out to get what he could for himself, and devil take the hindmost. At every touch of adversity they fell apart, each on his own; there was human pity and kindness, but not a trace of community spirit. The pioneer had horse sense, and card sense, and money sense, but not a particle of social sense. The pioneers were individualists. And they did stand the gaff.

This was the human stuff of America. It was not the stuff one would have chosen to make a nation or an admirable national character. And Americans today are the most reckless and lawless of peoples. We are also the most imaginative, the most temperamental, the most infinitely varied people. We are the kindest people on earth; kind every day to one another and sympathetically responsive to every rumor of distress. It is only in America that a passing car will stop to lend a stranded stranger a tire-tool. Only Americans ever made millions of small personal sacrifices in order to pour wealth over the world, relieving suffering in such distant places as Armenia and Japan.

Everywhere, in shops, streets, factories, elevators, on highways and on farms, Americans are the most friendly and courteous people. There is more laughter and more song in America than anywhere else. Such are a few of the human values that grew from individualism while individualism was creating this nation.

IV. Antigone's Daughters

Jean Bethke Elshtain

Jean Bethke Elshtain's "Antigone's Daughters," reprinted from the April 1982 Democracy, *is a refreshing essay which questions the wisdom of feminists who closely align themselves with the state. Besides demonstrating a deep knowledge and understanding of contemporary feminism, Elshtain gives us an insight into feminism: "Maternal thinking, like Antigone's protest, is a rejection of amoral statecraft and an affirmation of the dignity of the human person."*

This essay advances a note of caution. It argues that feminists should approach the modern bureaucratic state from a standpoint of skepticism that keeps alive a critical distance between feminism and statism, between female self-identity and a social identity tied to the public-political world revolving around the structures, institutions, values, and ends of the state. The basis for my caution and skepticism is a sober recognition that any political order in our time which culminates in a state is an edifice that monopolizes and centralizes power and eliminates older, less universal forms of authority; that structures its activities and implements its policies through unaccountable hierarchies; that erodes local and particular patterns of ethnic, religious, and regional identities; that standardizes culture, ideas, and ideals; that links portions of the population to it through a variety of dependency relationships; that may find it necessary or convenient to override civil liberties and standards of decency for *raison d'état* or executive privilege; and that, from time to time, commits its people to wars they have had neither the opportunity to debate fully nor the right to challenge openly.

For feminists to discover in the state the new "Mr. Right," and to wed themselves thereby, for better or for worse, to a public identity inseparable from the exigencies of state power and policy would be a mistake. This is a serious charge. I shall defend and develop my argument by considering the ways in which certain important feminist thinkers, at times somewhat casually and carelessly, have presumed the superiority of a particular sort of public identity over a private one. I shall trace out the logic of these arguments, indicating what a fully public identity for women would require, including the final suppression of traditional female social worlds. Finally, I shall reclaim for women a social identity that locates them very much in and of the wider world but positions them against overweening state power and public identity defined in its terms. My aim is to define and to defend a female identity and a feminist perspective that enables contemporary women to see themselves as the daughters of Antigone. To recognize that women as a group experience their social worlds differently from men as a group complicates feminist thinking, deepens female self-awareness, and calls attention to the complexity and richness of our social experiences and relations.

The feminist protest of the past several decades has largely concentrated on the ways—official and unofficial, ideological and practical—in which women have been excluded from equal participation in public life and equal share in official power in government and business. Responding to constraints that curbed their participation as citizens and limited expression of their individual autonomy, the end of feminist protest was conceived as the full incorporation of women into the power, privileges, and responsibilities of the public arena. The stated aim of the largest feminist political organization, the National Organization for Women (NOW), founded in October 1966, is to gain "truly equal partnership with men." To this end, NOW's Bill of Rights contains a list of proposals and demands required to attain such equal partnership. These demands include the establishment of government sponsored twenty-four-hour child-care centers, abortion on demand, equal pay for equal work, aggressive recruitment of women for top positions in all political and business hierarchies, and so on. Each demand requires action by the federal government to promote women's interests and to achieve NOW's version of sex equality. The presumption behind these demands, as stated by Betty Friedan's *The Feminine Mystique,* is that contemporary woman suffers a particular assault against her identity by being housebound; the man, however, with other "able, ambitious" fellows, enters the success-driven ethos of the American public world and keeps "on growing."[1] Friedan contrasts, and devalues, the activities and identities of women in their "comfortable concentration camps" with the exciting, fulfilling, and presumably worthwhile world of the successful professional male.[2] In her more recent *The Second Stage,* Friedan remains innocent of any intractable tensions between simultaneous commitments to full intimacy and mobile success on market terms. She evades any serious questioning of her rosy, upbeat feminist project by transcending (her favorite word) every conflict that poses an apparent clash of interests, values, or purposes, or

[1]Betty Friedan, *The Feminine Mystique* (New York: Dell Books, 1974), p. 201.

[2]Ibid., p. 325.

that seems to present obstacles to her vision of feminism's "second stage."[3]

Liberal feminists have not been alone in urging that private woman join public man. Susan Brownmiller, a radical feminist, presumes that all the central features of the current male-dominated power structure will remain intact indefinitely; therefore, women must come to control these structures fifty-fifty. Armies, for instance,

> must be fully integrated, as well as our national guard, our state troopers, our local sheriffs' offices, our district attorneys' offices, our state prosecuting attorneys' offices—in short the nation's entire lawful power structure (and I mean power in the physical sense) must be stripped of male dominance and control—if women are to cease being a colonized protectorate of men.[4]

Women should prepare themselves for combat and guard duty, for militarized citizenship with a feminist face.

Similarly, one fundamental presumption underlying more deterministic modes of Marxist feminism is the insistence that women will never be "liberated" to join hands with those men whose identities bear the teleologic seed of the future revolutionary order—the proletariat—until they are sprung from the ghetto of the home and wholly absorbed in the labor force, there to acquire an overriding public identity as a member of the class of exploited workers. The realm of intimacy is recast, crudely, as the world of reproduction, an analogue of the productive process.

These moves to transform women into public persons, with a public identity that either primarily or exclusively defines them and takes precedence in cases of conflict with private lives, were embraced or implicitly adopted by the most widely disseminated statements of feminist politics. As a feminist project this ideology required "the absorption of the private as completely as possible into the public."[5] Women, formerly the private beings, would be "uplifted" to the status of a preeminently public identity to be shared equally with men. Though this overstates the case for emphasis, it reflects accurately the main thrust of feminist thought and practice—particularly that of mainstream, liberal feminism—from the late 1960s through the 1970s. What

[3]Betty Friedan, *The Second Stage* (New York: Summit Books, 1981).

[4]Susan Brownmiller, *Against Our Will: Men, Women and Rape* (New York: Simon and Schuster, 1975), p. 388.

[5]Robert Paul Wolff, "There's Nobody Here But Us Persons," in Carol Gould and Marx Wartofsky, eds., *Women and Philosophy* (New York: G. P. Putnam, 1976), pp. 140–41.

was conspicuously missing from the discussion was any recognition of the potential dangers inherent in calling upon the state as an instrument for sexual emancipation. Concentrating only upon the good purposes to be served, feminists did not bring into focus the possibilities for enhanced powers of state surveillance and control of all aspects of intimate social relations.

In practice, the demand for a shift in the social identities of women involves their full assimilation into a combined identification with the state and the terms of competitive civil society, terms which have permeated all aspects of public life due to the close entanglements between government and corporations. The modern state, however, is the locus of structured, "legitimate" public life. It is this state feminists look to to intervene, to legislate, to adjudicate, to police and to punish on their behalf.

This process emerges in stark relief in an *amicus curiae* brief filed by NOW with the Supreme Court that argues that the all-male draft violates the constitutional rights of women. The brief asserts that "compulsory universal military service is central to the concept of citizenship in a democracy" and that women suffer "devastating long term psychological and political repercussions" because of their exclusion from such service.[6] Eleanor Smeal, president of NOW, insists that barring women from the military and from combat duty is based "solely on archaic notions of women's role in society."[7] Whatever one's position on women and the draft, NOW's stance and the stated defense for it embodies the conviction that women's traditional identities are so many handicaps to be overcome by women's incorporation into male public roles.

What all feminist protests that inveigh against women's continued identification with the private sphere share is the conviction that women's traditional identities were wholly forced upon them—that all women have been the unwitting victims of deliberate exclusion from public life and forced imprisonment in private life. That is, women were not construed as agents and historic subjects who had, in their private identities as wives, mothers, and grandmothers, played vital and voluntary roles as neighbors, friends, social benefactors, and responsible community members. Though these latter roles are not necessarily

[6]Linda Greenhouse, "Women Join Battle on All-Male Draft," *New York Times*, March 22, 1981, p. 19. We do have plenty of evidence on the devastating damage done men and women who served in a variety of capacities in Vietnam.

[7]Ibid.

gender related, historically they have been associated with women. Holding up the public world as the only sphere within which individuals made real choices, exercised authentic power or had efficacious control, the private world, in turn, automatically reflected a tradition of powerlessness, necessity, and irrationality. The darker realities of the public world, with the notable exception of its exclusion of women, went unexplored just as the noble and dignified aspects of women's private sphere were ignored.

Feminists who celebrated "going public" could point to the long history of the forced exclusion of women from political life and participation—whether the franchise, public office, or education and employment—as evidence that women's private identities were heavy-handed impositions by those with superior power.[8] They could also recall a tradition of political thought in which great male theorists located women outside of, and frequently at odds with, the values and demands of politics and the sphere of public action. In contrast, another strain of feminist thought, best called "difference feminism," questioned the move towards full assimilation of female identity with public male identity and argued that to see women's traditional roles and activities as *wholly* oppressive was itself oppressive to women, denying them historic subjectivity and moral agency.[9] They could point to a first-person literature in which women defined and appropriated a particular female identity, rooted in private activities and relations, as a source of individual strength and social authority. They suggested that feminists should challenge rather than accept the present public world. And, rather than chastizing Western political thinkers for their failure to incorporate women into their scheme of things, why not question that very scheme with its devaluation of the traditional world and ways of women?

At this point it is important to take the measure of that public identity into which "liberated" women are to be inducted. Contemporary American public identity is a far cry indeed from Jefferson's noble

[8]My argument should not be taken as a denial that women, historically, *have* suffered in specific ways. It is, however, a denial that this suffering has been so total that women are reduced to the status of objects—whether in the name of feminism or in the name of defenses of male supremacy.

[9]Examples of "difference feminism" include: Carol Gilligan, "In a Different Voice: Women's Conception of Self and Morality," *Harvard Educational Review* 47 (1977), pp. 481–517; some of the essays in the volumes *Women, Culture and Society*, ed. Michelle Rosaldo and Louise Lamphere (Stanford University Press, 1974); and *Discovering Reality: Feminist Perspectives on Epistemology, Metaphysics, Methodology and the Philosophy of Science* (Amsterdam: Dordrecht-Reidel, forthcoming 1982).

republican farmer or Lincoln's morally engaged citizen, the "last best hope on earth." Instead we find a public life, political and economic, marked by bureaucratic rationalization and culminating in the state's monopoly of authority in most vital fields of human activity. This process of rationalization and centralization, in the words of Brian Fay,

> refers to the process by which growing areas of social life are subjected to decisions made in accordance with technical rules for the choice between alternative strategies given some set of goals or values. The characteristic features of these sorts of decisions are the quantification of the relevant data, the use of formal decision procedures, and the utilization of empirical laws; all of these are combined to form an attitude of abstraction from the traditional qualitative, and historically unique features of a situation in order to settle the question at hand "objectively." This sort of instrumental rationality is intimately connected with control over the various factors at hand, such that, by the manipulation of certain variables in accordance with some plan, some goal is best achieved.[10]

The aims are efficiency and control and powerful bureaucracies have been set up to implement these aims. Bureaucrats operate in conformity to certain impersonal, abstract, and rational standards: this is the price of entry into the predominant public identity available to anyone, male or female. It is the world Hegel called "civil society," in which individuals treat others as means to some end and carry out actions to attain self-interest in public.

For women to identify fully with the present public order is for them to participate (and there is pathos if not tragedy in this) in the suppression of an alternative identity described by Dorothy Smith, a feminist sociologist, as "the concrete, the particular, the bodily," an identity with which women have traditionally been defined and within which, for better *and* worse, they have located themselves as social and historic beings.[11] This world, once taken for granted and now problematic, exists in contrast to the abstracted "mode of ruling," the ways of acting of the powerful. Women's historic social identity, at odds with extreme versions of abstract individualism, public-oriented behavior aimed at good for others but not reducible to interest for self. The problem, as Jane Bennett points out in a recent study, is that women, as the "exem-

[10]Brian Fay, *Social Theory and Political Practices* (London: George Allen and Unwin, 1975), p. 44.

[11]Dorothy E. Smith, "A Sociology for Women" in *The Prism of Sex: Essays in the Sociology of Knowledge*, ed. Julia A. Sterman and Evelyn Torton Beck (Madison, Wisconsin: University of Wisconsin Press, 1979), pp. 135–188.

plars/defenders of civic virtue," were pressed to sacrifice individual goals altogether in order to preserve "a particular type of public good."[12]

Feminist protest that seeks the elimination of this sphere of the concrete, particular, smaller social world—viewing only the sacrifices forced upon women, not the good attained by women—is one response to identities grown problematic under the pressures of social rationalization and modernization. A second response, where growth is a measure of the anger and despair of its adherents, is the militant reaffirmation of a rigid feminine identity, one that aims to leave all the political stuff to men who are better equipped for the task—ironically, of course, such feminine women are actively promoting this passive end. Somewhat lost in the cross-fire between hostile camps is a third alternative, which I shall call "social feminism," that opposes the rush toward a technocratic order and an overweening public identity and repudiates, as well, the standpoint of ardent feminine passivity.

The third way, a feminist *via media,* begins with a female subject located within a world that is particular, concrete, and social, and attempts to see it through her eyes. If one begins in this way, one cannot presume, with the feminists I discussed earlier, that this world is automatically one from which all women should seek, or need, to be wholly liberated. The French feminist writer, Julia Kristeva, observed in an interview: "Feminism can be but one of capitalism's more advanced needs to rationalize."[13] Those feminisms that embrace without serious qualification the governing consciousness and norms of social organization of the current public world serve in precisely this way.

To sketch my alternative requires that I begin from the standpoint of women within their everyday reality. Is it possible to embrace ideals and values from the social world of women, severed from male domination and female subordination? I am convinced this is possible only by not viewing women's traditional identities as devoid of vitality, as being tainted by relations of domination. What follows is my effort to reclaim for women, construed as social actors in the world, an identity that pits them against the imperious demands of public power and contractual relations, one that might serve as a locus for female thinking, acting, and being as transformed by social feminist imperatives. This locus is not some solid rock, not an ontological definition of female

[12]Jane Bennett, "Feminism and Civic Virtue," unpublished paper (1981).

[13]Julia Kristeva, "Women Can Never Be Defined," in Elaine Marks and Isabelle de Courtivron, eds., *New French Feminisms: An Anthology* (Amherst: University of Massachusetts Press, 1980), p. 141.

"being"; rather, it is a series of overlapping intimations of a subject in the process of defining herself both with and against the available identities, public and private, of her epoch.

The female subject I have in mind is an identity-in-becoming, but she is located historically and grounded in tradition; she belongs to a heritage at least as old as Antigone's conflict with Creon. This powerful myth and human drama pits a woman against the arrogant insistencies of statecraft. Recall the story: the *dramatis personae* that matter for my purposes are Creon, King of Thebes, and his nieces, Antigone and her sister, Ismenê, daughters of the doomed Oedipus. Creon issues an order in the higher interests of state that violates the sacred familial duty to bury and honor the dead. Antigone, outraged, defies Creon. She defines their conflict with clarity and passion.

> Listen, Ismenê:
> Creon buried our brother Eteoclês
> With military honors, gave him a soldier's funeral,
> And it was right that he should; but Polyneicês,
> Who fought as bravely and died as miserably,—
> They say that Creon has sworn
> No one shall bury him, no one mourn for him
> But his body must lie in the fields, a sweet treasure
> For carrion birds to find as they search for food.
> That is what they say, and our good Creon is coming here
> To announce it publicly; and the penalty—
> Stoning to death in the public square
> There it is,
> And now you can prove what you are:
> A true sister, or a traitor to your family.[14]

Ismenê, uncomprehending, asks Antigone what she is going to do, and Antigone responds: "Ismenê, I am going to bury him. Will you come?" Ismenê cries that the new law forbids it. Women, she cries, cannot fight with men or against the law and she begs "the Dead/To forgive me." But Antigone, determined, replies: "It is the dead, not the living, who make the longest demands." Harshly, she orders Ismenê off with the words: "I shall be hating you soon, and the dead will too," for what is worse than death, or what is the worst of deaths, is "death without honor." Later, Antigone proclaims, "There is no guilt in rever-

[14]Sophocles, *The Oedipus Cycle*, "Antigone," trans. Dudley Fitts and Robert Fitzgerald (New York: Harvest Books, 1949), p. 186.

ence for the dead" and "there are honors due all the dead." This primordial family morality precedes and overrides the laws of the state. Creon must be defied, for there are matters, Antigone insists, that are so basic they transcend *raison d'état*, one's own self-interest, even one's own life.

Creon's offense is his demand that political necessity justifies trampling upon a basic human duty, an imperative that lies at the heart of any recognizably human social life. In her loyalty to her slain brother and to family honor, Antigone asserts that there are matters of such deep significance that they begin and end where the state's right does not and must not run, where politics cannot presume to dictate to the human soul. In "saving" the state, Creon not only runs roughshod over a centuries-old tradition, he presumes to override the familial order, the domain of women. In refusing to accept *raison d'état* as paramount, Antigone sets the course for her rebellion and pits the values of family and particular loyalties, ties, and traditions against the values of statecraft with its more abstract obligations. In her rebellion, Antigone is as courageous, honorable, and determined as Creon is insistent, demanding, and convinced of the necessity of his public decree.

Sophocles honors Antigone in her rebellion. He sees no need to portray a chastened Antigone, having confronted Creon but having failed to sway him, finally won over to the imperatives of *raison d'état*, yielding at last to Creon's fears of law-breakers and anarchy. Strangely, Antigone has not emerged as a feminist heroine. It is equally strange that a magisterial Greek thinker who would eliminate altogether the standpoint of Antigone is sometimes honored by feminists for his "radical" rearrangements without apparent regard to gender. I refer to Plato of *The Republic*, a Plato dedicated to eradicating and devaluing private homes and particular intimate attachments (principally for his Guardian class). Such private loyalties and passions conflicted with single-minded devotion to the city. Plato cries: "Have we any greater evil for a city than what splits it and makes it many instead of one? Or a greater good than what binds it together and makes it one?"[15]

To see in Plato's abstract formulation for rationalized equality (for that minority of men and women who comprise his Guardian class) a move that is both radical and feminist is to accept public life and identity as, by definition, superior to private life and identity. Indeed, it is to

[15]Plato, *The Republic*, trans. Allan Bloom (New York: Basic Books, 1968), Book V/460E-462D, p. 141.

concur in the wholesale elimination of the private social world to attain the higher good of a state without the points of potential friction and dissent private loyalties bring in their wake. This view accepts Plato's conviction that "private wives" are a potentially subversive element within the city. Plato cannot allow women their own social location, for that would be at odds with his aim for a unified city. Instead, he provides for women's participation under terms that deprivatize them and strip them of the single greatest source of female psychological and social power in fifth- and fourth-century Athens—their role in the household; their ties with their children. Effectively, he renders their sexual identities moot. In whose behalf is this dream of unity, and female public action, being dreamed?

The question of female identity and the state looks very different if one picks up the thread of woman's relationship to public power from the standpoint of an Antigone; if one adopts the sanctioned viewpoint of the handful of thinkers whose works comprise the canon of the Western political tradition; or if one tells the tale through the prism of unchecked *realpolitik,* from astride the horse of the warrior, or from the throne of the ruler. The female subject, excluded from legitimate statecraft unless she inherited a throne, is yet an active historic agent, a participant in social life who located the heart of her identity in a world bounded by the demands of necessity, sustaining the values of life-giving and preserving.

This sphere of the historic female subject generated its own imperatives, inspired its own songs, stories, and myths. It was and is, for many if not all, the crucible through which sustaining human relations and meaning are forged and remembered. It is easy to appreciate both the fears of traditionalists and the qualms of radicals at the suppression of this drama of the concrete and the particular in favor of some formal-legalistic, abstract "personhood," or to make way for the further intrusion of an increasingly technocratic public order. To wholly reconstruct female social identity by substituting of those identities available through the public order would be to lose the standpoint of Antigone, the woman who throws sand into the machinery of arrogant public power.

But how does one hold on to a social location for contemporary daughters of Antigone without simultaneously insisting that women accept traditional terms of political quiescence? The question answers itself: the standpoint of Antigone is of a woman who dares to challenge public power by giving voice to familial and social imperatives and duties. Hers is not the world of the *femme couverte,* the delicate lady, or the coy sex-kitten. Hers is a robust voice, a bold voice: woman as guardian of the prerogatives of the *oikos*, preserver of familial duty and honor, protector of children, if need be their fierce avenger. To recapture that voice and to reclaim that standpoint, and not just for women alone, it is necessary to locate the daughters of Antigone where, shakily and problematically, they continue to locate themselves: in the arena of the social world where human life is nurtured and protected from day to day. This is a world women have not altogether abandoned, though it is one both male-dominant society and some feminist protest have devalued as the sphere of "shit-work," "diaper talk," and "terminal social decay." This is a world that women, aware that they have traditions and values, can bring forward to put pressure on contemporary public policies and identities.

Through a social feminist awareness, women can explore, articulate, and reclaim this world. To reaffirm the standpoint of Antigone for our own time is to portray women as being able to resist the imperious demands and overweening claims of state power when these run roughshod over deeply rooted values. Women must learn to defend without defensiveness and embrace without sentimentality the perspective that flows from their experiences in their everyday material world, "an actual local and particular place in the world."[16] To define this world simply as the "private sphere" in contrast to "the public sphere" is to mislead. For contemporary Americans, "private" conjures up images of narrow exclusivity. The world of Antigone, however, is a *social* location that speaks of, and to, identities that are unique to a particular family, on the one hand; but, on another and perhaps even more basic level, it taps a deeply buried human identity, for we are first and foremost not political or economic man but family men and women. Family imagery goes deep and runs strong, and all of us, for better or worse, sporadically or consistently, have access to that imagery, for we all come from families even if we do not go on to create our own. The family is that arena that first humanizes us or, tragically, damages us. The family is our entry point into the wider social world. It is the basis of a concept of the social for, as Hegel recognized, "the family is a sort of training ground that provides an understanding of another-oriented and public-oriented action."[17]

What is striking about political theory in the western tradition is the very thin notion of the social world so much of that theory describes. All aspects of social reality that go into making a person what he or she

[16]Smith, "A Sociology for Women," p. 168.

[17]Bennett, "Feminism and Civic Virtue."

is fall outside the frame of formal, abstract analyses. In their rethinking of this tradition, many feminist thinkers, initially at least, locked their own formulations into an overly schematic public-private dichotomy, even if their intention was to challenge or to question it.[18] Those feminists who have moved in the direction of "social feminism" have, in their rethinking of received categories, become both more historical and more interpretive in their approach to social life. One important female thinker whose life and work form a striking contrast to the classical vision and to overly rigid feminist renderings of the public and private, particularly those who disdain anything that smacks of the traditionally "feminine," is Jane Addams. Addams embodies the standpoint of Antigone. A woman with a powerful public identity and following, who wielded enormous political power and influence, Addams's life work was neither grandly public nor narrowly private. Instead, she expressed the combined values of centuries of domestic tradition, and the dense and heady concoction of women's needs, and she brought these to bear on a political world that held human life very cheap indeed.

Addams recognized, in uncritical celebrations of heroic male action, a centuries-long trail of tears. What classical political theorists dismissed as ignoble—the sustenance of life itself—Addams claimed as truly heroic. Rather than repudiating human birth and the world surrounding it as a possible source of moral truth and political principle, Addams spoke from the standpoint of the "suffering mothers of the disinherited," of "women's haunting memories," which, she believed, "instinctively challenge war as the implacable enemy of their age-long undertaking."[19] At one point she wrote:

> Certainly the women in every country who are under a profound imperative to preserve human life, have a right to regard this maternal impulse as important now as the compelling instinct evinced by primitive woman long ago, when they made the first crude beginnings of society by refusing to share the vagrant life of man because they insisted upon a fixed abode in which they might cherish their children. Undoubtedly women were then told that the interests of the tribe, the diminishing food supply, the honor of the chieftain, demanded

[18]I consider myself guilty on this score. See one of my earlier formulations on the public-private dilemma, "Moral Woman/Immoral Man: The Public/Private Distinction and its Political Ramifications," *Politics and Society* 4 (1974), pp. 453–473. I try to restore a richness this initial foray dropped out in *Public Man, Private Woman: Women in Social and Political Thought* (Princeton: Princeton University Press, 1981).

[19]Jane Addams, *The Long Road of Woman's Memory* (New York: Macmillan Co., 1916), p. 40.

> that they leave their particular caves and go out in the wind and weather without regard to the survival of their children. But at the present moment the very names of the tribes and of the honors and the glories which they sought are forgotten, while the basic fact that the mothers held the lives of their children above all else, insisted upon staying where the children had a chance to live, and cultivate the earth for their food, laid the foundations of an ordered society.[20]

A feminist rethinking of Addams's category of the social, resituating it as an alternative to privatization and public self-interestedness, would allow us to break out of the rigidities into which current feminist discourse has fallen. Seeing human beings through the prism of a many-layered, complex social world suffused with diverse goods, meanings, and purposes opens up the possibility for posing a transformed vision of the human community against the arid plain of bureaucratic statism. This communitarian ideal involves a series of interrelated but autonomous social spheres. It incorporates a vision of human solidarity that does not require uniformity and of cooperation that permits dissent. The aim of all social activity would be to provide a frame within which members of a diverse social body could attain both individual and communal ends and purposes, without, however, presuming some final resolution of these ends and purposes; a social world featuring fully public activities at one end of a range of possibilities and intensely private activities at the other.

If this communal ideal is to be claimed as a worthy ideal for our time, a first requirement is a feminist framework that locates itself in the social world in such a way that our current public, political realities can be examined with a critical and reflective eye. One alternative feminist perspective, a variation on both "difference" and "social" feminism that helps us to do this is called "maternal thinking" by its author, Sara Ruddick.[21] According to Ruddick, mothers have had a particular way of thinking that has largely gone unnoticed—save by mothers themselves. That is, women in mothering capacities have developed intellectual abilities that wouldn't otherwise have been developed; made judgments they wouldn't otherwise have been called upon to make; and affirmed values they might not otherwise have affirmed. In other words, mothers engage in a discipline that has its own characteristic virtues and errors and that involves, like other disciplines, a conception

[20]Ibid., pp. 126–27.

[21]Sara Ruddick, "Maternal Thinking," typescript. A shortened version has appeared in *Feminist Studies* (Summer 1980), but I draw upon the original full-length draft.

of achievement. Most important for the purposes of feminist theory, these concepts and ends are dramatically at odds with the prevailing norms of our bureaucratic, and increasingly technological, public order.

Ruddick claims that one can describe maternal practices by a mother's interest in the preservation, the growth, and the social acceptability of her child. These values and goods may conflict, for preservation and growth may clash with the requirements for social acceptability. Interestingly, what counts as a failure within the frame of maternal thinking, excessive control that fails to give each unique child room to grow and develop, is the *modus operandi* of both public and private bureaucracies. Were maternal thinking to be taken as the base for feminist consciousness, a wedge for examining an increasingly over-controlled public world would open up immediately. For this notion of maternal thought to have a chance to flourish as it is brought to bear upon the larger world, it must be transformed in and through social feminist awareness.

To repeat: the core concepts of maternal achievement put it at odds with bureaucratic manipulation. Maternal achievement requires paying a special sort of attention to the concrete specificity of each child; it turns on a special kind of knowledge of this child, this situation, without the notion of seizure, appropriation, control, or judgment by impersonal standards. What maternal thinking could lead to, though this will always be problematic as long as mothers are socially subordinated, is the wider diffusion of what attentive love to all children is about and how it might become a wider social imperative.

Maternal thinking opens up for reflective criticism the paradoxical juxtapositions of female powerlessness and subordination, in the overall social and political sense, with the extraordinary psycho-social authority of mothers. Maternal thinking refuses to see women principally or simply as victims, for it recognizes that much good has emerged from maternal practices and could not if the world of the mother were totally destructive. Maternal thinking transformed by feminist consciousness, hence aware of the binds and constraints imposed on mothers, including the presumption that women will first nurture their sons and then turn them over for sacrifice should the gods of war demand human blood, offers us a mode of reflection that links women to the past yet offers up hope of a future. It makes contact with the strengths of our mothers and grandmothers; it helps us to see ourselves as Antigone's daughters, determined, should it be necessary, to chasten arrogant public power and resist the claims of political necessity. For such power, and such claims, have, in the past, been weapons used to trample upon the deepest yearnings and most basic hopes of the human spirit.

Maternal thinking reminds us that public policy has an impact on real human beings. As public policy becomes increasingly impersonal, calculating, and technocratic, maternal thinking insists that the reality of a single human child be kept before the mind's eye. Maternal thinking, like Antigone's protest, is a rejection of amoral statecraft and an affirmation of the dignity of the human person.

V. Government Is Women's Enemy

Sharon Presley and Lynn Kinsky

Sharon Presley and Lynn Kinsky have been active in individualist feminism for many years and have been especially influential in making feminism a topic of discussion in the current libertarian movement. Presley was instrumental in founding the Association of Libertarian Feminists—the only organizational expression of individualist-feminism in the 20th century. As a writer and lecturer, she has placed particular emphasis upon bringing undeservedly obscure women, such as Suzanne La Follette, into the public light. Her perspective on feminism combines libertarianism with humanism.

Kinsky was one of the founders of the long-lived and successful Reason *magazine. Her early articles in* Reason *and her active participation in libertarian events laid groundwork for present discussions of individualist-feminism.*

The following article is a general statement of feminism from a libertarian perspective.

> I ask no favors for my sex. I surrender not our claim to equality. All I ask of our brethren is that they will take their feet off our necks, and permit us to stand upright on the ground which God has designed us to occupy.
>
> —Sarah Grimké, *Letters on the Equality of the Sexes and the Condition of Women*, Boston, 1838.

The above words of early feminist Sarah Grimké are as good an answer now as they were then to the question, "What do feminists want?" We want, as women, as persons, to be free.

Feminism is a proposition that insists that no one exists for anyone else; that government, commerce, technology, education, etc., all exist as tools for people to use as they decide, not the other way around. Feminism rejects any system that keeps people tied to roles, that depends on a hierarchical oppressor-oppressed relationship in order to function.

Feminists want women to be free—free of the domination of men, free to control their bodies and psyches as they see fit, free to make their own decisions about their own lives independent of the coercive domination of others.

Unfortunately, inconsistency has crept into the modern women's movement. While rejecting patriarchal attitudes and dominating ways of interacting on a *personal* level, women's liberationists will too often ask for government favors and handouts such as free child-care centers or free abortions. *Yet turning to the government just changes the sort of oppression women face, not the fact.* Instead of being overburdened as mothers or wives we become overburdened as taxpayers, since child-care workers, doctors, etc., have to be paid by someone unless they are to be enslaved also! Turning to the government to solve our problems just replaces oppression by patriarchs we *know*—father, husband, boss—with oppression by patriarchs we don't know—the hordes of legislators and bureaucrats who are increasingly prying into every nook and cranny of our lives!

But there is a nonauthoritarian alternative—a philosophy that not only has goals compatible with the psychological goals of feminism, but methods more compatible with these goals than the alternatives usually touted. So it is particularly appropriate that the first woman in history to receive an electoral vote—Tonie Nathan—is an advocate of this philosophy: libertarianism.

The essence of libertarianism is the belief that all social interactions should be voluntary, that no one has the right to rule another, that individuals have the right to live their lives in any manner they see fit as long as they don't initiate force or fraud against others.

Libertarians want to repeal laws, not pass them. They are not interested in stopping people from smoking pot, having abortions, *or* from spending their own money as they see fit. Libertarians just want to leave people alone. They believe that there *are* voluntary nonauthoritarian alternatives to coercive government services and institutions that will work, even in our modern complex society.

Libertarian feminists believe that we can't achieve a nonauthoritarian society by authoritarian methods. If our goals are personal autonomy and individual freedom, we can't achieve these goals by taking away individuals' rights to choose for themselves. If we pass laws that force *our* values on others, we are no better than men who have forced *their* values on us through legislation. We merely substitute our tyranny for the tyranny of men. Women's liberationist Susan Brownmiller advocating anti-obscenity laws is no better than Conservative James Buckley advocating abortion laws.

Government Is Women's Enemy

> Oh! that we could learn the advantage of just practice and consistent principles! that we could understand, that every departure from principle, how speciously soever it may appear to administer to our selfish interests, invariably saps their very foundation! that we could learn

that what is ruinous to some is injurious to all, and that whenever we establish our own pretentions upon the sacrificed rights of others, we do in fact impeach our own liberties and lower ourselves in the scale of being!
—Frances Wright, *Course of Popular Lectures,* New York, 1830.

Not only on a moral and psychological level, but on a practical level as well, it would be bitterly ironic for women to turn to government for solutions to their problems. Government has harmed women far more than it has helped them. Government has, in many cases, *created* the problems in the first place and still continues to perpetuate them through unnecessary and harmful legislation.

Child Care Centers

The issue of child-care centers is a prime example of why government is an enemy, not a friend of women. Government regulations have *created* the child-care crisis! Zoning laws, unnecessary and pointless "health and safety" restrictions, required licensing that is difficult to obtain—all combine to assure that people will not be able to get together to provide low-cost child care on their own.

Then when the government sees the lack of child-care facilities (caused by government restrictions), it steps in to fill the void with stolen money at costs far in excess of what perfectly adequate private child care could be provided for. Typically a large portion of the cost of child-care centers goes to line the pockets of the bureaucratic administrators or to pay rent on unnecessarily expensive buildings—as a recent scandal in New York City shows so well. (Outrageously inflated rents far beyond the normal market value were paid for broken-down slum buildings owned by landlords with friends at City Hall.) But parents don't need these bureaucrats and expensive buildings to provide loving care for children.

Worse yet, after forcing parents and children into the role of charity cases, the government is also in a position to control the development of children just as it does in the public schools. Government officials intend that these "child development centers" (as they like to call child-care centers) will be places where young children can be psychologically conditioned to what the administrators think are healthier attitudes.

> There is serious thinking among some of the future oriented child development research people that maybe we can't trust the family alone to prepare young children for this new kind of world which is emerging . . . In the first 18 months of life, the brain is growing faster

than it ever will again. It is then also more plastic and available to appropriate experience and corrective interventions.
—Reginald Lowrie, President of the Joint Commission on the Mental Health of Children

Do you trust *government officials* to intervene in the lives and minds of your children?

Public Schools

If you wonder what kind of attitudes these government officials have in mind and what kinds of "corrective interventions" they plan, just look at the public school system. Public schools not only foster the worst of traditionalist sexist values but inculcate docility and obedience to authority with sterile, stifling methods and compulsory programs and regulations. Government has obtained frightening power over the lives of children in public schools through the use of psychological testing and "counseling," secret (and often viciously subjective) files that follow children throughout their school years, and—worst of all—compulsory drug programs for allegedly "hyperactive" children. All in the name of helping children, the government draws its net tighter and tighter. (That these programs are truly harmful rather than helpful is well documented in *The Myth of the Hyperactive Child, and Other Means of Child Control,* by Peter Schrag and Diane Divoky.)

These programs in the public schools are popular and widespread. It is unrealistic to assume that they won't be incorporated into government child-care centers, too. And never forget that no matter how much control you think you have over child-care centers or schools, the strings are always attached. What the government finances, it ultimately controls.

Abortion and Contraception

The government's record on abortion and contraception is no better. Such controls could not have been instituted without the power of government in the first place. And alleged "reforms" notwithstanding, controls and restrictions still exist. The much-touted 1973 Supreme Court decisions that supposedly brought "legalized abortion" still allow the government great latitude in dictating when and the conditions under which abortions may be performed; and the places where contraceptives may be sold are still limited. Whether you can even see contraceptives or ads for them is also still heavily restricted by local, state, and federal laws. But unlike the politicians of the Republican and

Democratic Parties, who weasel their way past the issues, the Libertarian Party calls for total repeal of abortion and contraception laws, not just wishy-washy "reforms." Libertarians believe that abortion is a matter of individual conscience and choice, and that the State has no right to tell women how they may use their own bodies.

Other Government Discrimination Against Women

Much of the discrimination that women face in today's society has been enshrined and institutionalized through law and other government processes. So-called "protective" labor legislation has kept women out of certain jobs and encouraged private job discrimination. Marriage, divorce, and property laws all discriminate against women.

In the area of sexuality, government discrimination against women is particularly blatant: laws against prostitution try to dictate how women will use their own bodies, and usually only the woman prostitute, not her male customer, is prosecuted. "Sexual delinquency" charges are brought against young girls far more often than against boys. Lesbians and single mothers are discriminated against in child-custody and adoption cases.

And most blatant of all, rape cases are treated differently from other assault cases: conviction is much harder to obtain because evidence is required that is not required for non-sexual assaults. Often not only must the victim produce a "corroborating witness," but she must also demonstrate *her* innocence as well as the rapist's guilt!

What Is To Be Done

> The modern conviction, the fruit of a thousand years of experience, is, that things in which the individual is the person directly interested, never go right but as they are left to his own discretion; and that any regulation of them by authority, except to protect the rights of others, is sure to be mischievous.
>
> —John Stuart Mill, *On the Subjection of Women*, London, 1869.

Many feminists will say "but what we need are better laws and better politicians." Libertarians agree that the laws must change. Discrimination built into the laws, such as in the instances cited above, must go. Government is obligated to treat all citizens equally. Those laws that restrict the freedom of women to make choices about their bodies, about their lives and the lives of their dependent children, about their sexual relationships with others, must go. But while libertarian feminists uncompromisingly believe in the repeal of such restrictive laws against women, they do not believe that passing laws to obtain or extend special government privileges and handouts will solve the other problems of women. The history of government shows all too well that corruption, boondoggling, inefficiency, wastefulness, and authoritarian control are inherent in the political system. On both a moral and a practical level, women are far better off without government "solutions."

We need to develop nonauthoritarian alternatives, both as substitutes for government institutions and services already in existence, and as an example to others that voluntary action does work. For instance, an excellent example of feminist voluntary action right now is the rape crisis centers. Angered by the lack of interest or inability of the police and courts to deal sensitively with the problem of rape, women in many communities have formed rape crisis centers to provide help and support for rape victims and to try and dispel the many myths about the crime of rape. The various self-help medical clinics are another good example of a non-governmental solution to a problem, and schools, child-care centers, and other important services also exist on private, voluntary community bases already. Libertarians believe that many additional services can also be provided if the government will just get off our backs. We are learning to break free of Big Brother politically as well as psychologically. We don't need him either way.

Suggested Readings

Avrich, Paul. *An American Anarchist: The Life of Voltairine de Cleyre.* Princeton, N.J.: Princeton University Press, 1978.

De Cleyre, Voltairine. *Selected Works*. New York: Mother Earth, 1914.

La Follette, Suzanne. *Concerning Women* (1926). New York: Arno Press, 1972.

Lane, Rose Wilder. *The Discovery of Freedom: Man's Struggle Against Authority*. New York: The John Day Co., 1943.

Marsh, Margaret S. *Anarchist Women 1870–1920.* Philadelphia: Temple University Press, 1981.

Mill, John Stuart. "On the Subjugation of Women" (1869) in *Three Essays: On Liberty, Representative Government, the Subjugation of Women.* New York: Oxford University Press, 1975.

Paterson, Isabel. *The God of the Machine*. Caldwell, Idaho: Caxton, 1964.

Spencer, Herbert. *Social Statics*. London: John Chapman, 1851, pp. 155–171.

Wollstonecraft, Mary. *A Vindication of the Rights of Women* (1792). New York: Source Book Press, 1971.

WOMEN AND SEX

VI. An "Age of Consent" Symposium

Lillian Harman

As the daughter of Moses Harman, editor of the free-love periodical Lucifer the Light Bearer, *Lillian Harman was born into the feminist crusade. At the age of 16, she was imprisoned in the Oskaloosa County Jail in Kansas for her non-state, non-church marriage to E. C. Walker. Her articles in* Lucifer, Liberty *and other individualist-anarchist periodicals were clear calls for a woman's right to self-ownership.*

Harman's concern with age-of-consent laws must be understood in the social context of the late 1800s. Feminist and social purity reformers were intimately linked by various common goals. Ironically, because of the purity reformers' emphasis on eugenics, their efforts promoted birth control in America. Since their goal was purity and not sexual freedom, however, they also cried out for censorship, the prosecution of those who frequented prostitutes, and raising the age of consent. In contrast, individualist feminists such as Lillian Harman pursued sexual freedom rather than "purity" and were often victimized by laws supported by the mainstream of feminists. The following article, which demonstrates this schism, is reprinted from Liberty.

It may confidently be asserted that all friends of Liberty are agreed as regards these three general propositions:

1. The existing system of sexual relations is very imperfect.
2. What is right or is wrong for a member of one sex under given conditions is right or is wrong for a member of the other sex under analogous conditions.
3. All persons, regardless of sex, should be protected from violence, extra-legal or legal.

Touching the first proposition, libertarians find themselves in agreement with authoritarians so far as the fact of imperfection is concerned, but they disagree widely, often fundamentally, as to the constituent elements of that imperfection. Likewise libertarians and authoritarians—at least, the more progressive contingent of the latter—are at one concerning the desirability and justice of the "single standard" in sex ethics, but here again the two schools are often vitally at variance when it comes to the consideration of what *is* right or wrong in the relations of the sexes. Finally, while authoritarians agree with libertarians that the individual should be protected from extra-legal violence, there are frequently irreconcilable differences of opinion when it is attempted to frame a definition which shall properly describe such violence, and, in addition to this difficulty in the way of reaching an agreement, there is the failure of the average authoritarian to recognize that under the present marriage system violence is legally sheltered, and his ineradicable propensity to commit legal violence in his blundering endeavors to prevent or punish extra-legal violence, or what he considers such.

The "Arena's" Crusade

For some time now the "Arena" has been trying to arouse a wider public interest in the age-of-consent laws of the various States, and in the January issue there is a symposium participated in by Aaron M. Powell, Helen H. Gardener, Frances E. Willard, A. H. Lewis, D. D.; O. Edward Janney, M. D.; Will Allen Dromgoole, and Emily Blackwell, M. D. The editor also continues his article on "Wellsprings and Feeders of Immorality," this being the second paper and dealing with "Lust Fostered by Legislation." The age of consent varies from ten years to eighteen, being the latter only in Kansas and Wyoming. In all the States association with a girl before she has reached the age prescribed in the statutes of the State in which she lives is rape, regardless of her consent to the association. The limit is ten years in three States, twelve years in four, thirteen years in three, fourteen years in nineteen, fifteen years in one, sixteen years in twelve, seventeen years in one, and eighteen years in two. Included in this enumeration are the territories and the District of Columbia. The demand of the reformers who are represented in this symposium, and of those for whom they speak, is that the limit shall be raised to at least eighteen years. There are some who make themselves heard through the press who wish to make it twenty-one years, and a few would put it still higher. But for the purposes of the present examination I will confine myself to the demand of the "Arena" writers.

The problem is a difficult one to deal with in the existing condition of society, where the most outrageous wrongs are possible because the people are economically enthralled and are the slaves of the grossest religious and moral superstitions. It is at once manifest that the ignorance fostered by the dominant powers in church, society, and the State is responsible for at least nine-tenths of the suffering resulting from the association of the sexes, both in and out of marriage. This is easily demonstrated, but the limits of this paper forbid the introduction of the evidence here. Suffice it to say that it is impossible to do justice by establishing a hard and fast line in this matter of age-of-consent laws. To say that the right of choice and determination should be withheld from all young women until they are eighteen is to utter an absurdity. Some are more developed, physically and mentally, at fifteen than others are at eighteen or twenty, or even when older. There are many exceptionally bright girls who know more at fifteen or sixteen than the mass of womankind do at fifty. Why such as these should have their lives wrecked by punishing their lovers for rape it will be exceedingly difficult for the "Arena" crusaders to show. The favorite argument of the advocates of the eighteen-year limit is that those who cannot be trusted with the management of their property until they are eighteen should not be trusted with the guardianship of their own bodies. But does the establishment of one arbitrary rule justify the establishment of another? Is individual capacity not to be considered at all? That one man never knows enough to take care of his business is not a valid reason why another who has been a good business man since he was a youth should be held in a lifelong minority. It is a well-known fact that thousands of parents permit their minor sons and daughters to attend to their own business affairs, and there is no doubt that the vast majority of the young people so trusted are better for their early introduction to the responsibilities of life, and it is equally certain that multitudes more would have been likewise benefited by similar opportunities to hew out their own fortunes had their parents been wise enough to open the way for them. But it is not true that girls and boys under eighteen never have had and have not now any control over their property. By the *Code Napoléon* a person of either sex may become an executor or executrix at seventeen, and at sixteen the minor may devise one-half his property. In some of our States the minor may choose a guardian at twelve and in others at fourteen. In New York a girl of sixteen may will and bequeath her personal estate, as may a boy of eighteen, and they may consent to marriage at the same age. Recurring to the question of majority rights often given by parents to their sons, it should be noted that in some States—possibly in all—a father may give notice by publication that he will appear in court at a given time to ask that his son, naming him, may be legally invested with the rights of a man, so far as independence from parental control is concerned, before he has reached the age of twenty-one. Only a few days ago I read such a notice in a Kansas paper.

Those acquainted with our school system are aware that many teachers are under eighteen years of age. Is it possible that these young women whom the State accepts as competent to teach and train her children are not competent to control their own persons? And then look at the thousands of girls under the age named who are earning their own livelihood in industry, business, and journalism. Why insult these by the gratuitous assumption that they are not competent to guard their persons from invasion when not assailed by physical violence? Dr. Janney thinks that the inequality in mental capacity of girls is a good reason why those who are in advance should wait until they are eighteen for their sex-liberty. This, he intimates, will give time for the others to catch up, and thus he would avoid the possibility of a wrong being done to a few of the immature ones by inflicting a certain wrong on all the more advanced who choose to live their own lives in their own way. If it be said that a similar wrong is inflicted on the man or woman who is capable of managing his or her own property interests before majority is reached, but who is denied that opportunity because all young people are not sufficiently intelligent, it is answered that the alleged parallel is far from perfect. As before said, many parents nullify the evil effects of that arbitrary law by giving their children an opportunity to help themselves early in life. Many of our youth do not feel the operation of the majority law at all except when they desire to vote before the age of twenty-one is reached. But in the case of the age-of-consent law such individual relief would not be easy to obtain, no matter how intelligent and humane the parents or the girl might be. With our numerous Societies for Meddling with Everybody's Business, the lover would probably be hanged or at least imprisoned for rape, and this in spite of the fact that the girl, her parents, and all others immediately interested were perfectly satisfied with their own arrangements.

I clearly recognize the fact that the child is not capable of judging for herself, but it is preposterous to hold that girls of fifteen and upwards are all children in thought, or such even in a majority of instances. This is an age of rapid development, and there are large numbers of young women in their teens who know much more about themselves and are far better qualified to be their own protectors than were their mothers when five or ten years older. Were it not for our State-enforced ignorance of sexual matters and the anti-natural teachings of a reactionary church, there would be precious few of our young women who would need the protection of the government to the extent of guarding them against themselves. Probably, all things considered, including the dense misinformation of the masses, the most reasonable present settlement of this age-of-consent question would be to fix the "age" at puberty.

A Peculiar Omission

Before proceeding to notice in detail some of the arguments of the contributors to the symposium, it will be well to call the attention of the fair-minded reader to a remarkable omission made by all who have written in the "Arena" on this subject. Everyone has tacitly assumed or explicitly stated that there is no legal protection or relief for the girl after she has reached the age of consent. If before that she consorts with a man, either through the compulsion of force or fear or in virtue of such "consent" as her mind may be able to give, she is outraged in the eye of the law, and her assailant is guilty of rape. But, if the "age" has been reached, she is no longer subject to outrage, and her assailant is not guilty of rape, if she consents. This is true, but the reformers should not have left the impression that her associate has committed *no* offence under the law, for such an impression is misleading. In many of the States association under promise of marriage is a misdemeanor, and in some it is a felony. In some States association with an unmarried, previously "chaste" woman involves the offence of seduction even without promise of marriage. In New York abduction consists in taking a girl under sixteen for purposes of marriage, prostitution, or intercourse, or inveigling and enticing an unmarried woman under twenty-five into a house of ill-fame or elsewhere for prostitution or intercourse. Seduction of an unmarried woman under promise of marriage involves imprisonment, or punishment by fine, or both. In most of the States, if not all, the father or other near relative of the woman seduced may bring action, and in some the woman may do so herself. We should all have had more faith in the desire and intention of the symposiasts to be fair if they had stated these facts with the particularity that they have shown in laying before the people the age-of-consent laws of the States. Not to say anything about it at all was still worse.

The Defenceless Position of The Wife

Opposite the first page of the symposium there is a group of portraits of the contributors, and under it Mr. Flower has put the label, "Some Defenders of the Home." I have read all the articles very carefully, and have failed to find a single word which would reveal to the uninitiated reader the startling fact that there is not a law on the statute-books of a single State of this Union which recognizes the possibility that the husband can commit a rape upon the wife. Looking in the law-books, I find it often and expressly stated that *the prostitute can be raped, but that the wife cannot*. So far as the husband is concerned, the wife is without defence. He can go to the brothel and commit a crime which will, if he is prosecuted, send him to the penitentiary; but, if he comes home the same night and commits the same crime on his wife, he will not be troubled by the law. Is it not strange that these "defenders of the home" forgot to say anything about so important a matter as this?

Miss Willard alone speaks of the necessity of making a wife the arbiter of her own destiny, but even she does not venture to tell the world what the law has put in the way of the accomplishment of that result.

Helen Gardener "Dares" The Opposition

I will pass over Mr. Powell's contribution, as it is chiefly a statement of the present status of the consent laws, and stop for a moment at Helen H. Gardener's, not because the latter contains any argument requiring an answer, but merely to show the readers of Liberty, by means of a quotation or two, the weightiness of some of the pleas for the surrender of the self-hood of the young women of America. This will do for a beginning:

> When I am asked to present an argument against lowering the age of consent, or when I am requested to write the reasons why that age should be raised to at least eighteen years, it impresses me very much as if some one were to ask me gravely if I would be so kind as to think up some fairly plausible grounds upon which one might base an objection to the practice of cutting the throats of his neighbor's children whenever that neighbor happened not to be at home to protect them; or to furnish a demurrer to the act of inoculating the community with small-pox as a matter of ordinary amusement.

That is a curiosity of argument which may well be left to answer itself. Miss Gardener wants to know if there is a legislator who believes that he has a right to assist in keeping the age of consent below eighteen years who will set forth his reasons, be they of a scientific, religious, social, or legal nature. I am not a legislator, but I have ventured to give some of my reasons for believing that the age of consent should not be raised to eighteen years, and I will now advance a few more. I do not believe that the State has a right to step between the young woman under eighteen and her lover, whether she does or does not choose to enter into legal marriage with him. Understand me, I say young woman; I am not speaking of children who have not reached puberty. Such interference is antagonistic to healthful social growth. It deranges the orderly process of development. Girls trained by intelligent mothers will be immensely more benefited than injured by relations that they desire, and the more liberty coupled with responsibility that we have the less there will be of sexual relations that are *not* desired. As for the girls whose mothers are not intelligent, their fate cannot be worse than it is now, and there is the reasonable chance that it will be greatly improved. The example of responsible freedom is almost immeasurably powerful. Regarding the scientific objections to the prohibition of sexual association until the age of eighteen is reached, they are numerous, but may be condensed into the single affirmation that there are very many young women whose nervous and physical systems are greatly injured, if not ruined, before their eighteenth birthday is reached by enforced abstinence from love associations. Others, again, do not feel the need of such relations before twenty or twenty-five, and some never. Let there be no cast-iron rule for all. We want no social procrustean beds. The world has been dosed nigh unto death by quacks who have thought that the race was damned unless everybody did just as they, the quacks, told them to do. We need liberty in domestic affairs just as much as in religion or politics, as Miss Gardener should know.

"The Sanctity of Motherhood"

Miss Willard observes that, "unless women had been at some time objects of barter, no such law could have been made." It seems to me that laws of this kind are evidences of the growing respect for woman which is a characteristic of this age. Faulty though they are, they show that the law-maker has desired to protect helpless infancy, while not interfering with the right of choice of young womanhood. The effect of those laws, whatever the intention of those who enacted them, has been to help place woman on her feet as an independent being, capable of acting for herself. That is, let it always be understood, when the limit has not been placed too high. The efforts of Miss Willard and her associates will, if crowned with success, necessarily weaken the sense of responsibility of womankind, and thus defeat the very purpose they have in view,—the protection of women from invasion. Another very important fact is persistently ignored by the age-of-consent agitators, and that is that the laws against rape remain to protect woman, and to avenge her if she is outraged—unless her husband is the criminal. When the age-of-consent laws are raised above fourteen or fifteen, the armies of "reform" have faced to the rear instead of to the front. The Roman law did not distinguish between rape and seduction or adultery, and the accused was not allowed to show that the association was with the consent of the woman, no matter what her age. The advocates of this *pseudo* reform are trying to force us back toward that savagely cruel code, and at least one of these "reformers," Rev. Mr. Lewis, would go every step of the way. He says: "It is not enough that the age of consent be 'raised.' *It must be erased.*" The italics are his. By this he means that the hour can never come in the life of any woman when she will be free to love outside of marriage and to express her love. It means that, no matter how old the woman may be and how capable of choosing for herself her mode of life, her lover will be punished for rape. I thank Rev. Mr. Lewis for letting use see the end of the road upon which he and his fellow-coercionists invite us to enter. I am glad, for the honor of humanity, that it is a Christian minister who makes this atrocious proposition.

When Miss Willard italicized the declaration that "the sanctity of motherhood must be respected to such degree as shall make a wife the unquestioned arbiter of her own destiny," was she thinking of the shameful fact that a wife is the only woman who can be outraged with impunity, and that no wife in the land is free from the danger of such outrage if her husband is not too much of a man to take advantage of the power with which the law has invested him? If she was thinking of this, why did she not say what she meant? And does she think that the wife is the unquestioned arbiter of her own destiny when she cannot legally free herself from her husband if he has not happened to commit some offence which the law recognizes as a valid cause for divorce? How can she be the arbiter of her own destiny when the law and the public opinion that Miss Willard shares deny to her the right to express her love for other than the man who legally holds her as the instrument of his desires? Has it never occurred to the head of the W.C.T.U. that an unmarried woman should also have an unquestioned right to the control of herself? And that among these unmarried women are the ones to whom she, by raising the age of consent to eighteen years, wishes to deny the right of choice, which is the heart and essence of self-government?

The Christian Minister's Special Pleading

Rev. Mr. Lewis represents in this symposium the intolerance of religion as well as the intolerance of morality. He is satisfied that the age-of-consent laws and all other evil things connected with sex and its expression (that is, evil in his eyes if not so in fact) had their origin in the phallic worship of the ancients. I have not here the space at my command to dispose of his misrepresentations of that venerable cult, nor is it necessary to the purpose of this article, but I must let him see in what a fragile glass house he dwells, if, indeed, he does not already realize the fact. Referring to the double standard of sexual morality, Mr. Lewis says:

> Too much cannot be said against this double standard. The Hebrew religion, and Christianity, which is its spiritual efflorescence, condemn such unjust distinction.

Let us see. By the Mosaic law, if a man had outraged a betrothed woman, he was put to death; but, if she was not betrothed, he must marry her and pay her father a fine of fifty shekels. In other words, in the first instance he had offended against the rights of the other man and must die, but in the second instance he must pay her father for his interference with his patriarchal rights, and the victim is compelled to spend her life with the man who has invaded her. Would Mr. Lewis say that there was no "distinction" in this method of dealing with the ravisher, and is he prepared to advocate a law compelling American women to marry their assailants? But this is only the beginning. Both the Jewish and Christian scriptures know nothing of the equality of woman with man; both place her in a position of inferiority and subjection to him. "Thy desire shall be to thy husband, and he shall rule over thee." According to the Levitical law, motherhood was a sin that must be expiated by a birth offering at the advent of each child, and, if the child was a girl, the sinfulness was supposed to be twice as great as when the child was a boy, and she was "unclean" and must continue her "purifying" for twice as long a time. Wholesale kidnapping and rape are commanded by God's priests in the Old Testament, while in the matter of divorce the husband is given a free hand by both the Old and the New, but the wife has no remedy whatever. "When a man hath taken a wife, and marries her, and it come to pass that she find no favor in his eyes, . . . then let him write her out a bill of divorcement, and give it in her hand, and send her out of his house." See also Deut. xxi., 10–14, where the man is given authority to send away in the same unceremonious manner the "wife" he has captured in war. Jesus modified this only to the extent of confining the husband to one cause for dismissing the wife. But in neither dispensation was the wife authorized to put away her husband. Can Mr. Lewis see no "unjust distinction" in this discrimination?

In the Decalogue the wife is put in the same category with cattle and slaves as a chattel. To perceive the "distinction" which the New Testament makes between men and women, read Colossians iii, Ephesians v, 1 Corinthians xiv, 1 Peter ii, 1 Timothy ii, and 1 Corinthians vii. Of course this is a slight digression from the discussion of the age-of-consent problem, but, as one of the champions of increased restriction of woman's initiative has seen fit to try to make capital for his pet religious superstition out of the question at issue, it was deemed expedient to follow him in his wandering and expose the hollowness of his claims.

Some Definitions That Do Not Define

Dr. Janney attempts definition; for instance, he says that "an immoral act becomes criminal when done in violation of a law which defines the crime." It becomes *illegal* under those circumstances, but the law cannot make an act criminal which is not so *per se.* To be criminal it must be an act of invasion without the consent of the invaded. The doctor continues: "Thus unchastity is criminal up to the 'age of consent'; after that, it is immoral, but not criminal." What confusion! It is not the unchastity that is criminal, but the invasion of the person of the child. Neither is "unchastity" necessarily immoral after that time; it depends entirely upon conditions, for we know that by "unchastity" Dr. Janney means intimate relations outside of marriage. In the next paragraph the doctor, advocating the extension of the "age" limit, says: "Several more years will be provided, during which the unchaste act is not merely immoral, but criminal." Here we are again met with the insulting assumption that free association is necessarily unchaste association, while the error of definition in the matter of criminality is repeated. If the legislature can make that a crime which is not so in itself, then all that would be necessary to make the writing and printing of Dr. Janney's article crimes would be the enacted opinion of the majority of the members of the legislatures of Maryland and Massachusetts that said writing and printing were crimes.

Why Women Are Ignorant of Their Peril

Describing the nature and deadly effects of certain diseases, Dr. Janney says: "It is safe to say that a girl of fourteen or sixteen years knows nothing of the existence of such diseases in men. It is something that does not enter into her thoughts." How much more will she know at eighteen, if she is handicapped with a mother and father who have failed to instruct her before she has reached her sixteenth year? A system of miscalled education that leaves girls thus defenceless at that age or an earlier or a later one is condemned by that fact, and the religious and moral instructors who sanction the prohibition of the circulation of physiological and medical works that would, if put into the hands of the young, prevent very much of this lamentable ignorance have no call to denounce those friends of liberty and growth who hold that light, and not law, is the only efficient protector of the young as well as of the more advanced in years.[1] But what will Dr. Janney do to protect the young wife of the diseased man? Does the girl of sixteen or twenty who marries know anything more about these diseases than does the girl who is not married? The chances are that she knows less, if anything, and this will possibly explain somewhat of her haste to enter into a legal relation where she cannot refuse to consort with the man she has chosen, even if she finds him a mass of corruption. Assuredly the free woman is in a better position to protect herself from such dangers than is the wife who cannot make effective defence against outrage save through a costly suit for divorce, and not then if her licensed assailant has committed no offence which the law does not sanction, as it does this. By the way, Miss Gardener had something to say about "licensed lechery," in connection with the age-of-consent laws; but this is the only "licensed" crime of the kind of which I have heard,—this legal subjection of the wife to the husband, in the spirit of the good old Bible injunction, "as the church is subject unto Christ, so let the wives be to their own husbands in *everything*," regardless of the state of his or their health. Dr. Janney should do a good deal of hard thinking before he writes again.

A Protest Against Gratuitous Insults

In conclusion, I wish to protest against the phraseology of most, if not all, of these conventional moralists. Miss Willard, to illustrate, speaks of the girl of ten being "held responsible equally with her strong, relentless, and doughty assailant for the sale of herself in a crime of which two only are capable." But, if two persons are capable of contracting for this relation, it cannot be a crime; you may call it unchaste, or immoral, or vicious, but a crime it cannot be. In the case of the child and the man, however, one of them not being able to contract, it can be neither a crime nor an immoral act on her part, for she does not invade him, and, as she presumably does not understand the nature of the act, it is not possible to conceive of it as an immoral action, so far as she is concerned. She may be severely injured physically and in her nervous system, but that does not imply moral obliquity. There is

[1]Since the above was written, the Woman Suffrage Association has been in convention in Atlanta, and it had a jubilee over the news that the bill raising the age of consent to twenty-one years, introduced by the Hon. Mrs. Holly in the Colorado assembly, had been passed by that body of wiseacres. The suffragists telegraphed their congratulations to Mrs. Holly. Why did the legislature not raise the "age" to sixty years and be done with it? Why stop at trifles, or be influenced in the least by considerations of good sense and justice?

but one criminal in the case, and that is the invader, the man. Why, then, look upon her in any different light from that in which you would view the victim of a highway robber or burglar? She is simply a sufferer from assault, not a participant in immorality or crime.

If Rev. Mr. Lewis and Dr. Janney are to be believed, woman is nothing but an incarnation of chastity; and, when she is smirched or becomes unorthodox in her sex nature and its manifestations, she is forever done for,—she has no other virtues or merits to redeem her or recommend her to our mercy. Man has many good qualities as well as bad ones, and so, even if he has been or is irregular or vicious in his sex associations, he is not lost; he can do much to win the toleration, the praise, or perhaps the enthusiastic laudation of his fellows, including even the women who have not "sinned," or been known to sin, which is the same thing to Mr. Grundy and his wife. Dr. Lewis refers to woman's conventional chastity as her "one badge of womanhood." Think of what that implies! A woman's service in the cause of humanity is nothing; her arduous labors for the support of herself and her parents and children are nothing; her devotion to her country in the hospital is nothing; her literary or artistic productions are nothing; her brains are valueless,—nothing about her is worth a moment's consideration but her conformity to a sexual code which may or may not be better than any other which man has invented. Her supposed faithfulness to this code is the "only badge of her womanhood"! Heavens! what would be left to the world of the achievements of men, if their sexual unorthodoxy had cancelled all their intellectual and ethical services? Where would be our inventions, our letters, our art, our science? Dr. Lewis insults the self-respecting women of the world, and they should sting him into shame and repentance with their unanimous and indignant affirmation that a true woman is something besides a bundle of sex nerves; they should tell him that they value themselves too highly to be thrown into a paroxysm of despair by a mistaken—if it is a mistaken—use of one function of their natures. Mr. Layton W. Crippen, fellow of the Society of Arts and member of the Japan Society, in a lecture at the Hotel Waldorf, New York, said that it was quite impossible to reconcile art and morality in the manner so often attempted. The real solution of the difficulty is in recognizing that goodness consists in more than mere "virtue"; in the words of the Kabbalah, it is composed of virtue and truth and beauty. So of the character of woman; her goodness consists in more than a mere fashionable adherence to a code of sex ethics, and she is not "ruined" by even real imprudence, if she have the strength of character to profit by her mistakes.

Dr. Janney calls sex association outside of the conventional limits "degradation." It may or may not be degradation, just as association within marriage may or may not be degradation. All depends on other factors than the license granted or withheld by the State, or the formula repeated or not repeated by priest or magistrate. The essential verities do not depend for their validity on any such ephemeral things as States and churches. There is no reason why liberty should degrade love, and no reason why a political or religious machine should legitimatize or sanctify prostitution and invasion; but there are many reasons why liberty should make sane and responsible the relations of the sexes, and why legal and ecclesiastical tyranny should do the very opposite. These are not *à priori* assumptions; they are valid generalizations from millions of facts recorded in the history of mankind.

The "Double Standard" of "Honor"

Once more Dr. Janney. He tells us that "no possession is so precious to a woman as her honor"; "it is infinitely more valuable to her than gold, houses, lands, or jewels; more valuable to her than even life itself." "Rather should the age of consent be placed above eighteen years than under it. Let chastity be valued above money." No fault can be found with the last sentence, but what does the doctor think of the women who marry for money and position and homes? But let that pass; he will not fail to see the pertinency of the question, I think. Nothing could well be more insulting to womanhood than this writer's cool assumption that woman's honor contains but one constituent element,—her chastity, as he calls it, which, after all, may be nothing more than her cowardice, or her superstitious reverence for traditions, or her coldness, or her ill-health, or her worldly prudence, or her happy family life leaving nothing at present to be desired. A man's honor is not entirely dissociated from the capacity and wish to tell the truth, from the desire to be honest in his business engagements, from his capacity to respect the rights of others and to be a gentleman in the broadest and best meaning of the word. Why should a woman's "honor" be held by the self-vaunted moralists to be less inclusive than that of her brother? Is it not as honorable to tell the truth, to be financially honest, to respect the rights of one's neighbors, to be womanly in the noblest sense, as it is to conform to a sexual code imposed by others? Why should a young woman be denied her right of choice merely because it is feared that she may possibly make a mistake in her love relations and so lose her "honor," when, in fact, she may be sexually unconventional, and yet be in all respects honorable to a degree? Let us be done with this nauseating cant which ignores every factor but one that contributes to complete womanhood, that one factor being sexual "purity," which is so often counterfeited by mere conventional conformity that the rational thinker places no value on the verbal counters with which is is attempted to give it universal currency.

Give us liberty, and chastity, purity, and morality will take care of themselves, because all will then have an opportunity to be healthfully chaste, pure, and moral instead of traditionally, customarily, or legally conventional—in the gaze of the world.

VII. Irrelevancies

Bertha Marvin

Bertha Marvin was one of the most frequent women contributors to Liberty. *The majority of her articles addressed the subject of women and love, particularly in the context of marriage. The following is a review of Gissing's* The Odd Women, *which Marvin used as a vehicle to express her condemnation of contemporary sexual standards as applied to women.*

I was glad to find George Gissing's face on the fly-leaf of this copy of "The Odd Women." It suits the book. I have read nothing else from his pen and am told that the other books would please me less. His face is sad, as if his life were a gray one. Poverty was a strong element in making it so. I do not know, but have the impression of that kind of hard times as his fate. And I do not know why I should be reminded of Ruskin when I think of him—for there seems no likeness whatever. There may be in a negative way. You can see at once that he lacked utterly what the Germans call "Humor." But Ruskin did have buoyancy, a quite different thing, but a saving grace which may rescue some moments from despair.

There is a satisfying quality in "The Odd Women," not the satisfaction of completeness, but of reality. It is realistic, in so far as the characters are full of imperfections and foibles. It *is* dramatic, because the eternal conflict in the *now* between what has been and what is to be, is shown in full force; but is is not *apparently* dramatic, there being few sharp effects or critical incidents. It is more full of thought than of action; but there is no preaching. I did not know, when I put the book down, just what George Gissing thereby wished to say; but I was filled with a realizing sense that he had drawn people as they were and life as it is in that phase. And no one had acted very well or risen to an occasion. Everyone dismally failed at times, in contrast with what, in our sweet days of dreaming, we expect of people; but each had been all he could be, and that I saw. I did not think that the author had definitely wished to teach anything, but to lay before us a page of life. If one has previously been impressed with the fact that marriage offers special opportunities for tyranny, one notices its exemplification in Monica's fate. Widdowson's tyranny is perfectly consistent. Any tense and coherent nature, tasting only of narrow joys, cramped and stiffened and stunted by the accepted traditions of the past, becomes, inevitably, in such a crisis, tyrannical. The miserable sickness of jealousy and its still more miserable madness is forcefully presented. The final outbreak of his fury brings no sense of artificial suddenness. He had never questioned his right to Monica as a wife. And what this unquestioning acceptance of a law of possession might make of him, if suddenly brought face to face with an imagined "unfaithfulness," was a reckoning with his own temperament and creed which had never been required of him. "He had waited, longed, for marriage, through half a lifetime." He had offered himself as a husband, in perfect good faith. He could promise this young girl a life full of comfort and pleasant gratification of manifold tastes, of absolute security against want or care, in exchange for her hitherto passive existence of denial and deprivation. He meant to be tender and "indulgent." His assumption that her choices, in detail, would be similar to his own; that a life of routine, without social event or social stimulus, without friendships, or enthusiasms, or any stirring or kindling to growth, would suit her just as it suited him, was hardly an unnatural assumption. We, all of us, ignore the fact that, except in the elemental necessities, human beings are more unlike than like. It will ever be natural for us to believe that others have just the same wants as we have—or that, if they have others, these last are unreasonable.

Monica never said to herself: I am marrying for a roof and bread and clothes and for the comfortable assurance of these for all my future. She was unformed and hated her days as they were. Widdowson offered her his love and she enjoyed the sense of being loved. Moreover, she even admired him and, having never felt a fire in her heart toward anyone, man or woman or child, the mild or negative quality of her attraction did not seem to her insufficient or questionable. Nor did her marriage in its reality on the physical plane, offend her. Perhaps the instinct of the race, working through her, took care of that, precluding any temperamental rebellion of her distinctive personality. Her battle was solely against the denial of freedom.

"The girl was docile, and for a time he imagined that there would never be conflict between his will and hers. . . . His devotion to her proved itself in a thousand ways; week after week he grew, if anything, more kind, more tender; yet in his view of their relations he was unconsciously the most complete despot, a monument of male autocracy. Never had it occurred to Widdowson that a wife remains an individual, with rights and obligations independent of her wifely condition. Everything he said presupposed his own supremacy; he took for granted that it was his to direct, hers to be guided. A display of energy, purpose, ambition, on Monica's part, which had no reference to domestic pursuits, would have gravely troubled him; at once he would have set himself to subdue, with all gentleness, impulses so inimical to his idea of the married state. . . . 'Woman's sphere is the home, Monica. Unfortunately, girls are often obliged to go out and earn their living, but this is unnatural, a necessity which advanced civilization will altogether abolish. You shall read John Ruskin; every word he says about women is good and precious. If a woman can neither have a home of her own, nor find occupation in anyone else's, she is deeply to be pitied; her life is bound to be unhappy. I sincerely believe that an educated woman had better become a domestic servant than try to imitate the life of a man.' "

I have been thinking that there are people who would say that George Gissing took life quite too seriously. When too much tragedy enters any life, the remark has a cruel sound. I do not see how the sadness and heaviness of Monica's fate or of Rhoda Nunn's could have been averted. One is glad to have Monica die, since one does not see how she could ever achieve a self-sustaining life. And Rhoda Nunn could never have been instrumental in the work of infusing any other spirit into her lover than a delight in conquest. Rhoda *could* take up life again, grown immeasurably through her disappointment and disillusion. But taking up life again is not happiness at first hand,—a better, perhaps; one may even feel sure that it is better,—but a part of taking life seriously.

I was often reminded, by the sharpness of contrast, of Ernst von Wolzogen's "Das dritte Geschlecht." There is a certain community of interest between "the third sex" and "the odd women." In "Das dritte Geschlecht" there is a free union which melts into a marriage of convenience, and a new birth of the somewhat frivolous (?) Lilli von Robiceck who charms all men unduly. All these problems are touched with a lighter hand, but never in a weak way. I think that Ernst von Wolzogen always finds room and scope for the poetry of life, and, with all his deftness of touch, never admits any phase of existence quite apart from it.

Monica did not drift into a marriage for refuge and support directly from her apprenticeship in the drapery establishment of Messrs. Scotcher & Co. Its thirteen and a half hours' work every week day and sixteen on Saturday, and its bread and cheese Sunday diet might easily be impelling forces. In her case something intervened; but it could not reach her at that phase in her evolution.

"Monica could not become quite at ease. This energetic woman had little attraction for her. She saw the characteristics which made Virginia enthusiastic, but feared rather than admired them. To put herself in Miss Nunn's hands might possibly result in a worse form of bondage than she suffered at the shop; she would never be able to please such a person, and failure, she imagined, would result in more or less contemptuous dismissal."

Until the last, I did not feel at all drawn to Rhoda Nunn. While her enthusiasm appealed to me, her hotheadedness repelled me as all people repel me who, in their haste and heat, walk over good and valuable human kind, with a denial of any worth or beauty that is not in line with their high-handed ambitions. That is, Rhoda Nunn was an enthusiast, and admirable as such; but not lovable. Perhaps ambitious is almost an unkind word to apply to her; but her ambitions were not aspirations. And there were negative causes for her zeal over new work for women; because "immorality" in sex was intolerable to her and the thought of sex almost unpleasant. That, taken by itself, is an unfair—because inadequate—characterization of her. She did have, also, a recognition that there was a world's work and that she wanted to help in it. But she had lost something out of her conception of the beauty of life and she denied this loss. She could have an enthusiasm about the world's work, but there was a strain of unheartedness about her. Mary Barfoot had lost nothing, for, although she was restricted in her sympathies and did not include in her work "the lower classes," she never *deliberately* excluded from her compassion, never hardened her heart, never shut away any part of herself as unworthy. And her acknowledged, definitized, self-approved limitation of sympathies jarred upon me less than Rhoda Nunn's shortcomings. I cannot understand why. Perhaps it was because her exclusions had no moral element that I could admire her in spite of them.

As regards her special work, she aimed to "draw from the over-stocked profession of teaching as many capable young women as she could lay hands on, and to fit them for certain of the pursuits nowadays thrown open to their sex. She held the conviction that, whatever man could do, woman could do equally well—those tasks only excepted which demand great physical strength."

Into this work she invites Monica, but when Rhoda Nunn lays the plan before her, there is hesitation.

"Then of a sudden, as if she had divined these thoughts, Rhoda assumed an air of gaiety, of frank kindness.

" 'So it is your birthday?—I no longer keep count of mine, and couldn't tell you without a calculation what I am exactly. It doesn't matter, you see. Thirty-one or fifty-one is much the same for a woman who has made up her mind to live alone and work steadily for a definite object. But you are still a young girl, Monica. My best wishes!'

"Monica emboldened herself to ask what the object was for which her friend worked.

" 'How shall I put it?' replied the other, smiling. 'To make women hard-hearted.'

" 'Hard-hearted?—I think I understand.'

" 'Do you?'

" 'You mean that you like to see them live unmarried.'

"Rhoda laughed merrily.

" 'You say that almost with resentment.'

" 'No—indeed—I didn't intend it.'

"Monica reddened a little.

" 'Nothing more natural, if you had done. At your age, I should have resented it.'

" 'But'—the girl hesitated—'don't you approve of anyone marrying?'

" 'Oh, I'm not so severe!—But do you know that there are half a million more women than men in this happy country of ours?'

" 'Half a million!' echoed Monica.

"Her naïve alarm again excited Rhoda to laughter.

" 'Something like that, they say. So many *odd* women—no making a pair with them. The pessimists call them useless, lost, futile lives. I, naturally,—being one of them myself,—take another view. I look upon them as a great reserve. When one woman vanishes in matrimony, the reserve offers a substitute for the world's work. True, they are not all trained yet—far from it, I want to help in that—to train the reserve.'

" 'But married women are not idle,' protested Monica earnestly.

" 'Not all of them. Some cook and rock cradles.' "

Miss Barfoot's work had its disappointments. Among others, a girl whom she had released from much hardship, suddenly disappeared and was discovered living with a married man. She resisted all efforts to bring her back, and when Monica was brought to the notice of these friends, Bella Royston had been lost sight of for a year. Then came a letter from her. Miss Barfoot showed it to her co-worker.

"Rhoda took the sheet and quickly ran through its contents. Her face hardened, and she threw down the letter with a smile of contempt.

" 'What do you advise?' asked the elder woman, closely observing her.

" 'An answer in two lines—with a cheque enclosed, if you see fit.'

" 'Does that really meet the case?'

" 'More than meets it, I should say.'

"Miss Barfoot pondered.

" 'I am doubtful. That is a letter of despair, and I can't close my ears to it.'

" 'You had an affection for the girl. Help her, by all means, if you feel compelled to. But you would hardly dream of taking her back again?'

" 'That's the point. Why shouldn't I?'

" 'For one thing,' replied Rhoda, looking coldly down upon her friend, 'you will never do any good with her. For another, she isn't a suitable companion for the girls she would meet here.'

" 'I can't be sure of either objection. She acted with deplorable rashness, with infatuation, but I never discovered any sign of evil in her. Did you?'

" 'Evil? Well, what does the word mean? I am not a puritan, and I don't judge her as the ordinary woman would. But I think she has put herself altogether beyond our sympathy. She was twenty-two years old,—no child,—and she acted with her eyes open. No deceit was practised with her. She knew the man had a wife, and she was base enough to accept a share of his—attentions. Do you advocate polygamy? That is an intelligible position, I admit. It is one way of meeting the social difficulty. But not mine.'

" 'My dear Rhoda, don't enrage yourself.'

" 'I will try not to.'

" 'But I can't see the temptation to do so. Come and sit down, and talk quietly.—No, I have no fondness for polygamy. I find it very hard to understand how she could act as she did. But a mistake, however wretched, mustn't condemn a woman for life. That's the way of the world, and decidedly it mustn't be ours.'

" 'On this point, I practically agree with the world.'

" 'I see you do, and it astonishes me. You are going through curious changes, in several respects. A year ago you didn't speak of her like this.'

" 'Partly because I didn't know you well enough to speak my mind. Partly—yes, I have changed a good deal, no doubt. But I should never have proposed to take her by the hand and let bygones be bygones. That is an amiable impulse, but anti-social.'

" 'A favorite word on your lips just now, Rhoda. Why is it anti-social?'

" 'Because one of the supreme social needs of our day is the education of women in self-respect and self-restraint. There are plenty of people—

men chiefly, but a few women also of a certain temperament—who cry for a reckless individualism in such matters. They would tell you that she behaved laudably, that she was *living out herself*—and things of that kind. But I didn't think you shared such views.'

" 'I don't, altogether.—"The education of women in self-respect." Very well. Here is a poor woman whose self-respect has given way under grievous temptation. Circumstances have taught her that she made a wild mistake. The man gives her up, and bids her live as she can; she is reduced to beggary. Now, in that position a girl is tempted to sink still further. The letter of two lines and an enclosed cheque would as likely as not plunge her into depths from which she could never be rescued. It would assure her that there was no hope. On the other hand, we have it in our power to attempt that very education of which you speak. She has brains and doesn't belong to the vulgar. It seems to me that you are moved by illogical impulses—and certainly anything but kind ones.'

"Rhoda only grew more stubborn.

" 'You say she yielded to a grievous temptation. What temptation? will it bear putting into words?'

" 'Oh, yes, I think it will,' answered Miss Barfoot, with her gentlest smile. 'She fell in love with the man.'

" 'Fell in love!' Concentration of scorn was in this echo. 'Oh, for what isn't that phrase responsible!'

" 'Rhoda, let me ask you a question on which I have never ventured. Do you know what it is to be in love?'

"Miss Nunn's strong features were moved as if by a suppressed laugh; the color of her cheeks grew very slightly warm.

" 'I am a normal human being,' she answered, with an impatient gesture. 'I understand perfectly well what the phrase signifies.'

" 'That is no answer, my dear. Have you ever been in love with any man?'

" 'Yes, when I was fifteen.'

" 'And not since,' rejoined the other, shaking her head and smiling. 'No, not since?'

" 'Thank heaven, no!'

" 'Then you are not very well able to judge this case. I, on the other hand, can judge it with the very largest understanding.—Don't smile so witheringly, Rhoda.—I shall neglect your advice for once.' "

Some extracts from one of her monthly addresses to her girls will give the spirit and tenor of Miss Barfoot's work and plans. The subject announced was "Woman as an Invader." "They point to half-a-dozen occupations which are deemed strictly suitable for women. Why don't we confine ourselves to this ground? Why don't I encourage girls to become governesses, hospital nurses, and so on? . . . To put the truth in a few words, I am not chiefly anxious that you should *earn money*, but that women in general shall become *rational and responsible human beings*. Follow me carefully. A governess, a nurse, may be the most admirable of women. I will dissuade no one from following those careers who is distinctly fitted for them. But these are only a few out of the vast number of girls who must, if they are not to be despicable persons, somehow find serious work. Because I myself have had an education in clerkship, and have most capacity for such employment, I look about for girls of like mind, and do my best to prepare them for work in offices. And (here I must become emphatic once more) I am *glad* to have entered on this course. I am *glad* that I can show girls the way to a career which my opponents call unwomanly. . . . A womanly occupation means, practically, an occupation that a man disdains. And here is the root of the matter. I repeat that I am not first of all anxious to keep you supplied with daily bread. I am a troublesome, aggressive, revolutionary person. I want to do away with that common confusion of the words womanly and womanish, and I see very clearly that this can only be effected by an armed movement, an invasion by women of the spheres which men have always forbidden us to enter. . . . We live in a time of warfare, of revolt. If woman is no longer to be womanish, but a human being of powers and responsibilities, she must become militant, defiant. She must push her claims to the extremity.

"An excellent governess, a perfect hospital nurse, do work which is invaluable; but for our cause of emancipation they are no good; nay, they are harmful. Men point to them, and say: Imitate these, keep to your proper world. Our proper world is the world of intelligence, of honest effort, or moral strength. The old types of womanly perfection are no longer helpful to us. . . . They are no longer educational. We have to ask ourselves: What course of training will wake women up, make them conscious of their souls, startle them into healthy activity? It must be something new, something free from the reproach of womanliness. I don't care whether we crowd out the men or not. I don't care *what* results, if only women are made strong and self-reliant and nobly independent. The world must look to its concerns. Most likely we shall have a revolution in the social order greater than any that yet seems possible. Let it come, and let *us* help its coming. When I think of the contemptible wretchedness of women enslaved by custom, by their weakness, by their desires, I am ready to cry: Let the world perish in tumult rather than things go on in this way!

"Our abusive correspondent shall do as best he can. He suffers for the folly of men in all ages. We can't help it. It is very far from our wish to cause hardship to anyone, but we ourselves are escaping from a hardship that has become intolerable. We are educating ourselves. . . . Because we have to set an example to the sleepy of our sex, we must carry on an active warfare, must be invaders. Whether woman is the equal of man, I neither know nor care. We are not his equal in size, in weight, in muscle, and, for all I can say, we may have less power of brain. That has nothing to do with it. Enough for us to know that our natural growth has been stunted. The mass of women have always been paltry creatures, and their paltriness has proved a curse to men. So, if you like to put it in this way, we are working for the advantage of men as well as for our own. Let the responsibility for disorder rest on those who have made us despise our old selves."

VIII. Prostitution

"Danielle"

A contemporary poster reads: "Prostitution is a combination of sex and free enterprise. Which are you against?"

Although prostitution would seem to be a clear-cut issue within feminism—if it is a woman's body, it is her right to sell it—the issue has been obscured by cultural prejudices against sex and political prejudices against capitalism. In the decades surrounding the turn of the century, mainstream feminists generally supported purity crusades in which the purpose of the law was not to protect rights, but to enforce virtue. These feminists wished to scourge society of such evils as alcohol and prostitution. More radical feminists, who were less concerned with respectability, demonstrated more sympathy for the prostitute but no tolerance for prostitution as a profession. Prostitution, they argued, was an evil created by the capitalist system which left women no economic alternative. This was asserted even when other alternatives were obviously available to the prostitute. These biases persist within feminism and it is rare to see a defense of prostitution which simply states it is a woman's right.

The following article was originally issued as a discussion paper by the Association of Libertarian Feminists. The author is a former prostitute who writes under the pseudonym of "Danielle."

A woman has the right to control her own life and body. Few feminists today would dispute that statement. But what about prostitution? Some feminists still argue that prostitution has no place in a non-sexist society, since "prostitutes are exploited by men."

And some prostitutes *are* exploited by men: women who have been coerced to become prostitutes by husbands or pimps, or who fear physical or other retribution should they try to leave "the life."

But what about those women who become prostitutes voluntarily? Many different types of women with different backgrounds go into the profession. They often do not wish to become "rehabilitated" into secretaries or clerk-typists for $150 or less a week. They may have been workers in these fields before they turned to prostitution. Some women work at both professions—moonlighting as prostitutes. Some prostitutes have college educations that they've been unable or unwilling to use on the job market.

Their prime motivation for choosing a life of prostitution is usually money and material goods. Prostitutes are capitalists; they operate within a free-market (albeit black-market) situation. Many operate as individual entrepreneurs, with the freedom to set their own hours, to come and go as they please, and to take time off when they choose. This freedom means taking an economic risk, but it also gives the prostitute an incentive to earn as much as she likes. If she doesn't work, she earns no money; if she works hard, she earns a great deal.

Women who choose such a life voluntarily have turned their backs on the security of a conventional life and a conventional job. They do *not* feel exploited. In the words of one prostitute: "The customer comes and he pays me $50 for an hour. What have I given up? An hour of my time, the use of my body. What has he given up? Fifty dollars! Who is exploiting whom?"

Even feminists who support a woman's right to be a prostitute often feel that prostitution has nothing to do with the majority of women. True, only a small number of women are legally defined as prostitutes. But who among us has never considered marrying for money? Mama says that it's just as easy to fall in love with a rich man as a poor one. (At least, that's what my mother said.) Why is it all right to marry for money, for security, for status—and legally punishable to be a prostitute?

Furthermore, in both cases a woman is subject to laws that are set up to protect male domination of women. Laws against "loitering" and "common nightwalking" are not just anti-prostitute, they are anti-woman as well, and they are used by the police to harass solitary women who may or may not be prostitutes. The wife of a minister in Miami was arrested, under one of these laws, when she was on the way to the grocery store. A social worker in New York was held in jail overnight, even though she was able to show that she worked for a prestigious church.

The press calls a great deal of attention to the way that pimps abuse prostitutes. But married women also have little or no legal protection against their protectors. Most states still hold that it is legally impossible for a husband to rape his wife, and it is well known that battered wives often appeal in vain for help to the police and the courts. Laws concerning prostitutes are part of the general legal position of all women: they are at the same time especially protected and especially punished.

Legally entrenched male domination victimizes the prostitute even more than the married woman. The law does not protect her against crimes committed against her. Rather, she needs protection against the law, and her only real protection is anonymity. She loses this form of protection if she brings any kind of case involving coercion to court—rape, robbery, physical abuse, or anything else.

It is impossible for her to prosecute a rapist. A woman who is a known prostitute will be laughed out of the police station. If she is lucky enough to get the case to come to court, people will appear out of the woodwork to testify about her means of earning a living. She will be considered as inviting rape because of her profession.

A prostitute has no legal recourse if she is robbed on the job. One cannot report, as stolen, money that was not supposed to be legally yours in the first place.

Women who have been forced in some way to enter, stay in, or leave prostitution are victims, not only of the coercers, but also of the legal system. Prostitutes who want to "go straight" but who fear reprisals can often get a case in court and win it—if they are willing to turn in their coercer and then relocate in an attempt to escape reprisals. Prostitutes who wish to stay in the business but who wish to get rid of a pimp are really damned if they do, damned if they don't. Sometimes the only way to get rid of a pimp is to turn him in to the police—but then the prostitute loses her anonymity.

An argument in favor of keeping prostitution illegal is that it is always associated with a criminal subculture. And prostitution at present does have many kinds of crime flourishing alongside it. But, if prostitution were not illegal, real crime (involving force or fraud) would diminish. Any time a commodity that people want is made illegal, there's going to be real crime associated with it, preying on the illicit status of whatever's involved. One has only to look at the "Noble Experiment" of Prohibition in this country to recognize this point.

What solution can libertarian feminists endorse? Arguments have been made for legalization of prostitution, which is being tried in some counties in Nevada. Legalization sets legal conditions under which prostitution can be practiced: laws ranging from licensing to requiring regular health checks for VD to creating zones where prostitution is legal. Proponents argue that some of the laws would be to protect women. Others argue that prostitution, if it is to be treated like any other business, must have restrictions, as does any other business operating today.

The last thing that women need is more laws that ostensibly protect them. Laws making licensing mandatory mean that the government is to decide who can be a prostitute and who can't, and unlicensed prostitutes would still be illegal. And government standards are often arbitrary. One of the laws in Nevada that "protects" women is a regulation that permits only women to own brothels. The brothels there are still really owned by men. Men simply use their wives or girlfriends as fronts. And what of it? It's a useless law.

Legalization proponents tell us that prostitutes must go for regular health checks to prevent the spread of VD. First of all, very few prostitutes don't already do this on their own. To have a disease is bad business. Secondly, over 90% of the VD in this country is spread by non-prostitutes between the ages of 16 and 25. Therefore, if health care is to be promoted at the expense of rights, the logical step after licensing prostitutes and requiring health checkups for them is to force everyone to go for regular checkups. Does the government really have the right to tell you to go to the doctor?

As to the argument that prostitution should be regulated like any other business, the libertarian position is, of course, that *no* business should be regulated by the government.

The situation in Nevada is a sad one. Not only are all prostitutes required to work in brothels (no independent operators allowed), but they are also subject to harassing laws such as the one prohibiting a licensed prostitute from being on the street after 9 p.m., even if she's only going to the drugstore for cosmetics. And if a woman decides to work outside the system, she can still be arrested for prostitution.

Legalization just exchanges the existing set of laws for another, and is neither a feminist nor a libertarian solution. The only real solution to these problems is decriminalization—wiping all existing laws off the books. The prostitute then would be able to practice her profession while being able to bring those who perpetrate force or fraud against her to court without fear of legal reprisals. Thieves who masquerade as prostitutes would also be brought to light and prosecuted. The repeal of laws against women walking the streets at night unescorted would be beneficial to all women.

The repeal of laws against prostitution would help all people who are trying to be free to pursue their own, uncoercive life-styles.

Suggested Readings

Hamowy, Ronald. "Medicine and the Crimination of Sin: 'Self-Abuse' in 19th Century Medicine." *Journal of Libertarian Studies.* Summer, 1977.

Harman, Moses. *Love in Freedom.* Chicago: Light Bearer Library, 1900.

Sachs, Emanie S. *The Terrible Siren: Victoria Woodhull, 1838–1927.* New York: Harper, 1928.

Sears, Hal D. *The Sex Radicals: Free Love in High Victorian America.* Lawrence, Kans.: Regents Press, 1977.

Stern, Madeleine B., ed. *The Victoria Woodhull Reader.* Weston, Mass.: M&S Press, 1974.

Walkowitz, Judith R. *Prostitution and Victorian Society.* Cambridge: Cambridge University Press, 1980.

WOMEN AND MARRIAGE

IX. Marriage Contract

Lucy Stone and Henry Blackwell

Lucy Stone (1818–1893) firmly opposed the loss of legal status for women inherent in 19th-century marriages. Upon marriage, women frequently lost their rights to property, contracts, wages, protection by the law from wife-beating, and parental jurisdiction. Although she resisted marriage with Henry Blackwell, Stone finally agreed to the ceremony under two significant conditions: the marriage included a contract which repudiated the degrading marital laws and refused to abide by them. In case of dispute, both parties agreed to enter arbitration rather than appeal to the law. Moreover, Lucy Stone maintained her maiden name and for generations thereafter women who did not substitute their husbands' surnames for their own were known as "Lucy Stoners."

While acknowledging our mutual affection by publicly assuming the relationship of husband and wife, yet in justice to ourselves and a great principle, we deem it a duty to declare that this act on our part implies no sanction of, nor promise of voluntary obedience to such of the present laws of marriage, as refuse to recognize the wife as an independent, rational being, while they confer upon the husband an injurious and unnatural superiority, investing him with legal powers which no honorable man would exercise, and which no man should possess. We protest especially against the laws which give to the husband:

1. The custody of the wife's person.
2. The exclusive control and guardianship of their children.
3. The sole ownership of her personal, and use of her real estate, unless previously settled upon her, or placed in the hands of trustees, as in the case of minors, lunatics, and idiots.
4. The absolute right to the product of her industry.
5. Also against laws which give to the widower so much larger and more permanent an interest in the property of his deceased wife, than they give to the widow in that of the deceased husband.
6. Finally, against the whole system by which "the legal existence of the wife is suspended during marriage," so that in most States, she neither has a legal part in the choice of her residence, nor can she make a will, nor sue or be sued in her own name, nor inherit property.

We believe that personal independence and equal human rights can never be forfeited, except for crime; that marriage should be an equal and permanent partnership, and so recognized by law; that until it is so recognized, married partners should provide against the radical injustice of present laws, by every means in their power.

We believe that where domestic difficulties arise, no appeal should be made to legal tribunals under existing laws, but that all difficulties should be submitted to the equitable adjustment of arbitrators mutually chosen.

Thus reverencing law, we enter our protest against rules and customs which are unworthy of the name, since they violate justice, the essence of law.

X. Legal Disabilities of Women

Sarah Grimké

Sarah Grimké (1792–1873) was the older sister of Angelina Grimké and a radical in her own right. As one of Theodore Weld's "70"—an anti-slavery group which lectured widely and often at personal peril—Sarah Grimké broke many of the social conventions governing women. Her distinctive approach to women's rights was legal theory. The following essay (in the form of a letter to the Boston Female Anti-Slavery Society), undoubtedly her most famous, compares the legal status of woman to that of the slave. This comparison was offensive to many of her fellow abolitionists who wished to separate the issues of women's rights and slavery. Even the enlightened Theodore Weld pleaded with her to abandon the woman's cause until the slave was free. Again and again, Sarah and Angelina Grimké defended their crusade. "I know the opposition to our views arises in part from the fact that women are habitually regarded as inferior beings," Sarah wrote to Weld, "but chiefly I believe from a desire to keep them in unholy subjection to man, and one way of doing this is to deprive us of the means of becoming their equals by forbidding us the privileges of education." Sarah Grimké persisted in her attempt to educate women as to their own status through her lectures, letters, and pamphlets.

There are few things which present greater obstacles to the improvement and elevation of woman to her appropriate sphere of usefulness and duty, than the laws which have been enacted to destroy her independence, and crush her individuality; laws which, although they are framed for her government, she has had no voice in establishing, and which rob her of some of her *essential rights.* Woman has no political existence. With the single exception of presenting a petition to the legislative body, she is a cipher in the nation; or, if not actually so in representation governments, she is only counted, like the slaves of the South, to swell the number of law-makers who form decrees for her government, with little reference to her benefit, except so far as her good may promote their own. I am not sufficiently acquainted with the laws respecting women on the continent of Europe, to say anything about them. But Prof. Follen, in his essay on 'The Cause of Freedom in our Country,' says, 'Woman, though fully possessed of that rational and moral nature which is the foundation of all rights, enjoys amongst us fewer legal rights than under the civil law of continental Europe.' I shall confine myself to the laws of our country. These laws bear with peculiar rigor on married women. Blackstone, in the chapter entitled 'Of husband and wife,' says:—

> 'By marriage, the husband and wife are one person in law; that is, *the very being, or legal existence of the woman* is suspended during the marriage, or at least is incorporated and consolidated into that of the husband under whose wing, protection and cover she performs everything.' 'For this reason, a man cannot grant anything to his wife, or enter into covenant with her; for the grant would be to suppose her separate existence, and to covenant with her would be to covenant with himself; and therefore it is also generally true, that all compacts made between husband and wife, when single, are voided by the intermarriage. A woman indeed may be attorney for her husband, but that implies no separation from, but is rather a representation of, her love.'

Here now, the very being of a woman, like that of a slave, is absorbed in her master. All contracts made with her, like those made with slaves by their owners, are a mere nullity. Our kind defenders have legislated away almost all our legal rights, and in the true spirit of such injustice and oppression, have kept us in ignorance of those very laws by which we are governed. They have persuaded us, that we have no right to investigate the laws, and that, if we did, we could not comprehend them; they alone are capable of understanding the mysteries of Blackstone, &c. But they are not backward to make us feel the practical operation of their power over our actions.

> 'The husband is bound to provide his wife with necessaries by law, as much as himself; and if she contracts debts for them, he is obliged to pay for them; but for anything besides necessaries, he is not chargeable.'

Yet a man may spend the property he has acquired by marriage at the ale-house, the gambling table, or in any other way that he pleases. Many instances of this kind have come to my knowledge; and women, who have brought their husbands handsome fortunes, have been left, in consequence of the wasteful and dissolute habits of their husbands, in straitened circumstances, and compelled to toil for the support of their families.

> 'If the wife be indebted before marriage, the husband is bound afterwards to pay the debt; for he has adopted her and her circumstances together.'

The wife's property is, I believe, equally liable for her husband's debts contracted before marriage.

> 'If the wife be injured in her person or property, she can bring no action for redress without her husband's concurrence, and his name as well as her own: neither can she be sued, without making her husband a defendant.'

This law that 'a wife can bring no action,' &c., is similar to the law respecting slaves. 'A slave cannot bring a suit against his master, or any other person, for an injury—his master, must bring it.' So if any damages are recovered for an injury committed on a wife, the husband pockets it; in the case of the slave, the master does the same.

> 'In criminal prosecutions, the wife may be indicted and punished separately, unless there be evidence of coercion from the fact that the offence was committed in the presence, or by the command of her husband. A wife is excused from punishment for theft committed in the presence, or by the command of her husband.'

It would be difficult to frame a law better calculated to destroy the responsibility of woman as a moral being, or a free agent. Her husband is supposed to possess unlimited control over her; and if she can offer the flimsy excuse that he bade her steal, she may break the eighth commandment with impunity, as far as human laws are concerned.

> 'Our law, in general, considers man and wife as one person; yet there are some instances in which she is separately considered, as inferior to him and acting by his compulsion. Therefore, all deeds executed, and acts done by her during her coverture (i.e. marriage,) are void, except it be a fine, or like matter of record, in which case she must be solely and secretly examined, to learn if her act be voluntary.'

Such a law speaks volumes of the abuse of that power which men have vested in their own hands. Still the private examination of a wife, to know whether she accedes to the disposition of property made by her husband is, in most cases, a mere form; a wife dares not do what will be disagreeable to one who is, in his own estimation, her superior, and who makes her feel, in the privacy of domestic life, that she has thwarted him. With respect to the nullity of deeds or acts done by a wife, I will mention one circumstance. A respectable woman borrowed of a female friend a sum of money to relieve her son from some distressing pecuniary embarrassment. Her husband was from home, and she assured the lender, that as soon as he returned, he would gratefully discharge the debt. She gave her note, and the lender, entirely ignorant of the law that a man is not obliged to discharge such a debt, actually borrowed the money, and lent it to the distressed and weeping mother.

The father returned home, refused to pay the debt, and the person who had loaned the money was obliged to pay both principal and interest to the friend who lent it to her. Women should certainly know the laws by which they are governed, and from which they frequently suffer; yet they are kept in ignorance, nearly as profound, of their legal rights, and of the legislative enactments which are to regulate their actions, as slaves.

> 'The husband, by the old law, might give his wife moderate correction, as he is to answer for her misbehavior. The law thought it reasonable to entrust him with this power of restraining her by domestic chastisement. The courts of law will still permit a husband to restrain a wife of her liberty, in case of any gross misbehavior.'

What a mortifying proof this law affords, of the estimation in which woman is held! She is placed completely in the hands of a being subject like herself to the outbursts of passion, and therefore unworthy to be trusted with power. Perhaps I may be told respecting this law, that it is a dead letter, as I am sometimes told about the slave laws; but this is not true in either case. The slaveholder does kill his slave by moderate correction, as the law allows; and many a husband, among the poor, exercises the right given him by the law, of degrading woman by personal chastisement. And among the higher ranks, if actual imprisonment is not resorted to, women are not unfrequently restrained of the liberty of going to places of worship by irreligious husbands, and of doing many other things about which, as moral and responsible beings, *they* should be the *sole* judges. Such laws remind me of the reply of some little girls at a children's meeting held recently at Ipswich. The lecturer told them that God had created four orders of beings with which he had made us acquainted through the Bible. The first was angels, the second was man, the third beasts; and now, children, what is the fourth? After a pause, several girls replied, 'WOMEN.'

> 'A woman's personal property by marriage becomes absolutely her husband's, which, at his death, he may leave entirely away from her.'

And further, all the avails of her labor are absolutely in the power of her husband. All that she acquires by her industry is his; so that she cannot, with her own honest earnings, become the legal purchaser of any property. If she expends her money for articles of furniture, to contribute to the comfort of her family, they are liable to be seized for her husband's debts: and I know an instance of a woman, who by labor and economy had scraped together a little maintenance for herself and a do-little husband, who was left, at his death, by virtue of his last will and testament, to be supported by charity. I knew another woman, who by great industry had acquired a little money which she deposited in a bank for safe keeping. She had saved this pittance whilst able to work, in hopes that when age or sickness disqualified her for exertion, she might have something to render life comfortable, without being a burden to her friends. Her husband, a worthless, idle man, discovered this hid treasure, drew her little stock from the bank, and expended it all in extravagance and vicious indulgence. I know of another woman, who married without the least idea that she was surrendering her rights to all her personal property. Accordingly, she went to the bank as usual to draw her dividends, and the person who paid her the money, and to whom she was personally known as an owner of shares in that bank, remarking the change in her signature, withdrew the money, informing her that if she were married, she had no longer a right to draw her dividends without an order from her husband. It appeared that she intended having a little fund for private use, and had not even told her husband that she owned this stock, and she was not a little chagrined, when she found that it was not at her disposal. I think she was wrong to conceal the circumstance. The relation of husband and wife is too near and sacred to admit of secrecy about money matters, unless positive necessity demands it; and I can see no excuse for any woman entering into a marriage engagement with a design to keep her husband ignorant that she was possessed of property. If she was unwilling to give up her property to his disposal, she had infinitely better have remained single.

The laws above cited are not very unlike the slave laws of Louisiana.

> 'All that a slave possesses belongs to his master; he possesses nothing of his own, except what his master chooses he should possess.'
>
> 'By the marriage, the husband is absolutely master of the profits of the wife's lands during the coverture, and if he has had a living child, and survives the wife, he retains the whole of those lands, if they are estates of inheritance, during his life; but the wife is entitled only to one third if she survives, out of the husband's estates of inheritance. But this she has, whether she has had a child or not.' 'With regard to the property of women, there is taxation without representation; for they pay taxes without having the liberty of voting for representatives.'

And this taxation, without representation, be it remembered, was the cause of our Revolutionary war, a grievance so heavy, that it was thought necessary to purchase exemption from it at an immense expense of blood and treasure, yet the daughters of New England, as well as of all the other States of this free Republic, are suffering a similar injustice—but for one, I had rather we should suffer any injustice or oppression, than that my sex should have any voice in the political affairs of the nation.

The laws I have quoted, are, I believe, the laws of Massachusetts, and, with few exceptions, of all the States in this Union. 'In Louisiana and Missouri, and possibly, in some other southern States, a woman not only has half her husband's property by right at his death, but may always be considered as possessed of half his gains during his life; having at all times power to bequeath that amount.' That the laws which have generally been adopted in the United States, for the government of women, have been framed almost entirely for the exclusive benefit of men, and with a design to oppress women, by depriving them of all control over their property, is too manifest to be denied. Some liberal and enlightened men, I know, regret the existence of these laws; and I quote with pleasure an extract from Harriet Martineau's Society in America, as a proof of the assertion. 'A liberal minded lawyer of Boston, told me that his advice to testators always is to leave the largest possible amount to the widow, subject to the condition of her leaving it to the children; but that it is with shame that he reflects that any woman should owe that to his professional advice, which the law should have secured to her as a right.' I have known a few instances where men have left their whole property to their wives, when they have died, leaving only minor children; but I have known more instances of 'the friend and helper of many years, being portioned off like a salaried domestic,' instead of having a comfortable independence secured to her, while the children were amply provided for.

As these abuses do exist, and women suffer intensely from them, our brethren are called upon in this enlightened age, by every sentiment of honor, religion and justice, to repeal these unjust and unequal laws, and restore to woman those rights which they have wrested from her. Such laws approximate too nearly to the laws enacted by slaveholders for the government of their slaves, and must tend to debase and depress the mind of that being, whom God created as a help meet for man, or 'helper like unto himself,' and designed to be his equal and his companion. Until such laws are annulled, woman never can occupy that exalted station for which she was intended by her Maker. And just in proportion as they are practically disregarded, which is the case to some extent, just so far is woman assuming that independence and nobility of character which she ought to exhibit.

The various laws which I have transcribed, leave women very little more liberty, or power, in some respects, than the slave. 'A slave,' says the civil code of Louisiana, 'is one who is in the power of a master, to whom he belongs. He can possess nothing, nor acquire anything, but what must belong to his master.' I do not wish by any means to intimate that the condition of free women can be compared to that of slaves in suffering, or in degradation; still, I believe the laws which deprive married women of their rights and privileges, have a tendency to lessen them in their own estimation as moral and responsible beings, and that their being made by civil law inferior to their husbands, has a debasing and mischievous effect upon them, teaching them practically the fatal lesson to look unto man for protection and indulgence.

Ecclesiastical bodies, I believe, without exception, follow the example of legislative assemblies, in excluding woman from any participation in forming the discipline by which she is governed. The men frame the laws, and, with few exceptions, claim to execute them on both sexes. In ecclesiastical, as well as civil courts, woman is tried and condemned, not by a jury of her peers, but by beings, who regard themselves as her superiors in the scale of creation. Although looked upon as an inferior, when considered as an intellectual being, woman is punished with the same severity as man, when she is guilty of moral offences. Her condition resembles, in some measure, that of the slave, who, while he is denied the advantages of his more enlightened master, is treated with even greater rigor of the law. Hoping that in the various reformations of the day, women may be relieved from some of their legal disabilities, I remain,

Thine in the bonds of womanhood,

Sarah M. Grimké

XI. Cupid's Yokes

Ezra H. Heywood

Cupid's Yokes *is surely the most controversial pamphlet issued from the individualist-feminist movement. Its author, Ezra Heywood, was a champion of unpopular causes. As an abolitionist, he was one of the few who opposed the Civil War as a massive violation of life and liberty. As a labor activist, he insisted on linking the labor cause with free love, thus alienating the young Benjamin Tucker who withdrew from Heywood's* The Word *(1872–1893). Gradually* The Word *focused more and more on free-love issues such as birth control and the abolition of legal marriage. Even as a free-love advocate, Heywood pushed his ideas to the limit by openly flouting the Comstock laws which defined birth control information as obscenity and prohibited it from being distributed through the mail.* Cupid's Yokes *advocated birth control and resulted in Heywood's arrest. This was merely one of a series of encounters between Heywood and Comstock. The spirit of rebellion which characterized Heywood's insistence upon sexual freedom can be symbolized by the contraceptive device he advertised in* The Word *under the label "The Comstock Syringe." Predictably, he was arrested for this advertisement.*

The following is an edited version of Cupid's Yokes *representing the first portion of the essay. Footnotes have been deleted.*

Love in its dual manifestations, implies agreement, he who loves and she who reciprocates the inspiration therein are quickened, neither to hurt the other, nor evade any moral or pecuniary obligation which the incarnate fruits of their passion may present. When a man says of a woman, "She suits me"—that is, she would be to him a serviceable mate,—he does not often as seriously ask if *he* is likely to suit *her;* still less, if this proposed union may not become an ugly domestic knot which the best interests of both will require to be untied. Whether the number outside of marriage, who would like to get in, be greater or less than the number inside who want to get out, this mingled sense of esteem, benevolence, and passional attraction called Love, is so generally diffused that most people know life to be incomplete until the calls of affection are met in a healthful, happy and prosperous association of persons of opposite sex. That this blending of personalities may not be compulsive, hurtful, or irrevocable; but, rather, the result of mutual discretion—a free compact, dissolvable at will—there is needed, not only a purpose in Lovers to hold their bodies subject to reason; but also radical change of the opinions, laws, customs, and institutions which now repress and inebriate natural expressions of Love. Since ill-directed animal heat promotes distortion rather than growth; as persons who meet in convulsive embraces may separate in deadly feuds,—sexual desire here carrying invigorating peace, there desolating havoc, into domestic life,—intelligent students of sociology will not think the marriage institution a finality, but, rather, a device to be amended, or abolished, as enlightened moral sense may require.

When the number of opinions for and against a given measure are equal, it is called "a tie vote," and is without force and void, unless the speaker of the assembly throws his "casting vote," thereby giving to his side a majority of one, and enabling the measure to become a "law," binding, not only of those who favored, but also on those who opposed it! Not to note the manifest injustice and absurdity of such "an act," in the popular connubial assembly of bride and groom both vote one way,—that is, to "have" each other,—while the binding, or casting, vote is given by a "speaker," called priest or magistrate, who is supposed to represent society so far as it is a Civil act, and God so far as it is a sacrament or religious matter. But, since neither society nor deity has ever "materialized" at weddings in a manner definite enough to become responsible for what Lovers may do or suffer in their untried future, we have no further use for a "speaker" in our nuptial congress, and must search elsewhere for the moral obligations which Lovers, by their tie vote to be "one," incur. In its desire to "confirm this amity by nuptial knot," society forgets that Lovers are Lovers by mutual attraction which does not ask leave to be, or to cease to be, of any *third* party; that its effort to "confirm" Love by visible bonds tends to destroy Magnetic Forces which induce unity; and that Lovers are responsible only for what they, themselves, do, and the fruits thereof. Since the words "right" and "duty" derive their ethical qualities from our relations to what is essentially reasonable and just,—to the nature of things,—legislative "acts" neither create nor annul moral ties. As "alone we are born, alone we die, and alone we go up to judgment," so no one can escape from himself; but each must administer the Personal and Collective interests which he or she embodies. Being the authors and umpires of their rights and duties, the sexes weave moral ties by free and conscientious intimacy, and constantly give bonds for their mutual good behaviour. Cause and effect are as inseparable in human actions as in the general movements of Nature; choose as you please, the results of the choice you are the responsible author of. Relieving one from outer restraint does not lessen, but increases this Personal Accountability: for, by making him *Free,* we devolve on him the necessity of self-government; and he must respect the rights of others, or suffer the consequences of being an invader. In claiming freedom for myself, I thereby am forbidden to encroach. When man seeks to enjoy woman's person *at her cost,* not a Lover, he is *a libertine,* and she a martyr. How dare woman say she loves man, when seeking her own good at his expense? Perfect Love "casts out fear," and also sin; if derived from the Greek *sinein,* to injure, the word sin implies invasion, injury; thus gratification of sexual desire in a way that *injures* another is *not* Love, but sin. Though they have a right to enjoy themselves at their own cost yet, if their passion is hurtful, a sense of duty to themselves and others should teach Lovers continence.

Having its root in the Latin *vir,* a man, the radical import of the word virtue is manly strength: usage invests it with intelligence to know and power to resist wrong. One cannot choose without comparing the objects of choice; without judging for himself what is right, and personally placing himself at the disposal of Reason; hence, Virtue consists in ability to reason correctly, and force of will to obey Thought. But, since one cannot choose or act, when mental and physical movement is suppressed, Liberty, occasion, is the primary and indispensable condition of Virtue; while vice originates in stagnant ignorance, which the policy of repression enforces. The conscience, feeling, or impressions which precede and inspire thought announce the presence of ethical intelligence, and indicate how largely human actions are influenced by spiritual impulse. While, therefore, Liberty is the father, Conscience is the mother of Virtue. Chastity is power to choose between aesthetic health and disease, a power born of the same mental scope and activity which promote Virtue. Sexual passion is not so much in fault as reason; flesh is willing, but spirit is weak; the mind is unable to tell the body what to do. When the true relation of the sexes is known, ideas rule and bodies obey brain; purity of motive—just and ennobling action—follow the lead of free inquiry. The popular idea of sexual purity, (freedom from fornication or adultery, abstinence from sexual intercourse before marriage, and fidelity to its exclusive vows afterwards), rests on intrusive laws, made and sustained by men, either ignorant of what *is* essentially virtuous, or whose better judgment bows to Custom that stifles the cries of affection and ignores the reeking licentiousness of marriage beds. Is coition pure only when sanctioned by priest or magistrate? Are scandal-begetting clergymen and bribe-taking statesmen the sources of virtue? The lascivious deliriums prevalent among men, the destructive courses imposed on women, and the frightful inroads of secret vice on the vitality of youth of both sexes, all show the sexual nature to be, comparatively, in a savage state; and that even public teachers have *not begun* to reason originally on questions of Love, virtue, continence or reproduction.

While Passion impels movement in one person towards another, and tends to overleap *unnatural* barriers, its proposals are, nevertheless subject to rejection; created and nourished by the object of attraction, it is toned by Love which generates, but never annuls moral obligations. If intrusive, passion is hurtful; but, the person assailed, has a natural right of resistance; and, if a woman or girl, her effort in self-defence will be reinforced by disinterested strength around her. If men do not rally to protect a woman thus imperiled, it is because their sense of right is distorted by an idea that women belong to men, and that the person of this particular woman is, somehow, the property of the man who can overpower her. Our applause of an example of Love measures the contempt which right-minded people feel for a man who imposes himself, or the unwelcome fruit of his passions, on woman. She is "safe" among men, not through laws which deny Liberty, but by prevailing knowledge of the fact that Nature vests *in herself* the right to control and dispose of her own person. If Lovers err, it is due not to Liberty, but to ignorance, and the demoralizing effect of the marriage system. If free to go wrong, disciplined by ideas, they will work out their own salvation in the school of experience. The Free Love faith proclaims the fact that persons recognized in law as capable of making a sexual contract are, when wiser by experience, morally able to dissolve that contract; and that Passion is not so depraved as to be incapable of redemption and self-government.

The essential principle of Nature, Love, is a law unto itself; but, resisted by custom, its natural intent and scope are not generally understood. We were all trained in the school of repression or inebriacy; and taught that, to express ourselves otherwise than by established rules, is sinful. To get out of one's body to think, to destroy all his old opinions, is almost necessary, to enable him to approach and investigate a new subject impartially. The grave tendencies of the Love question, its imperative force in human destiny, its momentous relations to government, religion, life, and property, demand revolution in social doctrines, and institutes, more beneficently severe than is yet fully conceived of. But, since nothing is fixed but natural right, the most radical method of treatment is the most truly conservative. Evils like libertinism and prostitution, which have baffled the wisest human endeavor, will yield only to increasing intelligence, and the irresistible forces of Conscience. I beg my readers, therefore, to bring to this subject honest intent to know truth and obey it. That the grand Principle of Love is potent with greater good than is realized in human affairs, is certain; that this noblest element of human being does not logically lead to the marital and social ills around us, is equally evident. The way out of domestic infelicity, then, must lie through larger knowledge of the nature of Love and of the rights and duties involved in its evolution.

Since the sexual union, (for life or until legally divorced), of one woman with several men—Polyandry; or that of one man with several women—Polygamy; or that of one man with one woman—Monogamy, is a conventional agreement between two or more individual contractors and a collective third, society, marriage, in either of its three historical forms, is a human device to tame, utilize, and control the sexual passion, which is supposed to be naturally ferocious and ungovernable. What Nature "hath joined," man need not attempt to "put asunder;" but, since the legalized marital relation is so chaotic and mischievous, (clergymen and legislators themselves often being the first to violate what they profanely assume to be a divine ordinance); and since Deity has never yet come forward to own that he is "the author and finisher" of marriage laws, it is better to attribute them to the erring men who enacted them, than to accuse Divine Wisdom of so much folly. Marriage, then, being the creature of *men's* laws, we have the same right to alter or abolish it that we have respecting any other human institution. The principles of Nature derived from a careful study of essential liberty and equity, are a safer guide than crude social codes which come to us from the ignorant and despotic past. Woman, who, being up first in the morning hours of history, played a winning hand in this marriage game, is again coming to the front; and, in the parliament of Reason, where the thought, impulse, attraction, and conscience of both sexes have free play, better methods of social intercourse and reproduction will be matured than exclusive *male* wisdom has yet invented. It is for the Free Love School to develop an order of sexual unity worthy to be called a sacrament, and which sensible people need not blush to share.

"Will you have me?" is the prayer by which man seeks partnership in the being of woman; and she also has persuasive ways and means to pray to, and "capture," him. This would be well, were it not a compulsory choice of evils, and were they able to determine, in advance, the grave interests of offspring, industry, business, health, temperaments, and attractions, which mutually concern them, and on the adjustment of which depends their future weal or woe. Girls become pubescent at about 12, and boys at 14, though girls, then, are much older, sexually, than boys: from these ages young people are capable of all the pleasures and miseries of passional experience. But, since sexual union for life is extremely hazardous for both parties,—it being impossible to correct the fatal mistake of marriage without the commission of crime by one or the other,—they are usually left to illicit intercourse, or to exhaust their vitality in secret vices. Even when married,—coming into this new relation without knowledge of its uses or of self-control,—they prey on each other, and a few years of wedded life and child-bearing may leave the wife an emaciated wreck of her former self, and the husband very much less, a man, than Nature designed him to be. Though *bewildered* moralists advise early marriage, they well know how often puny offspring rebuke the alliance, teaching indiscreet parents that coition should have stopped short of reproduction. Those who think the evil is not in the essential immorality of the marriage system, but in its abuses, denounce with just severity the legalized slavery of women therein. The absurdity consists in an effort to make the wife legally "equal" to the husband inside of nuptial bonds; it is an effort to make her an equal victim and an equal oppressor with him. Since marriage involves the loss of liberty, many of our best people, especially women, never marry, preferring to endure the ills of celibacy rather than fly to what may prove irretrievable ruin. Slavery is voluntary or involuntary; voluntary when one sells or yields his or her own person to the irresponsible will of another; involuntary when placed under the absolute power of another without one's own consent. The compulsive features of marital law are incidental and secondary to the marriage relation itself, which is unnatural and forced. Pen cannot record, nor lips express, the enervating, debauching effect of celibate life upon young men and women. Who supposes that, if allowed to freely consult their natural wits and good sense, they would tie themselves up in the social snarl of matrimony? Yet they are now compelled to choose between suicidal evils of abstinence and the legalized prostitution of marriage. Some, by clandestine intimacies, live below marriage; others, by personal defiance, and at the expense of social ostracism, attempt to live above it; but both are on the "ragged edge" of peril, as were "free negroes" who tried to live above or below the old slave system. The fierce blood-hounds put upon the track of fugitive slaves, were forerunners of the "dogs of war" which marriage now trains to hunt down its victims. A system so prolific of hypocrites and martyrs is compulsive in the most mischievous sense of that word, and will be abolished when free and virtuous people resolutely confront it.

Since marriage does not provide for the education of sexual desire or of its expression, but gives legal "right" and power to sin, every priest or magistrate, who "solemnizes" the rite, sells indulgences of a far more disastrous nature than those which scandalized the Romish Church. On account of her political, social, and pecuniary vassalage, woman is the chief martyr to the relentless license granted man; but cases are on record where the husband was effectually subdued by the tigress, with whom he went into the nuptial "paradise." Founded on the supposition that man's love is naturally ferocious, marriage attempts, by legal means, to furnish food for his savage nature; and we have but to lift the roofs of "respectable" houses to find the skeleton's of its feminine victims. It is because the marriage theory is unnatural and barbarous that it works out such shocking results. In the phrase "tyranny of lust," I have brought a good word into bad company, and must apologize for its misuse; for lust properly means desire, prayer, exuberant strength. So, likewise, the popular view of Love gives a devilish intent and drift to the divinest of words. Advocates of marriage cling to the exploded doctrine of natural depravity, and Freethinkers, Spiritualists and Atheists, who scout theological perdition, think social hells of permanent necessity in human life. Nowhere does the human intellect so disgrace itself as in its cowardly half-ashamed, and hypocritical attitude in the presence of Free Love. When woman's thought comes forward in the discussion, we hope for better things. In the early struggle of history which led to the establishment of polyandry (as in later domestic conflicts), the ruling impulse of the women was not sexual desire, but, rather, spiritual superiority, intuitional strategy, by virtue of which they were masters of men in the realm of religious mysticism. On the contrary, the repulsive evidence of sexual depravity, in men, referred to in the notes below, indicate the savage use, now made of animal force, which is capable of beneficent expenditure. When man loves woman intelligently, what is now consuming passional heat, will make him a genial, civil, and serviceable being. The unreserved devotion, with which a lover gives himself and his fortune to his bride, discloses the possible divine life on earth. But when impulsive, self-forgetting love, overflowing the narrow limits of family enclosures, gives one's heart and purse to deserving girls and women, the now, seemingly, savage suitor becomes Providence incarnate. Charles Sumner, in his will, gave money to the daughters of the poet Longfellow, of Dr. S. G. Howe, and of the Rev. Dr. Wm. H. Furness, "in consideration of his profound regard for their estimable parents;" but cases have occurred, and will multiply, as civilization prevails, where men of no blood relation, and without a hint of sexual intimacy, give money and even estates, to girls and women, worthy of love and distinction, irrespective of their parents, ennobling themselves and human kind in so doing.

Though man may "propose," and woman "accept," a notion inhabits the average *male* head that the irresistibly attractive force of woman's nature makes *her* responsible for any mutual wrong-doing. Thinking woman at the bottom of all mischief, when a male culprit is brought into court, the French ask "Who is she?" If he said that Mrs. Elizabeth R. Tilton "thrust her love on him unsought," the Rev. Henry Ward Beecher thereby indicated how much there is in him of the "old Adam," who remarked to the "Lord God," interviewing him after he had indulged in the "forbidden fruit," "The woman whom thou gavest to be with me, she gave me of the tree, and I did eat." The insanity plea put forward in courts of law by aggrieved "husbands" who, as in the Sickles and McFarland case, murder men that are attracted to their "wives," also affirms, in a round-about way, the supposed inability of a man to control himself when under the spell of a woman's enchantment. Contrary to the old law which regarded the husband and wife as one, and the husband that one, when the twain sin, *she* is held responsible, and he is excused on the ground that he was over-persuaded, and too weak to withstand her wishes. From the Garden of Eden to Plymouth Church, skulking has been the pet method of man to escape from the consequences of sexual indiscretion. Beecher's confessions and "letters of contrition," with his later denials, sadly illustrate the pathetic penitence, the sniveling cowardice, and brazen-faced falsity with which "great men" endeavor to appease, cajole, and defy equivocal public opinion. The harsh judgments pronounced on women which abound in the literature of all ages, are equalled only by the evidences of ludicrous puerility which men display when confronted with their sexual "deeds done in the body." The tragic anarchy which now distracts social life originates first in the "legal" denial of the right of people to manage their own sexual affairs; and secondly in the supposed exemption from moral responsibility of either man or woman in Love.

The facts of married and single life, one would suppose, are sufficiently startling to convince all serious-minded people of the imperative need of investigation; especially of the duty of young men and women to give religiously serious attention to the momentous issues of Sexual Science. But, on the threshold of good intent, they are met by established ignorance forbidding them to inquire. It is even thought dangerous to discuss the subject at all. In families, schools, sermons, lectures, and newspapers its candid consideration is so studiously suppressed that children and adults know nothing of it, except what they learn from their own diseased lives and imaginations, and in the filthy by-ways of society. Many noble girls and boys, whom a little knowledge from their natural guardians, *parents and teachers,* would have saved, are now, physically and morally, utter wrecks. Where saving truth should have been planted, error has found an unoccupied field, which it has busily sown, and gathers therefrom a prolific harvest. The alleged increase of "obscene" prints and pictures caused both Houses of the U.S. Congress, March 1, 1873, to pass a bill, (or, rather an amendment of the Post Office Act of June, 1872), which was immediately signed by the President, said to be "For the suppression of Obscene Literature," and from which I make the following extract:—

> 148.—That no obscene, lewd, or lascivious book, pamphlet, picture, paper, print, or other publication of an indecent character, nor any article or thing designed or intended for the prevention or conception or procuring of abortion, nor any article or thing intended or adapted for any indecent or immoral use or nature, nor any written or printed card, circular, book, pamphlet, advertisement, or notice of any kind giving information, directly, or indirectly, where, or how, or of whom, or by what means either of the things before mentioned, may be obtained or made, nor any letter upon the envelope of which, or postal card upon which indecent or scurrilous epithets may be written, or printed, shall be carried in the mail; and any person who shall knowingly deposit, or cause to be deposited, for mailing or delivery, any of the hereinbefore-mentioned articles or things, or any notice, or paper containing any advertisement relating to the aforesaid articles or things, and any person who, in pursuance of any plan or scheme for disposing of any of the hereinbefore-mentioned articles or things, shall take or cause to be taken, from the mail any such letter or package, shall be deemed guilty of a misdemeanor, and, on conviction thereof, shall, for every offence, BE FINED NOT LESS THAN ONE HUNDRED DOLLARS NOR MORE THAN FIVE THOUSAND DOLLARS, OR IMPRISONMENT AT HARD LABOR NOT LESS THAN ONE YEAR NOR MORE THAN TEN YEARS, OR BOTH, IN THE DISCRETION OF THE JUDGE.

I credit Congress and President Grant with good intentions in framing this "law;" for, ignorant of the cause of the evils they proposed to correct, they were probably unaware of the unwarrantable stretch of despotism embodied in their measure, and of the abuse which would be made of it. A humane man, Dr. Lewis has not the savage disposition; the influence of "obscene literature" may be as depraving as he affirms; but his measures of repression are a clear invasion of natural right, and will serve only to hasten the downfall of marriage, which he writes to uphold. "Prohibition a Failure" is the title of a book, in which Dr. Lewis, by irrefutable logic, shows that the policy which he brings to the social question is indefensible and self-defeating when applied to the liquor traffic. When the Doctor as intelligently studies Social reform as he has temperance, he will blush to remember the heated words that have fallen from his pen. Regarding Anthony Comstock, representative of the Young Mens' Christian Association and the real author of the "law" quoted above, I regret to be unable to entertain so favorable an opinion. In a letter addressed to Hon. C. L. Merriam, M. C., dated Brooklyn, N.Y., Jan. 18, 1873, he says: "There were four publishers on the 2nd of last March; *to-day three of these are in their graves, and it is charged by their friends that I* WORRIED THEM TO DEATH. BE THAT AS IT MAY, I AM SURE THAT THE WORLD IS BETTER OFF WITHOUT THEM." This is clearly the spirit that lighted the fires of the Inquisition. Appointed special supervisor of the U.S. Mails (by what authority I am unable to learn); and, by religio-sectarian intolerance, constituted censor of the opinions of the people in their most important channel of inter-communication, he is chiefly known through his efforts to suppress newspapers and imprison editors disposed to discuss the Social Question. In Nov., B. L. 1, he procured the arrest and imprisonment of Victoria C. Woodhull and her editorial associates for publishing a preliminary ventilation of the "Brooklyn Scandal," which afterwards filled American newspapers. Subsequently, he caused the incarceration, during seven months, of George F. Train for publishing in his newspaper (The Train Ligue) certain quotations from the Christian Bible, touching the same "scandal" which the implicated churches employ Mr. Comstock to hush up. As I write this (Jan. 1, Y. L. 4), a note from another subject of his vengeance, John A. Lant, editor and publisher of the N.Y. Toledo Sun, dated Ludlow St. Jail, New York, Dec. 30, 1875, says: "Judge Benedict to-day sentenced me to imprisonment in Albany Penitentiary one year and six months. I will endeavor to send you a copy of the sentence. It is worth to us all it costs me." Mr. Lant's crime is sending through the mails his newspaper, containing criticisms of the "scandal," and of Rev. II. W. Beecher! Mr. Comstock's relation to Mr. Lant, as heretofore to Mrs. Woodhull and Mr. Train, is that of *a religious monomaniac,* whom the mistaken will of Congress and the lascivious fanaticism of the Young Mens' Christian Association have empowered to use the Federal Courts to suppress free inquiry. The better sense of the American people moves to repeal the National Gag-Law which he now administers, and every interest of public and private morality demands thorough discussion of the issue which sectarian pride and intolerance now endeavor to postpone.

"Beauty is a joy forever," and for all; the quality of beauty being to awaken admiration and esteem in observers to the extent of their ability to appreciate it. To be susceptible of beauty in one thing does not unfit, but rather prepares us to appreciate it in others. Love of the beautiful person, or of character, is not less involuntary and nonexclusive than in things. A man cannot love even one woman truly unless he is free to love what is lovable in all other women. The fact that sexual love is passional, as well as aesthetic, does not make it exclusive. The philosophic Irishman who liked to be alone, especially "when his swateheart was with him," expressed the natural privacy of Love, and also indicated the scientific fact that the affectional union of two creates a collective third personality, superior, in some respects, to either constituent factor. If from this mystical confluence of two beings there springs a child, even this Evolution of Love does not make either one of the three persons less accountable to self and truth, or less permeable by material and spiritual, human and divine influences which either may encounter. Monogamists hold that Love is possible only between one man and one woman, the word monogomy meaning *to marry to one only*. Yet, *so called* monogamists constantly violate that principle; for, if divorced by death, crime, or the courts, scarcely a man or woman hesitates to marry the second, third, or fifth time. Are they any the less "pure" in doing so? Certainly not; second, third, or subsequent marriages may be more healthful and harmonious than the first, for the good reason that at least one of the parties has had the benefits of experience. It is admitted that, if the previous partners in her bed are divorced by death or other cause, a woman may truly love and wisely marry the second or fifth man; but the purity of her love for the fifth man is not determined by the previous four being dead or divorced; were they all living and her personal friends, she can love the last man as truly as she loved the first. Consistent with the teachings of the Bible, which sanctions polygamy, Christians support missionaries in foreign lands, who welcome to church membership and the communion table, men who have a plurality of wives. David, the "man after God's own heart," compassed the death of Uriah to get possession of his wife, Bathsheba and "took more wives and concubines out of Jerusalem after he was come from Hebron," for God "gave him the house of Saul and the wives of Saul into his bosom." Though Solomon was very "promiscuously" married, Sunday-School children are yet taught to revere him as "the wisest man." The monogamic or one-love theory is both theoretically and practically rejected by modern Christians, (as likewise by "Infidels") and, if they will honestly follow Jesus,—who, while he did not directly condemn polygamy, was yet, theoretically, a woman's emancipationist—he will take them into his Free Love Kingdom of Heaven, where he says, "they neither marry nor are given in marriage."

Though the Jehovah-God of the Bible, disliking irresponsible divorce, "hateth putting away," he is a thorough polygamist; its Jesus-God as plainly favors the entire abolition of marriage. Out of the modern Christian Church have come three phases of sexual morality,—Shakerism, or the utter proscription of sexual intercourse; Mormonism, or sanctified polygamy; and Oneida-Perfection with its "free" love and omnigamy. While the question of marriage and property are to be settled on the basis of Reason, the Bible and other records of the past thought being only incidental evidence, the Oneida Community are nearer sound on these two points than any other Christian sect. I give, therefore, a brief abstract of their Love doctrine, mainly in the words of their Seer and pastor, Rev. J. H. Noyes. The kingdom of heaven supplants all human governments; in it the institution of marriage, which assigns the possession of one woman to one man, does not exist, the intimate union of Love extending to the whole body of believers. The pentecostal spirit abolishes exclusiveness in regard to women and children, as respecting property. The new commandment is that we love each other fervently, not in pairs, but *en masse;* as religious excitements act on amativeness, this is an indication of the natural tendency of religion to Love. The union of hearts expresses and ultimates itself in union of bodies. Love is attraction; seeking unity, it is desire; in unity, happiness. In unobstructed Love, or the free play of the affinities, sexual union is its natural expression. Experience teaches that sexual love is not restricted to pairs; second marriages annul the one-love theory and are often the happiest. Love is not burnt out in one honeymoon, or satisfied by one lover; the secret history of the human heart proves that it is capable of loving any number of times and persons, and that the more it loves the more it can love. This is the law of Nature, thrust out of sight and condemned by common consent, yet secretly known to all. Variety is as beautiful and useful in love as in eating and drinking. The one-love theory, based on jealousy, comes not from loving hearts, but from the greedy claimant. The law of marriage "worketh wrath;" provokes jealousy; unites unmatched natures and sunders matched ones; and making no provision for sexual appetite, causes disease, masturbation, prostitution, and general licentiousness. Unless the sexes come together *naturally*, desire dammed up breaks out irregularly and destructively. The irregularities and excesses of amativeness are explosions incident to unnatural separations of male and female elements, as in the explosion of electric forces. Mingling of the sexes favors purity; isolation, as in colleges, seminaries, monasteries, &c., breeds salacity and obscenity. A system of complex marriage, supplying want, both as to time and variety, will open the prison doors both to the victims of marriage and celibacy; to those in married life who are starved, and to those who are oppressed by lust; to those who are tied to uncongenial natures, and to those who are separated from their natural mates; and to those in the unmarried state who are withered by neglect, diseased by unnatural abstinence, or ploughed into prostitution and self-pollution by desires which have no natural channel. Carrying religion into life, pledging the earnings of each for the support of the whole, the Oneidans seek "not the union of two but the harmony of all souls."

Whether the Oneida scheme succeeds or fails, as an experiment it is doing great service to civilization; and New York State has the thanks of all intelligent reformers for permitting Perfectionism to illustrate its ideas of sexuality in its own way. But their conceited and self-righteous contempt for Socialists who "have no religion," and their belief that Liberty tends to demoralization,—"leads to hell,"—show the Oneidans to be ignorant of the source of the spirit of toleration and progress, which presided at their birth and has compelled marriage bigots to leave them unmolested. Making better use of religion than any other Christian sect, the Oneidans yet fail to learn the deepest lesson which Jesus taught, are mistaken in supposing that Free Love and Free Labor are possible only within their iron-clad scheme of Socialism, and that the first lesson of progress is to have one's Individuality broken on their religio-communistic wheel. Impelled with Paul to prove all things and hold fast to that which is good; inspired by the good old doctrine of Jesus, that each soul must *judge for itself what is right*, and be saved or "lost" on its own individual responsibility; declining to join the "bread-and-butter brigades" of Communism, Lovers will find their salvation in *Liberty* to choose,—to live on their own merits. The persistent growth of the "social evil" in defiance of all efforts to abate it, shows an irresistible tendency of people to associate even against law and custom; when they obey the higher law of Liberty, which makes social *choice sacred,* and Individual Integrity a duty, domestic life will gravitate towards unity, and Love become the potentially redeeming force which Nature intended it to be.

XII. Love, Marriage and Divorce

Stephen Pearl Andrews

Like many antislavery radicals, Stephen Pearl Andrews became active in the free-love movement, both in his own name and as a ghost writer for the infamous Victoria Woodhull. Much of Andrews' interest in women's rights undoubtedly derived from his wife, Esther B. Hussey, who was a doctor and suffragist, and from his friendship with women's rights pioneers Thomas and Mary Nichols.

In 1852, the columns of the New York Tribune *were opened to a discussion of marriage and divorce by Horace Greeley, its editor, and the noted social theorist, Henry James. Although Andrews was a prominent figure, he was excluded from this discussion on the grounds that his doctrines (favoring free divorce) were destructive to the public well-being and offended the public sense of decency. Andrews interpreted the exclusion differently: "Mr. Greeley found himself completely 'headed' and hemmed in by the argument, with the astuteness clearly to perceive that fact, while he had neither the dialectical skill to obscure the issues and disguise it, nor the magnanimity frankly to acknowledge a defeat." Andrews believed that the fundamental difference between Greeley and himself was a conflicting view of the individual in relation to government. Greeley maintained that the individual had to be supervised and restrained by government, while Andrews proclaimed the sovereignty of the non-invasive individual, capable of governing himself.*

The following exchange between Greeley and Andrews is extracted from Love, Marriage and Divorce and The Sovereignty of the Individual *(1853), edited by Andrews as a means of presenting his side, the suppressed side, of the discussion.*

A Parthian Arrow By Mr. Greeley

A HEART-BROKEN MANIAC.—We have just been put in possession of the particulars of a scene of sorrow seldom witnessed. A young lady, of this city, respectably connected and of fair reputation, nearly two years ago became acquainted with a man now residing in this place. The acquaintance soon ripened into a strong attachment, and, finally love, on her part. Under the promise of marriage, as she says, she was made to yield to his solicitations, and last autumn she gave birth to a child, which lived only two days. He disregarded his promises— avoided and frowned upon her. Here she was deprived of her lover and of her child. She felt that every eye was turned upon her with scorn—that those who saw her at her work, or met her in the street, knew her disgrace. Day by day, and week by week, her heart sank within her, paleness came to her cheeks, and her frame wasted away, till she is now almost a living skeleton. Wednesday morning she went to work in the mills, as usual, but soon returned, saying that she was sick. In a few hours she was a raving maniac, her reason gone, perhaps forever. Since then she has had a few rational intervals, in one of which she stated that she met that morning the one she calls her betrayer, and he frowned upon her and treated her with contempt. She could bear all the disgrace that attaches to her condition, if he would treat her kindly. But the thought that the one she has loved so dearly, and the one who made her such fair promises, should desert her at this time, and heartlessly and cruelly insult her, is too much for her to bear. Her brothers and friends are borne down with sorrow at her condition. What a picture! It needs no comment of ours. Public opinion will hunt down the heartless villain who betrayed her."—*Manchester* (N.H.) *Mirror*.

The above relation provokes some reflection on "the Sovereignty of the Individual," the right of every man to do pretty much as he pleases, etc., which the reader will please follow out for himself.

Reply By Mr. Andrews

The above missile *a tergo* from my valorous antagonist—after his retreat into the safety of a unilateral contest—is suggestive of many things, and might constitute the text for a whole bookful of commentary. It is the usual whine of blear-eyed and inveterate Tyranny, gloating over the fact that some one of his victims has got himself, or herself, into a worse fix by disregarding his behests, and attempting an escape from his infernal grip, than he or she was in before. The slave-hunter, amid the baying of his blood-hounds upon the warm scent of the track of an unhappy fugitive, growls out in the same manner his curses upon the inhumanity of the man who has preached Freedom to the Captive, charging upon him all the horrors of the sickening scene that is about to ensue. Should the friend who has whispered longings after emancipation into the greedy ear of the victim of slavery, afterward, through cowardice, or selfishness, or from any cause overmastering his devotion, shrink from going all lengths in uniting his fortunes with those of the slave—either by remaining with him in bondage, or taking his full share in the risks of the flight; and, if this desertion should rankle in the breast of the fugitive as the worst torment of his forlorn state, even when sore pressed by the devouring dogs, the case would be parallel in all ways to the one cited by Mr. Greeley.

Our transcendent Philosopher and Moralist of the *Tribune* can imply the most withering hatred of the "seducer" and "heartless villain," whom "public opinion" is invoked to "hunt down" for his crime, and whisper no word of rebuke for—nay, aggravate and hound on—that same Public Opinion in its still more reckless vengeance upon the unfortunate girl herself, by efforts to intensify "all the disgrace that attaches to her condition," which, terrible as it is now, she said, poor creature! she had the fortitude "to bear," but for the other element in her misery. That other element, the betrayal of her lover, in addition to the insane odium of the Public, Mr. Greeley charges upon the "seducer." I charge both one and the other cause of the poor girl's torture and insanity, just as boldly, upon Mr. Greeley himself, and the like of him. If the mental phenomena which led to her betrayal by her lover could be investigated, they would be indubitably traced back to the senseless rigors of that same Public Opinion; so that both causes of the wreck and insanity of one party, and of the endless remorse and torment of the other, as we must presume, flow from the same common fountain—a vitiated Public Sentiment, adverse to, and intolerant of, Freedom, or the Sovereignty of the Individual!

How exceedingly probable that, at the very moment this hapless girl's lover cast the repulsive glance that pierced her already wounded heart and overthrew her reason, his own heart was half bursting with the tenderest compassion. Placed in the dire alternative of renouncing affection, or else of abjuring his own Freedom perpetually, the instinct of self-preservation may have overborne, in his case, as it must and *will* overbear in many cases, the natural sentiments of Manhood and Gallantry, and Paternal Tenderness, all of which, unobstructed by a blundering Legislation and an ignorant Public Prejudice, would have prompted him to remain by her side, acknowledge her publicly, and succor and sustain her through all the consequences of their mutual love. *Remove from a man the arbitrary demand that he shall make more sacrifice than he feels to be just, and you neutralize, or evidently diminish, the temptation, on his part, to make less.* Demand pledges of him, on the contrary, under the penalty of the Penitentiary, against that over which he knows, by all his past experience, that he had no more control than he has over his Opinions or his Tastes, namely that his affections shall remain unchanged for life, that he will never love another woman, or that, if he does, he will crush that love as he would a viper, no matter though his own heart and others bleed to death in the effort—add to this that he shall change his whole methods of life, assume the care and direction of a Family Establishment, for which he may have no taste, but only repugnance, and take upon himself the liability of being required to support many lives, instead of the burdens already incumbent on him, beyond, it may be, already, his consciousness of power to bear up against the difficulties of surrounding competition and antagonism; and you put before him what may be, acting upon some natures, not the worst, as they are deemed, but the best as God made them—an insuperable obstacle to the performance of those acts of Justice which would be otherwise their natural and irrepressible impulse.

With some men and some women, the instinct for Freedom is a domination too potent to be resisted. An association with angels under constraint would be to them a Hell. The language of their souls is "Give me Liberty, or give me death." Such natures have noble and generous propensities in other directions. Say to a man of this sort, abjure Freedom or abjure Love, and, along with it, the dear object whom you have already compromised in the world's estimation, and who can foresee the issue of that terrible conflict of the passions which must ensue? In the vast majority of such cases, notwithstanding all, Generosity and Love conquer, and the man knowingly sacrifices himself and all future thought of happiness, in the privation of Freedom, the consciousness of which no Affection, no amount of the World's Good Opinion, no consideration of any kind, can compensate him for, nor reconcile him to. It would be strange, on the other hand, if the balance of motive never fell upon the other side; and then comes the terrible desertion, the crushing weight of public scorn upon the unprotected head of the wretched woman, and the lasting destruction of the happiness of all concerned, in another of the stereotyped forms of evil.

I do not deny that, among those men, nor, indeed, that the great majority of those men who seduce and betray women, are bad men; that is, that they are undeveloped, hardened, and perverted beings, hardly capable of compassion or remorse. What I do affirm is, that there are, also, among them, men of the most refined, and delicate, and gentle natures, fitted to endure the most intense suffering themselves while they inflict it—none but their own hearts can tell how unwillingly—on those they most dearly prize in the world; and that Society is in fault to place such men in such a cruel conflict with themselves, in which some proportion of the whole number so tried is sure to fall. I also affirm that, of the former class—the undeveloped, hardened, and perverted—their undevelopment, hardening, and perversion are again chargeable upon our false Social Arrangements, and, more than all else, perhaps, upon that very exclusion from a genial and familiar association with the female sex, now deemed essential, in order to maintain the Marriage Institution in "its Purity." And, finally, I affirm, that, while such men exist, the best protection that Woman *can* have against their machinations is more Development on her own part, such as can alone come from more Freedom, more Knowledge of the world, more Familiarity with Men, more ability to judge of character and to read the intentions of those by whom she is approached, more Womanhood, in fine; instead of a namby-pamby, lackadaisical, half-silly interestingness, cultured and procured by a nun-like seclusion from business, from Freedom of locomotion, from unrestrained inter-communication of thought and sentiment with the male sex, and, in a word, from almost the whole circle of the rational means of development.

He must be an unobservant man, indeed, who does not perceive the pregnant signs all around him that approximations toward the opinions now uttered by me are everywhere existent, and becoming every day nearer and more frequent.

"When People understand," says Lord Stowell, in the case of Evans *vs.* Evans, 1st Consistory Reports, p. 36, "that they *must* live together, they learn, by mutual accommodation, to bear that *yoke* which they know they *can not shake off;* they become good husbands and wives(!) from *the necessity of remaining* husbands and wives, for *necessity is a powerful master in teaching the duties which it imposes."* How antiquated does such a defense of any Institution begin to sound to our ears! It is equally good when applied to Despotism, to Slavery, to the Inquisition, or to any other of the Forms in which force and *Necessity* are brought to bear upon human beings to the destruction of their Freedom, and the ruin of their highest happiness. Indeed, it is the argument which, time out of mind, has been relied upon to sustain all those ancient abuses which are melting away before the Spirit of this Age. We are rapidly discarding Force, and recognizing the Truth, and Purity, and Potency of Love or Attraction, in Government, in Education, in Social Life, and everywhere.

The restraints of Marriage are becoming daily less. Its oppressions are felt more and more. *There are to-day in our midst ten times as many fugitives from Matrimony as there are fugitives from Slavery; and it may well be doubted if the aggregate, or the average, of their sufferings has been less.* There is hardly a country village that has not from one to a dozen such persons. When these unfortunates, flying from the blessings of one of our *peculiar* and *divine* institutions, hitherto almost wholly unquestioned, happen to be Women—the weaker sex—they are contemptuously designated "Grass-Widows;" as "runaway" or "free nigger" is, in like manner, applied to the outlaws of another "domestic" arrangement—Freedom in either case becoming, by a horrible social inversion, a badge of reproach. These severed halves of the matrimonial unit are, nevertheless, achieving respectability by virtue of numbers, and in America, at least, have nearly ceased to suffer any loss of caste by the peculiarity of their social condition. Divorce is more and more freely applied for, and easily obtained. Bastard children are now hardly persecuted at all by that sanctimonious Phariseeism which, a few generations ago, hunted them to the death, for no fault of theirs. The Rights of Women are every day more and more loudly discussed. Marriage has virtually ceased to claim the sanction of Religion, fallen into the hands of the civil magistrate, and come to be regarded as merely a civil contract. While thus recognized as solely a legal Convention, the repugnance for merely *Conventional* marriages *(Marriages de Convenance)* is yet deepening in the public mind into horror, and taking the place of that heretofore felt against a genuine passion not sanctified by the *blessing of the Church.* I quote from one of the most Conservative writers of the age when I say, that "it is not the mere ring and the orange blossom which constitute the difference between virtue and vice."

Indeed, it may be stated as the growing Public Sentiment of Christendom already, that the Man and Woman who do not LOVE have no right, before God, to live together as MAN and WIFE, no matter how solemn the marriage service which may have been mumbled over them. This is the NEGATIVE statement of a grand TRUTH, already arrived at and becoming daily louder and more peremptory in its utterance. How long, think you, it will be before the Converse, or POSITIVE, side of the same TRUTH will be affirmed, namely, that the Man and Woman who do LOVE, can live together in PURITY without any mummery at all—that it is LOVE that *sanctifies*—not the Blessing of the Church?

Such is my doctrine. Such is the horrid heresy of which I am guilty. And such, say what you will, is the eternal, inexpugnable TRUTH of God and Nature. Batter at it till your bones ache, and you can never successfully assail it. Sooner or later you must come to it, and whether it shall be sooner or later is hardly left to your option. The progress of Opinion, the great growth of the world, in this age, is sweeping all men, with the strength of an ocean current, to the acceptance of these views of Love and Marriage, to the acceptance of Universal Freedom—Freedom to Feel and Act, as well as Freedom to Think—to the acceptance, in fine, of THE SOVEREIGNTY OF EVERY INDIVIDUAL, TO BE EXERCISED AT HIS OWN COST. If our remaining Institutions are found to be adverse to this Freedom, so that bad results follow from its acceptance, then our remaining Institutions are wrong, and the remedy is to be sought in still farther and more radical changes.

Had there existed a Public Opinion already formed, based on Freedom, the poor girl in New Hampshire, whose sad history we have read in a paragraph, would probably not have been deserted or if she were, she would not have felt that "every eye was turned upon her in scorn, knowing her disgrace," visiting upon her a worse torture than any ever invented by savages, because, forsooth, *she had already been cruelly wronged!* A Christian people, indeed! "Her heart" would not have "sunk within her day by day and week by week." "Paleness" would not have "come upon her cheeks," and "her frame" have "wasted away until she was almost a living skeleton." She would not have become a raving maniac. "Her brothers and friends" would not have been "borne down with sorrow at her condition." Public opinion would not have been invoked "to hunt down" her betrayer, after first hunting down her; and, finally, her misfortune would not have been paraded and gloated over by a shameless public press, Mr. Greeley in the van, holding up the poor agonized, heart-riven, persecuted victim of the Infernalism of our Social Institutions, in warning to others against yielding to the purest, and holiest, and most powerful of the sentiments which God has implanted in the Human Heart—the joint force of the yearning after Freedom and after Love.

Mr. Greeley, the wrong that infests our social arrangements is deeper and more central than you have believed. It is not to be cured by superficial appliances and conservative nostrums. The Science of Social Relations must be known and applied. *You* do not know it. You refuse to study it. You do not believe that there is any such Science either known or possible. You persist in scratching over the surface, instead of putting the plow down into the subsoil of Social Reform. Very well, then, the world can't wait! You must drop behind, and the Army of Progress must even consent to proceed without your Leadership. I have been already a dozen times congratulated that I am helping to render you entirely "proper" and "orthodox." If you were quite sincere and more logical than you are, I could drive you clean back to the Papacy upon all subjects, where you have already confessedly gone upon the subject of Divorce—except that you relax a little in your rigor out of personal deference to Christ.

The truth will ere long be apparent that there is no middle ground upon which a man of sense can permanently stand, between *Absolut-*

ism, Blind Faith, and Implicit Obedience to authority, on the one hand, and on the other, "The Sovereignty of the Individual."

Suggested Readings

Ditzion, Sidney. *Marriage, Morals and Sex in America: A History of Ideas.* New York: Bookman Association, 1953.

Godwin, William. *Enquiry Concerning Political Justice.* 3rd ed. (1797). Edited by F.E.L. Priestley. Toronto: University of Toronto Press, 1946, pp. 499–514.

Goldman, Emma. *Anarchism and Other Essays* (1911). New York: Dover Reprints, 1969, pp. 233–245.

Harman, Lillian. *Marriage and Morality.* Chicago: Light Bearer Library, 1900.

Holcombe, Lee. "Victorian Wives and Property: Reform of the Married Women's Property Law, 1857–1882," in *A Widening Sphere: Changing Roles of Victorian Women.* Edited by Martha Vicinus. Bloomington: Indiana University Press, 1980.

Muncey, Raymond Lee. *Sex and Marriage in Utopian Communities: 19th Century America.* Bloomington: Indiana University Press, 1973.

WOMEN AND BIRTH CONTROL

XIII. Body Housekeeping

Angela Heywood

As one of the 19th century's most outspoken advocates of birth control and sexual freedom, Angela Heywood combined a fine theoretical mind with a bluntness that some found offensive. Most of her writing was published by The Word *(1872–1893) which she sporadically edited. The following article, published in the last issue of* The Word, *is an early defense of a woman's unconditional right to have an abortion based on her self-ownership. This article appeared at a time when a woman's right to abortion was a casualty of the rise of medical licensing in America. Angela Heywood's voice was virtually alone in advocating this basic right.*

What have *I* thought, said or done that anyone need be troubled about me? I come, in word expression, to establish man as man, not to demolish him. I am not proclaiming him a monster; I freight him not as disease,—leave that to the "Suffering Sisters." Not I, but Congress*men* force the sex issue. Is it "proper", "polite", for men, real *he* men, to go to Washington to say, by penal law, fines and imprisonment, whether woman may continue her natural right to wash, rinse or wipe out her own vaginal body opening,—as well as legislate when she may blow her nose, dray her eyes, or nurse her babe. Cold water prevents conception; will men therefore indite pumps and reservoirs? Whatever she may have been pleased to receive from man's own is his gift and her property. Women do not like rape, and have a right to resist its results. To cut a child up in woman, procure abortion, is a most fearful, tragic deed; but *even that* does not call for man's arbitrary jurisdiction over woman's womb. I read that—

> The increase in cases of sensual criminality, affecting present morality and future generations, suggests the consideration of a remedy that may be regarded as a kindness and mercy to the offender, who seems beyond the control of his carnal passions and, being administered with the wisdom of the highest medical skill and care, would doubtless be a protection to society and productive of beneficial results.—*Philadelphia Grand Jury in The Journal of Prison Discipline and Philanthropy, Jan. 1891, p.35*

This indicates that man is not so alarmed about preventing conception, for doth not CASTRATION accomplish it with a vengeance? In this proposal do not Peace Quakers rebuke the heistic statute? Are

Grand Jurors indeed meditating how to end the "pure" breed of Comstocks and Parkhursts? Mrs. Dr. Caroline B. Winslow, the late Chief Justice Waite's family doctor in Washington, said as Editor of *Alpha,* to a beautiful, young wife inquiring what she should do to prevent her having *many* children, her husband being of a warm, voluptuous nature, unable to retain his life element at her touch: Mrs. Winslow said,—

> "After all in all Maria, I scarce know what to say to thee unless thee shall use the valvet sponge."

Yes, the Comstock syringe without the guttapercha. Then what is all this Congressional, heistic ado about? The shorter path is for man to keep his "private parts" and semen property to himself, unless he can wisely invest it in future generations. Mediaeval hes locked up their attractive wive's sex power and left the key with priests; their successors, legislating obscenists, commit the business to Cook, Comstock and Parkhurst, but Gardner gets way with the key. Thus we find this aggressive cancer-plant on the body-politic and woman's body-self.

Superior to the immature animalism of Sir Phillip Sidney, Shakspeare (sic) and Byron, Whitman portrays man's creative power worthily in "A Woman Waits For Me"; verily we exclaim with Jewish fervor, Jehovah! But in addressing "The Common Prostitute" Whitman falls to the level of David, Solomon and Robt. Browning. If woman is ever a "prostitute" who makes her such? As her true mate in creative destiny man is incapable of the mawkish "sympathy". Whitman belittles himself in expressing to a so-called fallen women who really stands healthier than himself in the situation. She may be a "wreck" for having too trustingly served man, but does that entitle him to call her "prostitute"? I am obliged to feel that Whitman had *ir*responsible Solomon slyness in him, for he could not thus write to "My Girl" if he really sensed *how* she became "bad". Is he, indeed, a "libertine" (terrible is that name a part of accusing conditions), ready to "enjoy" her and skulk the costs thereof? Does he cure her of "prostitution", or does he leave her more of one? Was his "significant look" a *sly wink* after all? "My Girl" *has* poetry in her, but Whitman fails to hymn it. Prostitution is not so rare an attribute as to need furtherance in songs of poets. My revolt is that Whitman holds the girl before him deprecated. Man hath no need to deal with woman's vagina, her breasts or lips, if by so doing, in his own mind, she is hurt or defamed. Rather let him roll over on mother earth like a phrenzied (sic) stallion, and cry for mercy and cure. Unlike Athenian or Roman women, the American deems not to stand slave or mistress, but WOMAN.

The ground fact of woman's existence is her personality; knowledge left on me, with me, as me it is my right and duty to use. Let us not dispute in the near meeting which sex invites, but hold ourselves in the realm of Love where not hurt is, and infinite service is possible. If under sway of restrictive statutes, woman must stand still and quiver for want of wisdom to speak, allow her at least the sanctity of silence in whatever service she feels to render. Why this walk and talk in faith and practice if it is not both task and privilege for man and woman to find out what they are on this brown earth for? Law keeps up the old reign, the old disaster of hate; a new sign and saying I give unto you that ye love one another, have the joy, beauty and plenty resulting. Man so lot to himself and woman as to invole *violence* in these sacred nearings, *should have solemn meeting with, and look seriously at his own penis until he is able to be lord and master of it, rather than it should longer rule, lord and master, of him and of the victims he deflowers.* Is it not he who flows semen the criminal, rather than she who disposes of it? When man learns to cease CRIMINATING mothers, wives, daughters, in his rude "laws", puts thoughtful injunction on himself, stops his arrogant violation of woman, we can respect him as brother, sire, mate, Loving him as man, not as animal merely. St. Paul was kind enough to say that man is the head of woman; but this obscenist folly requires us to furnish brain for his,—put a *head* on man. Sex is not an unheard of or an unfelt fact in any one, and the sooner body housekeeping has rational mention the better. Intelligent acquaintance with, and clear knowledge of ourselves will replace the song of disease with the song of Health, and make home-thrift the rule, instead of the exception.

XIV. The Persecution of Moses Harman

Stanley Day

As one of the earliest advocates of birth control, Moses Harman (1830–1910) fought for freedom of the press as much as for women's rights, since the vehicle by which social purity reformers attempted to suppress birth control was censorship. Specifically, the Comstock laws (1873) prohibited the mailing of obscenity without defining what constituted obscene material; whatever the definition, however, contraceptives and birth control information were included. In opposition to this, Harman maintained, "Words are not deeds, and it is not the province of civil law to take preventative measures against remote or possible consequences of words." This attitude was translated into the policy under which Harman published Lucifer the Light Bearer *(1883–1907): He refused to edit letters to the editor which contained explicit language. Between 1887 and 1895, Harman was tried and convicted three times for the publication of letters to* Lucifer. *One of these letters is perhaps the earliest discussion in American journalism of forced sex in marriage as constituting rape. Harman's final arrest occurred in 1906 at the age of 75. The following article is reprinted from* Lucifer *and describes Moses Harman's imprisonment, when he spent time breaking rocks in the Illinois snow.*

"When the innocent is convicted the court is condemned."

In these days, when vital questions are probed to their very foundations, no honest man will shrink from any fact that analysis of his introspection into his physical, mental and moral nature reveals. The civilized world is networked with currents of investigation which a few years ago would have been smothered abjectly in *faith.* It is realized that between opposite extremes truth is found at the *juste milieu,* and an effort by the partisans of an extreme theory to suppress the publication of an opposing theory by force is as mischievious and wicked as it is lawless and dishonest. Error will always be exposed when truth is left free to combat it. And while the broad-minded investigator will go to both extremes and examine all sides of a question before settling down to a conviction, it is certain that, as long as men are free to choose whether they will investigate or not, no one has a right to complain that inquiries prosecuted by others are offensive to him. The forcible suppression of any sentiment however stultified or infatuated or of any language however harsh or offensive is so contrary to inborn American notions of freedom, fair play and justice that any attempt thereat calls forth prompt and indignant resentment.

The purpose of this writing is to show by a simple statement of facts some of the grotesque inconsistencies of an attempt to enforce in this country the suppressive methods of an inquisitorial censorship.

In 1881 the publication of a radical newspaper, LUCIFER, was commenced at Valley Falls, Kansas, the purpose being to provide a medium for the exchange and dissemination of radical thought and to stimulate progressive ideas in the social, economic, theological and philosophical fields of investigation. The merit of this unpretentious little paper lay in its fidelity to truth, and in extending hospitality to new ideas, and in candidly examining the value of their claims. No editors were ever more hearty, free or sincere than Moses Harman and his son George, and Edwin C. Walker.

While these men were quietly minding their own business and issuing LUCIFER weekly they were arrested February 23, 1887, on a charge of violating the Comstock postal law, and taken before United States Commissioner Wilson at Topeka, who held them to await the action of the grand jury, and upon executing bonds of $500 each to appear at the April term of court, they were allowed to go home.

Attending at the April term, they were told that nothing could be done with their case "on account of lack of appropriations," and again executing bonds to appear the following July, they went home.

At the July term they were told that the district attorney had decided not to present the charges to the grand jury "on account of the extreme heat," and for other frivolous reasons. Giving bonds to appear at the October term, they again went home.

This being forced to travel long distances fruitlessly, and to attend many terms of court accompanied by attorneys and bondsmen at considerable expense, was not the least oppressive of the many devices by which the prosecution exhibited its disposition to pester and annoy the defendants. Throughout the whole eight years of this outrageous persecution Mr. Harman has been compelled to give bonds a dozen or more times, a requirement as brutal as it was malicious, for one bond would have answered all reasonable requirement of the law. As the length of this narrative compels us to economize space, we cannot again refer in detail to each case in which a bond was required.

In October they again took the journey to court and were informed that they might return home and that they would be sent for if wanted.

A week after this adjournment it was discovered that they were wanted and they were accordingly sent for to come again to Topeka, where they were confronted with the most marvelous indictments ever incubated by a grand jury. These indictments, joint and several, charged the defendants with mailing a copy of each of five issues of their paper, to each of nine individuals, contrary to the statute. Ringing the changes and variations upon this theme amplified the indictments until they swelled up to 270 counts. The district attorney, like the drowning sailors, believing that some sort of ceremonial function was imperative at this juncture, required the defendants to execute another bond, which they did, and went home to unravel the intricacies of these complicated indictments.

Now, the purpose of an indictment is to inform the defendant what the charge against him is, but these indictments were drawn with the intention of concealing that information, and so effectual was the concealment that neither the defendants, their attorneys, the judge, nor even the district attorney himself could point to any one of the 270 counts which contained any intelligible accusation whatever against the defendants. So these indictments were quashed.

This would have been a good place for the prosecution to have stopped, but notwithstanding a remonstrance against the continuation of this farce, signed by one hundred of the best citizens of Valley Falls, the district attorney procured new indictments from a subservient grand jury.

By these new indictments, in 216 counts, the defendants were informed, for the first time, what articles they had published in LUCIFER that had set the indictment mill agoing and produced such a plethoric grist of counts, 486 in all, whereby so much filing of bail bonds was exacted. The articles which it was now pretended were so shocking as to require the persecution of the publishers were only four in number. As, subsequently, upon the trial, the district attorney admitted that he and the grand jury were mistaken as to two of these articles, and withdrew the charges relating to them, it will only be necessary for us to concern ourselves with the remaining two as to which the charge was pressed. These were (1) The now celebrated "Markland letter." (2) A letter written by Mrs. Celia B. Whitehead.

These letters are too lengthy to be reproduced in our present limited space. Readers who are unfamiliar with them will find fair counterparts of the Markland letter in a "Special Report on Diseases of the Horse," published and gratuitously circulated by the United States department of agriculture, and in a little pamphlet entitled "Our Suffering Sisters," issued by the International Medical Missionary Society. The Whitehead letter is an argument rather in favor of the law prohibiting contraceptics than otherwise.

The usual annoyance of arrest and bond filing followed.

Thus it will be seen that although charged with an indictable offense, it was two years after the pretended committing of the offense, and over a year after their first arrest, and then only by fighting for it, that the defendants could find out from the prosecution what the charge against them really was, and when they did find out they learned that the original indictments embraced some pretended offense which it was not deemed prudent to include in the second indictments.

In May, 1888, the defendants George Harman and Edwin C. Walker withdrew from the management of LUCIFER, and Moses Harman continued as sole editor. By reason of this withdrawal proceedings against the junior editors were *nolle prossed* on the trial. From this point, tnerefore, our narrative will concern itself solely with the conduct and fate of Moses Harman.

As soon as the charges took definite shape, LUCIFER'S friends clamored to know what it was all about, and on June 22 Mr. Harman reprinted the Markland letter in parallel columns with the 38th chapter of Genesis. This was done so that no one should be ignorant of the charge itself, nor of its frivolousness, that secrecy should not be added to the other disadvantages he would have to contend with, that it might be shown logically that, judged by the same tests which condemned the Markland letter, the Bible must necessarily be considered obscene, and furthermore, that something practical might be done to abolish such conditions as made possible the facts told in the Markland letter concerning the violation of a wife by a fiendish husband before her recovery from childbirth.

The other three indicted articles were republished July 20, August 3 and September 14, 1888, respectively, in especially large editions, thus demonstrating how difficult it is in this country to suppress thought, even though unprincipled men may be temporarily invested with power to hamper the press.

At the autumn term, 1888, the trial was put off until spring, because everybody was so interested in politics that the administration of justice in court was set aside as a matter of secondary importance.

Meanwhile discussion of the indicted articles had been growing very active, whereby the frivolities of the charges became more and more palpable, and sympathy with the persecuted editor more and more earnest and general, and moral and financial support was advanced for his relief.

At the spring term, 1889, defendant demurred to the indictment, and while this demurrer was pending Mr. Harman boldy advertised to send LUCIFER for one year with "Irene" for $1.75. The point of this lies in the fact that the author of "Irene," Mrs. Fowler, had just been indicted under the flimsy pretense that her book was obscene. The indictment against Mrs. Fowler was never brought to trial.

On May 24, 1889, Judge Foster rendered an opinion overruling the demurrer, in which he criticised the prosecution with merited severity, saying, "I have but little patience with those self-constituted guardians and censors of public morals who are always on the alert to find something to be shocked at, who explore the wide domain of art, science and literature to find something immodest and who attribute impurity where none is intended." On the other hand, he went so far aside from the real issues, and so far violated judicial impartiality, as to make a gratuitous and premature statement, implying that the Markland letter and the Whitehead letter excited impure thoughts in *his* mind, and so were really "obscene."

Mrs. Whitehead, long, well and widely known among progressive people as a woman of sterling character, was naturally indignant at the judge's imputation that she had written an obscene letter, and clipping her own and the Markland letter from LUCIFER, she mailed them to the judge with the request that he mark the parts in them which seemed to him indecent and return them to her. It might appear that, as the gravamen of the offense Mr. Harman was charged with was mailing these very articles, Mrs. Whitehead acted rashly in exposing herself to prosecution and inviting the judge to do likewise, but when we consider that all the obscenity there really was in the case lay in the prurient fancy of the judge and the prosecution, her act assumes a dignity far beyond any mere act of defiance.

Then followed a flood of criticism, and LUCIFER and other radical papers were filled with opinions from many as competent to write opinions as Judge Foster himself, even though not clothed with authority, and the judge and district attorney were overwhelmed with letters from all parts of the country. There was no doubt a strong sentiment throughout the country that Mr. Harman would not be honestly dealt with. This sentiment came from observation of the inconsistencies of the prosecution, as well as from a recollection of the outrage upon good old D. M. Bennett in a similar case. Under these criticisms the moral attitude of the prosecution became so contemptible that in the autumn the district attorney washed his hands of the business by continuing the case to April, 1890, before which time his term of office would expire.

The attempt at suppression had resulted in widespread notoriety for the indicted articles. They had been distributed by Mr. Harman and his friends until they were well known and thoroughly discussed by all the well-informed radicals in the country. Some thought that not merely were the articles not detrimental to public morals, but that to amend public morals their publication was an eminently meritorious act. Some maintained that while the constitution guaranteed freedom of speech, and liberty of sentiment, with no restraint as to form of expression, it was still injudicious to print articles which might be objectionable to good taste. But while all censured officials so false to their obligations as to persecute Mr. Harman for printing matter of his own selection in his own paper for those who wanted to read it, there were some who considered such a publication unnecessary, on the ground that inhumanities like that described in the Markland letter were so rare that it was not worth while to combat them as it might be if they were more frequent. For the enlightenment of this latter class, and to meet their objection, many instances like that narrated in the Markland letter were detailed by LUCIFER'S contributors, and among such contributions was a letter from Dr. O'Neill, describing a number of similar perversions.

Another arrest followed, February 18, 1890, on the O'Neill letter. Marshal Dillard, who had the warrant, was ordered to put Mr. Harman in jail in Valley Falls, and again in Topeka, but having no malice towards him, and full of confidence in him, he allowed him to go, unattended, on his promise to accompany him to Topeka next morning, but on arriving at Topeka the commissioner, to prevent his absconding, fixed bail at $1,000, and another bond was given.

On March 11 LUCIFER contained a letter from Mrs. Waisbrooker quite similar to the O'Neill letter. Of this the prosecution, with its usual consistency, took no notice.

On April 17 a pretended trial took place, of a character grossly discreditable even to the system of jurisprudence under which such an outrage is possible. Of this farce the following are some of the main features: The new district attorney, Mr. Ady, had assured Mr. Harman that he should have sufficient notice of trial to enable him to prepare properly. This assurance he dishonorably violated, hustling on the trial at a time when Mr. Harman was unprepared, and showing thereby an entire lack of any honest intention to try the issues in the case with fairness. On the day in question Mr. Harman's counsel, Mr. Overmeyer, was in the deepest family affliction. His wife was not expected to live throughout the day and his child was dangerously ill. He was in no condition to try such a case. Other counsel was on the way from New York, intending in good faith to try the case upon its merits. These facts were fully detailed in affidavits on a motion to adjourn the case for one day, but while the prosecution had loitered along for four years, it now insisted that one day was too long a time for such an aggravated case of "obscenity" to go unattended to. No fair judge would have denied such an application for an adjournment. The application was, however, sneeringly denied by Judge Foster, who said to Mr. Harman: "If you had been as diligent in looking up counsel as you have been in instructing me in my duties you would not now be unprepared." Thus Judge Foster got square for some fancied slight to his ineffable dignity. No one has ever been able to tell with certainty what it was that piqued the judge and led him to take this mean revenge. Possibly something may have been written to him by some of Mr. Harman's friends which excited his spleen. Possible it was the fact that just before the trial Mr. Harman had printed in LUCIFER the oath of office taken by the judge. If it was this latter act that the judge resented he would better have deliberated long enough to realize that from the mere printing of the oath there was no implication that the oath was likely be violated, but on the contrary, all the presumptions were that the judge would live up to his oath. The judge directed the trial to proceed at once, and assigned as counsel a lawyer entirely unfamiliar with the numerous details of the case, who, instead of setting up a proper defense and arguing on the law and the substantial merits, interposed the preposterous plea of insanity. Against this course Mr. Harman protested with earnest vigor, but his protest was treated as if it were mere contumacious disorder, and the judge presided over this hideous, wicked farce with as much gravity as if he were honestly trying the case.

It must have been gratifying to the judge that the conviction which ensued was upon just those articles which he had gratuitously characterized as obscene in his opinion a year before, but the obscenity of which he had omitted to explain to Mrs. Whitehead. As it was, the verdict was a compromise, three of the jurors being disposed to acquit.

Judge Foster imposed the most brutal sentence ever known in a case of this kind, five years' imprisonment and a fine of $300, and in doing so again manifested a pique and malignity which showed him entirely unfit to fulfill judicial functions. This manifestation of pique was accentuated by the fact that at the same term of court another defendant confessedly guilty of an offense of the same nature was allowed to go on payment of the minimum fine.

No stay was allowed, and Mr. Harman was at once committed to prison. His letters at this time are models of dignified protest against wrong. He remained in prison until August 30, when by virtue of a writ of error he was released, after seventeen weeks' imprisonment. A new bond was required.

On October 16, 1890, a curious proceeding was had before Judge Phillips, somewhat in the nature of a trial, on the O'Neill letter, yet without a jury. The defendant was examined before the judge for about an hour and adjournments were then had to December 29, when the law of the case was argued by counsel and submitted.

The appeal in the Markland letter case was adjourned at this time to the spring term of 1891.

January 15, 1891, Judge Phillips brought in a verdict of guilty against Mr. Harman, and without his being present in court sentenced him to one year's imprisonment. Comparing the Markland and the Whitehead letters on one hand with the O'Neill letter on the other hand it will be seen that the present case showed an improvement in judicial moderation. Another improvement was manifested, for, an appeal being taken, the monotonous formality of giving bonds was omitted, the marshal saying: "Go about your business as usual—when I want you I know there to find you."

In March, 1891, a writ of error as to the O'Neill letter case was allowed by Judge Caldwell, and another bond was required.

On June 1 Mr. Harman attended in court with counsel to argue the appeals, but adjournment was had to the latter part of November, when both cases were submitted to Judge Caldwell.

On April 15, 1892, while these appeals were yet undecided, a high-handed trick was played upon Mr. Harman. A whole edition of his paper was stopped in the postoffice at Topeka. This was the second time Mr. Harman's enemies had recourse to this rascally trick, the first time being in October, 1890.

Early in June, 1892, Judge Caldwell filed his decision, setting aside Judge Foster's sentence in the Markland letter case. Thus it appears, while Judge Foster was so eager for conviction that he could not wait one day for the purpose of having a fair trial, that after six years of atrocious outrage, fiendish persecution, hideous perversion of justice, and contemptible trickery, the case stood just where it did in the outset, in June, 1886, when the Markland letter was first published.

June 13 Judge Caldwell filed a decision sustaining the conviction by

Judge Phillips on the O'Neill letter and confirming the sentence, and a few days thereafter, to the eternal disgrace of our American judiciary, Moses Harman began a term of a year's imprisonment for exercising the American birthright of free speech.

On February, 16, 1893, on a petition for habeas corpus, Mr. Harman was discharged from imprisonment in the O'Neill letter case, upon the ground that the sentence of four months on each of three counts must either be held void for uncertainty, or else it must be held to mean that the sentences on all these three counts run concurrently, in which latter case the prisoner had more than served his term.

This left Mr. Harman with the old Markland letter case hanging over him—the case that was reversed and remanded "to be dealt with according to law."

After three years of inactivity and when everybody was in hopes this preposterous nonsense was so dead as to be incapable of resurrection, District Attorney Perry, who, with the change of administration, had been reappointed to succeed Mr. Ady, moved before Judge Phillips to correct the sentence and that an amended sentence be passed. This was very clearly inflicting two punishments for the same offense, but the district attorney seems to have had no shame and no moral sense to restrain him from making the contention that the previous proceedings were unlawful. The very proceeding that he instituted so dishonorably had not turned out as he expected, and so he declared it unlawful. The unlawfulness of the whole business was just what Mr. Harman and his friends had insisted upon from the outset. Had the case been "dealt with according to law" Mr. Harman would have been free from annoyance six years ago.

On June 1, 1895, Judge Phillips, the same judge who showed his incapacity for dealing with such cases "according to law" by his misfit sentence in the O'Neill letter case, undertook to correct the sentence inflicted by Judge Foster in the Markland letter case by the infliction of a new sentence, under which Mr. Harman was again arrested and at the present writing is lodged in the Kansas state prison at Lansing.

This is the history to date of one of the most flagrant violations of citizen rights ever perpetrated in this country. On a prosecution entirely groundless and unjustifiable an estimable old man, after being harassed unmercifully for eight years, has been swindled out of his liberty by a series of alleged trials which are a disgrace to our jurisprudence, and at least is in prison for having done an act for which humanity will long revere his memory.

That the publication of the Markland letter has resulted in great good no one who knows the facts can deny. But it ought not to be necessary in our civilization to make a martyr in order to take an advance step in the world's progress.

Mr. Harman in his persecution has the sympathy of all good men, and all to whom these presents may come are urged to respond in some form, spreading the light he has kindled, strengthening his hands for further conflict and helping to uplift humanity as he has done.

XV. If You Liked Gun Control . . .

Beverly J. Combs

"If You Liked Gun Control, You'll Love the Antiabortion Amendment" expresses the confusion of a woman whose respect for the First Amendment's separation of church and state extends to the Second Amendment's guarantee of the right to bear and keep arms. To Combs, the right to control her own body through abortion implies the right to protect her body against aggression. The tension she feels between her prochoice stand on abortion and her opposition to gun control is the tension between a conservative and a liberal ideology. The resolution of this tension is individualist-feminism; that is, a statement of self-ownership which includes both the right to control and the right to protect one's person. Gun control is, of course, a particularly important issue to women whose size makes them vulnerable to attack.

Combs is a descendant of several old and famous Virginia families and is a tenth-generation granddaughter of the American Indian princess Pocahontas.

For many years, conservatives have given considerable time and devotion to the cause of protecting the Second Amendment to the Constitution—the right to keep and bear arms. Equal time and devotion should now be given to the cause of protecting one of our rights under the First Amendment—the right to religious liberty. Most conservatives have chosen to go the other way, however, giving adamant support to the proposed antiabortion amendment, an amendment based solely on religious dogma—dogma not belonging to the Constitution of a free people. It is to those conservatives that I address this lament.

As a conservative, I stand opposed to any amendment infringing upon my present rights; as a woman, I stand opposed to any amendment restricting my right to protect my health; and, above all, as an American, I stand opposed to any amendment providing the means for religious tyranny to enter into the affairs of state.

It is, therefore, with no small amount of consternation that I watch you, my old conservative friends, so vociferously thumbing your noses at the first clause of the First Amendment—the separation of church and state.

What is even more dismaying is that you are destroying the First Amendment by marshaling the same tactics we used successfully to preserve the Second Amendment. Had I not once been on "the other side," perhaps the situation would not appear so perplexing.

"Nazis!" we shouted then, "First gun registration, then the brown shirts in the night."

"Nazis!" you shout now, "First abortion, then the ovens."

As I read the chapter "The Family" from Richard Grunberger's *The 12-Year Reich*, some of the words echoed an all too familiar tune: "the new regime proved its claim to be better protectors of family life by imposing harsh curbs on equality for women, abortion, homosexuality and (conspicuous) prostitution . . . immediately after the seizure of power of advertisement and display of contraceptives was banned . . . and all birth control clinics were closed down. Abortions were termed 'acts of sabotage' against Germany's racial future, involving commensurately heavy punishment . . . . "

But we must not pause too long to burden our minds with the facts; let us return to our slogans.

One of the slogans of the gun lobby is: "Why outlaw guns? The criminal will always be able to get a gun." Yes, he will, my friends—except under an absolute dictatorship. For example, it is not a difficult task for criminals to clandestinely manufacture guns and peddle them through the black market.

Now I ask you: "Why outlaw abortions? A woman will always be able to get an abortion." Yes, she will—except under an absolute dictatorship. For example, the rich will be able to go to another country for an abortion and the poor will still resort to their do-it-yourself or back-alley abortions.

We thought it an injustice for people to imply that only the ignorant or the violent keep guns. On the other hand, I think it is an equal injustice for you to imply that only the immoral or the uncaring seek abortion.

I recall, there was much slapping of the right thigh when some of us sat one night and listened to some "damned fool woman" state how it was "dreadful about all those big, grown men running around the country killing those poor little skeet." Recently when I listened to you state that under the proposed antiabortion amendment "the body and life of the mother are only involved indirectly," I was slapping the other thigh.

Further insulting my intelligence, you go on to say that meaningful life begins at conception. Does it, my friends? *Why?* Because you say so; furthermore, you can prove it by showing me a movie on the development of a fetus.

At this point, I think it is not impertinent to ask the question, "Where do babies come from?"

From *meaningless* life, you say. Oh?

You didn't say that? But you have just told me *meaningful* life begins at conception; hence, I must assume that the sperm before it unites with the egg to form a zygote is *meaningless* life.

Ah, wait a minute, I think I'm catching on. The sperm is part of a *man's* body; the ovum, part of a *woman's* body. But what if a man damages his half of the zygote before it unites with the woman's half, thus causing the eventual spontaneous abortion of a "meaningful life?"

Well, goes the reply, a man has a right to do what he wants concerning his own body (including the right to shoot a prowler if he decides such prowler *might* do him some bodily harm). Anyway, you're not talking about spontaneous abortion, you say.

I know you're not, that's why I am. For carried to its ultimate conclusion, your proposed antiabortion amendment should, I think, be called The Bedroom Amendment.

If it is logical to argue that the next step after the banning of handguns would be the banning of shotguns and rifles, is it not logical to argue that the next step after the banning of induced abortions would be an attempt to ban or forcibly control spontaneous abortions? Because abortion is a religious, sexual taboo, government must eventually intrude into the "affairs of the bedroom" if there is to be effective abortion control.

What are the causes of spontaneous abortion? In his article "Polluted Genes" (North American Newspaper Alliance) Jon Frederics points out that "a man's heavy drinking habits may lead to birth defects, spontaneous abortions, and other bodily abnormalities." Perhaps future research will show that many of our personal habits infringe upon "the welfare and rights of the unborn."

The future. What lies ahead for those of us who love liberty?

Man does not have the gift of being able to see into the future; therefore, he must study the history of mankind and draw from the lessons history teaches.

Studying the history of mankind leads me to believe that it is man's nature to revel in the barbarity of religious oppression. I can only conclude that you have laid the foundation for religious oppression if your proposed antiabortion amendment becomes a part of our Constitution. History teaches me many will come along to build on this foundation. What then of our guns, which we say we keep to defend our guaranteed freedoms? There will be no further use for them, for you yourselves will have destroyed individual liberty, from within.

But, you ask, what has all this to do with the killing of "innocent little babies?"

Nothing, as far as I can see. The issue in question is freedom. The proposed antiabortion amendment ignores the cornerstone of freedom: The individual—neither the church nor the state—must make the decisions concerning his own body. As the master makes the decisions concerning the slave's body, thus the dictatorial state makes the decisions concerning man's body.

If you insist, however, let us speak of the killing of innocent babies: the millions of babies that have been killed throughout history by man's wars and man's cruelty.

Ah, but this is all right, you say. Man may kill babies in the name of war, and besides, wars are fought in the name of religion.

Yes, some of them have been. But am I to believe that in the name of religion, a woman—perhaps sick, haggard, and worn or perhaps with greater purposes than motherhood—*must,* should be forced to go through with, pregnancy?

Of course. Unless man, in the name of religion, goes to war; then it is justifiable with the instruments of war—bombing and burning, disease and desolation, heartbreak and hell—to do this woman enough harm to cause her to abort.

When I listened closely to the argument of the pro-gun-control crowd, I decided what they meant was gun confiscation. Now I have listened closely to your antiabortion argument, and I have decided what you mean is this: sex is sin; pregnancy is a woman's punishment for her part in this sin.

Listen to yourselves: "Selfish women." "Virgin Mary didn't do that." "*For* a man having a gun. *Against* a woman having an abortion." "God will judge."

Oh, you can parade your grave concern for these innocent little "unborn children." But, my conservative friends, I think I know you better than that. I wonder what you would say to a bill that stated: "No firearm may be kept in any dwelling where one of the occupants therein is a minor."

It might save one child from a tragic accident. But you seem to be more concerned with the rights of the "unborn" child—from the moment of conception.

Seemingly obsessed with the phrase "moment of conception" and determined that I should abide by your religious dogma—dogma asserting that I was a person from the moment of conception—you antiabortionists try to pass legislation which in effect states that my soul entered my body at the moment of conception. Or am I to believe I was once a person without a soul?

Furthermore, not content with trying to write your own religious beliefs into the Constitution, you also try to distort the religious beliefs of my forefathers (and foremothers), apparently expecting me to believe that their views were the same as yours are.

In spite of your sanctimonious asseverations, however, I find evidence that many of our country's founders were inclined to be neither straitlaced nor superstitious: Thomas Jefferson doubted the virgin birth; Sarah Harrison refused to repeat the word "obey" at her marriage ceremony; John Randolph (of Roanoke) believed occasionally in God, frequently in Christ, and always in John Randolph; and although Elizabeth Blair had 19 children, I can only conjecture whether this was due to the presence of piety or the absence of the pill.

Nevertheless, you keep marching. Yet, it seems to me, you are trying to march in one direction while facing in the opposite direction.

Two hundred years ago, a few men defied a religious belief: the belief that a king had the divine right to rule over the common man. And as a result of their defiance, the common man in this country at last became equal to a king.

Equal to a king! Now the common man was to control his own destiny, his own body, his own thoughts.

One symbol, and more than a symbol, of this new equality was the gun. The right of the common man to own a gun (the right of the *people* to keep and bear arms) was acknowledged—he alone was to make the decisions concerning the protection of his own body.

The ideas held by these few men were new—revolutionary. Yes, these were gallant men, searching for better answers instead of echoing the old ways. What dreams they had of new health, new freedom, new courage to end some of the suffering that had long plagued this miserable human race.

But what is it I hear today—this brazen hypocrisy, this distain for women—where will it lead?

"In trying to legislate gun control, Congress is trying to legislate morals." "Congress can't legislate morals, the criminal won't obey the laws." "If a woman's not ready to pay, she shouldn't play."

> I see a woman, she stands in the doorway of a little shack. Around her are gathered several small children, dirty and sad; their little faces reflect none of the pleasures of childhood.
>
> At her sagging breast, a baby sucks, fighting for the nourishment which is not there.

> She looks away from her children, far away; her eyes mirror all the misery of the world.
>
> She will not be with us long, this one; Fate will soon carry her away.
>
> The kings! They will do something for her, someday—take up a church offering, or develop a new fertilizer, maybe.
>
> Poor wretched soul, had it but once drunk from the golden cup of liberty and tasted the sweet joy of being equal to a king.

Oh, we could have some splendid times together on this one; I will miss you as I go on alone. But as you turn and go the other way, farewell, old friends.

Suggested Readings

Dienes, C. Thomas. *Law, Politics and Birth Control.* Urbana, Ill.: University of Illinois, 1972.

Gordon, Linda. "Voluntary Motherhood: The Beginnings of Feminist Birth Control Ideas in the United States." *Feminist Studies.* Winter-Spring, 1973.

Heywood, Ezra. *Free Speech: Report of Ezra H. Heywood's Defense Before the United States Court, in Boston April 10, 11, 12, 1883.* Princeton, Mass.: Cooperative Publishing, 1883.

Ledbetter, Rosanna. *The History of the Malthusian League, 1877–1927.* Columbus: Ohio State University Press, 1976.

The Queen v. *Charles Bradlaugh and Annie Besant.* London: Freethought Publishing Company, n.d.

West, William L. "The Moses Harman Story." *Kansas Historical Quarterly.* Spring, 1971.

WOMEN AND CHILDREN

XVI. Relations Between Parents and Children

Clara Dixon Davidson

The following article was written by Clara Dixon Davidson, a contributor to Liberty *and the editor of a short-lived periodical,* L'Enfant Terrible *(1891–1892), which issued from San Francisco. This article was part of a lengthy debate among individualist anarchists on the status of children. Specifically, the debate revolved around whether children possessed individual rights or were the property of their parents.*

The wisdom of acts is measured by their consequences.

The individual's measure of consequences is proportionate to the circle of his outlook. His horizons may lie so near that he can only measure at short range. But, whether they be near or far, he can only judge of consequences as proximately or remotely touching himself. His judgment may err; his motive remains always the same, whether he be conscious of it or not.

That motive is necessarily egoistic, since no one deliberately chooses misery when happiness is open to him. Acts always resulting either indifferently or in furtherance of happiness or increase of misery, one who has power to decide and intelligence to determine probable consequences will certainly give preference to the course which will ultimately advance his own happiness.

The law of equal freedom, "Every one is free to do whatsoever he wills," appears to me to be the primary condition to happiness. If I fail to add the remainder of Herbert Spencer's celebrated law of equal freedom, I shall only risk being misinterpreted by persons who cannot understand that the opening affirmation includes what follows, since, if any one did infringe upon the freedom of another, all would not be equally free.

Liberty without intelligence rushes toward its own extinction continually, and continually rescues itself by the knowledge born of its pain.

Intelligence without liberty is a mere potentiality, a nest-full of unhatched eggs.

Progress, therefore, presupposes the union of intelligence and liberty: Freedom to act, wisdom to guide the action.

Equal freedom is the primary condition to happiness.

Intelligence is the primary condition to equality in freedom.

Liberty and intelligence acting and re-acting upon each other produce growth.

Thus growth and happiness are seen to be, if not actually synonymous, almost inseparable companions.

Where equal freedom is rendered impossible by disproportion in degrees of development, the hope of the higher units lies in the education of the lower.

Children, because of their ignorance, are elements of inharmony, hindrances to equal freedom. To quicken the processes of their growth is to contribute toward the equilibrization of social forces.

Then, liberty being essential to growth, they must be left as free as is compatible with their own safety and the freedom of others.

Just here arises my difficulty, which I freely admit. For the enunciation of this principle is the opening of a Pandora's box, from which all things fly out excepting adult judgment.

Who shall decide upon the permissible degree of freedom? Who shall adjust the child's freedom to its safety so that the two shall be delicately, flawlessly balanced?

The fecundity of these questions is without limit. Of them are born controversies that plague all the unregenerate alike, whether they be philosophers or the humblest truth-seekers.

Christians escape this toilsome investigation. Their faith in rulership simplifies all the relations of life. Their conduct need not be consistent with equal freedom, since obedience, not liberty, is the basis of their ideal society.

Reluctantly I admit that during infancy and to some extent in childhood others must decide what is for a child's welfare.

The human babe is a pitiably helpless and lamentably ignorant animal. It does not even know when it is hungry, but seeks the maternal breast as a cure-all for every variety of physical uneasiness; therefore the mother or nurse must inevitably decide for it even the quantity of nourishment it may safely receive and the length of time that may intervene between tenders of supplies. That these judgments are far from infallible is well known. One mother of five living children confessed to me that she had lost one child, starved it in the process of learning that her lactation furnished a substance little more nutritious than water.

Grown older, the babe does not know the danger of touching a red-hot stove. How should it know? It is without experience. The mother's impulse is to rescue the tender, white baby-hand. Is she wise in interposing this restraint? I think she is not. If the child is to have bayoneted sentries always on guard between it and experience, it can only grow surreptitiously. I say "bayoneted" advisedly, since the hand interposed between the baby and the stove not infrequently emphasizes its power with a blow which gives more pain than the burn would have given, while its value as experience may be represented by the minus sign.

The theory that it is the duty of parents to provide for the needs of their young children, and of children to obey their parents and, in their age, to support them, is so generally accepted that I shall rouse a storm of indignation by asserting that there are no duties.

While a cursory glance at the subject may seem to show a denial of equal freedom in the refusal of a parent to support his child, a more careful study will reveal the truth that, so long as he does not hinder the activities of any one nor compel any other person or persons to undertake the task which he has relinquished, he cannot be said to violate the law of equal freedom. Therefore his associates may not compel him to provide for his child, though they may forcibly prevent him from aggressing upon it. They may prevent acts; they may not compel the performance of actions.

It will, perhaps, be well to anticipate at this point a question sure to be asked during the discussion.

Is it not aggression on the part of parents to usher into existence a child for which they are either unable or unwilling to provide?

Much may be said in reply.

First: In any association differences of opinion would arise as to whether it was aggression or not; these differences would imply doubt, and the doubt would make forcible prevention, even if practicable, unjustifiable.

Second: This doubt would be strengthened by consideration of the fact that no one could be able to predict with certainty nine months previous to the birth of a child that at the time of its birth its parents would be unable to provide sustenance for it.

Third: it would be further strengthened by the knowledge that death is always open to those who find life intolerable, and, so long as persons seek to prolong existence, they cannot properly complain of those who thrust it upon them. A young babe does not question whether the milk it feeds upon flows from its mother's breast or from the udder of a cow, and should it, with dawning intelligence, feel disturbed in mind or distressed in body by reason of its relations toward its environments, it will, by then, have learned the art of dying.

And now, having opened a gulf which swallows up duty, shall I be able to allay the consternation of those who have substituted the worship of this for their repudiated worship of another unsubstantial God?

It has seemed to me that, generally speaking, people's love for their children is in inverse proportion to their love of God and duty. However this may be,—and I will admit that, although parallel and pertinent, it is not directly in the line of inquiry I am pursuing,—there is still left to us the certainty that increasing intelligence will more and more incline individuals to face the consequences of their own acts; not for duty's sake, but in order to help establish and preserve that social harmony which will be necessary to their happiness.

Even in the present semi-barbarous condition of parental relations it is exceptional, unusual, for parents to abandon their children, and the two distinct incentives to such abandonment will be removed by social evolution, leaving the discussion of the obligation of parents to care for their children purely abstract and rather unprofitable, since no one will refuse to do so.

The two motives to which I refer are poverty and fear of social obloquy. Married parents sometimes desert their children because they lack abundant means of subsistence; unmarried parents occasionally not only desert their offspring, but deny them, in order to escape the malice of the unintelligent who believe that vice is susceptible of transmutation into virtue by the blessing of a priest, and virtue into vice by the absence of the miracle-working words.

Recognition of the law of equal freedom would nearly remove the first, render the second more endurable, and finally obliterate both, leaving parents without motive for the abandonment of offspring.

That parents usually find happiness in provision for the welfare of their young is well known. Even the habits of the lower animals afford evidence sufficient to establish this position, and, for convenience, postulating it as a principle, I shall proceed to examine how far parents defeat their own aim by unintelligent pursuit of it.

Food is the first, because the indispensable, requisite to welfare, but unintelligent and indiscriminate feeding results in thousands of deaths annually and sows seeds of chronic invalidism in millions of young stomachs.

Clothing also is considered indispensable, and is so in rigorous climates, but the primary object of covering the body, which is surely to make it comfortable, is usually almost wholly forgotten in the effort to conform to accepted ideals of beauty,—ideals often involving peculiar departures from natural forms.

Shelter is a necessity which is often accompanied by such over-zealous inhospitality to fresh air as places choice between in-door and out-door life in uncertain balance.

But the sturdiest pursuits and the dreariest defeats and failures are found in educational endeavors.

The child comes into an unknown world. His blinking eyes cannot decide which is nearer, the lighted taper on the table or the moon seen through the window. He does not know that a Riverside orange is larger than the palm of his tiny hand until he has learned the truth by repeated efforts to grasp it. He has all things to learn: ideas of dimension, weight, heat, moisture, density, resistance, gravitation,—all things in their inter-relations and their relations to himself. And what bungling assistance he receives in the bewildering path through this tangle of truth!

He learns that God sends the rain, the hail, and the snow down from the sky; that his little sister was brought from heaven by an angel and deposited in a doctor's pill-bags. The tie of relationship between her and himself remains a mystery. Anthropomorphism lurks everywhere. The unseen hand moves all things. He asks many questions which his teachers cannot answer, and, unwilling to confess their ignorance, they constantly reiterate: "God did it," as if that were an answer.

Turning from unsuccessful inquiries concerning natural phenomena, perhaps the child perceives, in a dim way, his relations with the State, and, as God posed before him in the realm of philosophy and science, so do all replies to his questionings now end in omnipotent government.

"Why does no one prevent the man with a star from clubbing the other man?"

"Because he is a policeman."

"Who said that a policeman might strike people?"

"The government."

"What is the government?"

"The government is,——my son, you will learn when you are older."

"Who pays the policeman for clubbing the other man?"

"The government."

"Where does the government get the money?"

"You will learn when you are older."

Usually at the age of six years, or even earlier, a child's education is practically abandoned by its inefficient parents and entrusted to the church and the State.

The State uses money robbed from the parents to perpetuate its powers of robbery by instructing their children in its own interest.

The church, also, uses its power to perpetuate its power. And to these twin leeches, as "Ouida" has aptly designated them, to these self-interested robbers and murderers, are the tender minds of babies entrusted for education.

Herbert Spencer has shown that the status of women and children improves in proportion to the decline of militarism and the advance of industrialism.

The military spirit is encouraged in multifold ways by both church and State, and little children and women, in their pitiable ignorance, assist in weaving nets that shall trip their own unwary feet and those of other women and children to follow them.

A spirit of subordination is inculcated by both church and State, which contemplate without rebuke the brutalities of authority, excepting in some cases of extra-ordinary cruelty, and teach the helpless victims that it is their duty to submit.

The most commonplace tenets of these powers would seem absurd and outrageous if expounded to an unprepared adult mind and stripped of all those devices of language by which the various promptings of shame, good nature, ignorance, or deceit impel us to soften the truth.

Say to such an one:

"Murder by the State is laudable; murder by an individual is criminal.

"Robbery by the State is permissible; robbery by an individual is a serious offense against public welfare.

"Assault of the parent upon his child is justifiable; assault of the child upon the parent is intolerable."

He would not look upon you with the simple confidence of a puzzled child, attributing the apparent incompatibilities to the feebleness of his own understanding.

But to the child these bewildering social sophistries, flowing into his mind from sources that appeal to his trust, and presented with ambiguities of language that serve to increase its difficulties, must appear hopeless labyrinths of mystery.

Thus at every step from infancy to adult life the progress of the child is checked by the incapacity of those who desire to advance its welfare.

Inherited tendencies and the training which they themselves received incline parents to become inexorable masters and to commend most the conduct of that child which is easiest enslaved.

Parents beat their children, elder children beat younger brothers and sisters, and the wee ones avenge their wrongs vicariously by beating their dolls or their wooden horses.

Through individual revolts against the general barbarity, revolts of increasing frequency and power, humanity gradually evolves above actual application of its savage principles. But these revolts against savagery, when led by emotion, often result nearly as disastrously as savagery itself.

Reason must be the basis of all enduring social growth.

When reason shall have learned to rebel against inequalities in liberties, and when this mental rebellion shall have become quite general, then will people have passed beyond danger of relapse into savagery.

Then parent and child shall not be master and slave, a relation distasteful to reasoning people, but they shall be friend and friend. There will be no restraints imposed except such as are absolutely necessary, and these will not take the form of blows and will be removed as early as possible.

Examples of such restraints as I mean are:

Detention from the brink of a precipice or an open well or the track of a coming locomotive, or of one child from striking another.

Parents who recognize the fundamental principle of happiness through freedom and intelligence will, generally speaking, achieve results proportionate to the degree of their success in harmonizing their lives with this principle. The greater their intelligence the higher perfection will they reach in the interpretation and application of the law of equal freedom, and in preparing their children to attain harmonious relations with their environment.

SUPPLEMENTARY

How to make liars of children:

I have said that infants have all things to learn. It would seem, and would be, superfluous to repeat a fact so well known, were it not true that most people credit little children with so much more knowledge than they could possibly have acquired in the given time. I have heard, not once but many times, mothers accuse young children of falsehood when I fully believed that the apparent mis-statements were due in part to the little ones' weak grasp on the language which they attempted to speak and partly to misinterpretation of facts. Even grown-up people do not look upon the simplest incident from exactly the same point of view; yet they expect from mere babes perfection of accuracy, and, being disappointed in this unreasonable expectation, accuse them of falsehood, and not infrequently worry them into admitting faults which have, in reality, no meaning to their dim understandings. But after lying has come to have meaning, the little mind becomes indifferent to truthfulness, finding that punishment falls the same, whether it inspire truth or falsehood.

Thus the child is made a liar by its parents' ignorant endeavor to teach it regard for the truth.

But worse mistakes are made by those parents whose daily conversation with their children furnishes examples of untruthfulness. Who has not been frightened into obedience by tales of a bogie-man, a Chinaman, a black man, or a Santa Claus with his rattan,——stories which do triple injury by fostering cowardice, class-hatred, and lying?

To teach a child to steal:

Carefully lock away from him all fruits and sweets. Allow him no money for personal expenses. If you miss anything, accuse him of having taken it. If you send him out to make purchases, count the change with suspicious care when he returns. If he has lost a few pennies, accuse him of having spent them for candy. If you never buy candy for him, this will teach him a means of supplying himself, and probably your next accusation will be true.

Strike children and they learn to strike each other; scold them and they learn to quarrel; give them drums and flags and uniforms and toy guns and they desire to become professional murderers. Open their letters, listen to their conversations with their young friends, pry into their little secrets, invade their private rooms without knocking, and you make them meddlers and disagreeable companions.

I have said that it is not the duty of children to obey their parents or to care for them in old age.

The following facts bear on this position:

The life of a child is usually merely incident to the pleasure of its parents, and is often an accident deeply deplored by both. Even when conception is desired, it is still for the pleasure of the parents. If it were possible, which it is not, to conceive of a life given solely for its own happiness, its parents taking no pleasure either in the sexual relation or in the hope of offspring, the child could incur no responsibility by the opinions or the acts of its parents.

After its birth child does not say:

"Give me food, clothes, and shelter now in exchange for food, clothes, and shelter which I will give you in your old age," and, could he make such a contract, it would be void. A man cannot be bound by promises he made during his infancy.

The question of obedience I pass, since highly-evolved parents cannot be obeyed, because they will not command.

On careful thought the removal of the idea of duty will be seen to be less startling than it must at first appear to those who have accepted without question the dogmas of authority. Mr. Cowell has called my attention to the fact that the love which most people have for their parents or foster-parents is evidence that few wholly lack lovable attributes. During the long years of familiar companionship between parents and child ties are usually formed which cannot be broken while life lasts, not ties of duty but of affection; these render mutual helpfulness a source of pleasure. If they be lacking, a self-respecting parent would choose the shelter of an almshouse rather than the grudging charity bestowed by his child under the spur of a belief in duty.

XVII. The Speech of Polly Baker

In 1770, Abbé Raynal included the much-reprinted Speech of Polly Baker in his Philosophique et Politique *as an example of the severity of New England laws. Years later, while visiting Benjamin Franklin, the Abbé launched on a vigorous defense of the trial's authenticity only to be interrupted by an amused Franklin. "M. l'Abbé, I am going to set you straight," he said. "When I was young and printed a newspaper, it sometimes happened, when I was short of material to fill my sheet, that I amused myself by making up stories, and that of Polly Baker is one of the number." With this confession (reported by Thomas Jefferson and Philip Mazzei), Franklin swept away the mystery which surrounded Polly Baker and her famous speech, allegedly delivered before a Court of Judicature in Connecticut where she was being prosecuted for having an illegitimate child.*

It is believed that the speech was originally printed in the General Advertiser *of April 15, 1747, a London newspaper. Within the week, five London papers reprinted it and the speech was well upon its remarkable career. Freethinker Peter Annet included Polly Baker's defense in his* Social Bliss Considered *(1749), and the speech was periodically revived by American newspapers. When its authorship was revealed, not everyone appreciated the jest; John Adams, for example, referred to the speech as "one of Franklin's many 'Outrages to Morality and Decorum'." Among those taken in by Franklin's good humor was Ezra Heywood who, over a century later, enthusiastically reprinted "The Speech of Polly Baker" in* The Word *only to be advised of its apocryphal nature by William B. Greene.*

Although the speech is humorously presented, Franklin's sympathy is clearly with Polly Baker. This sympathy is consistent with Franklin's rather advanced sexual views and with his reputation as a libertine. The importance of the speech lies not in Franklin's intentions, however, but in the use to which it was put. The speech was widely reprinted and circulated as a plea for sexual freedom and for women's rights.

May it please the Honorable Bench to indulge me in a few words. I am a poor, unhappy woman who has no money to fee lawyers to plead for me, being hard put to it to get a tolerable living. I shall not trouble your Honors with long speeches, nor have I the presumption to expect that you may by any means be prevailed on to deviate in your sentence from the law, in my favor. All that I humbly hope is that your Honors will charitably move the Governor's goodness in my behalf, that my fine may be remitted. This is the fifth time gentlemen, that I have been dragged before your Court on the same account: twice I have paid heavy fines, and twice been brought to public punishment for want of money to pay these fines. This may have been agreeable to the laws, and I don't dispute it; but since laws are sometimes unreasonable in themselves, and therefore repealed, and others bear too hard in particular cases, therefore there is left a power somewhere, to dispense with the execution of them. I take the liberty to say that I think this law, by which I am punished, is both unreasonable in itself, and particularly severe with regard to me, who has always lived an unoffending life in the neighborhood where I was born, and I defy my enemies (if I have any) to say I ever wronged man, woman, or child.

Abstracted from the law, I cannot conceive (may it please your Honors) what the nature of my offense is. I have brought five children into the world, at the risk of my life. I have maintained them well by my own industry, without burdening the township, and would have done it better, if it had not been for the heavy charges and fines I have paid. Can it be a crime (in the nature of things, I mean) to add to the number of the king's subjects, in a new country that really wants people? I own it, I should think it a praiseworthy, rather than a punishable action. I have debauched no other woman's husband, nor enticed any youth. These things I never was charged with; nor has anyone the least cause of complaint against me, unless, perhaps, the Minister or Justice because I have had children without being married, by which they have missed a wedding fee. But, can this be a fault of mine?—I appeal to your Honors. You are pleased to allow I don't want sense; but I must be stupified to the last degree not to prefer the honorable state of wedlock to the condition I have lived in. I always was, and still am, willing to enter into it and doubt not my behaving well in it, having all the industry, fertility, and skill in economy, appertaining to a good wife's character. I defy any person to say I ever refused an offer of that sort. On the contrary, I readily consented to the only proposal of marriage that ever was made to me, which was when I was a virgin; but too easily confiding in the person's sincerity that made it, I unhappily lost my own honor, by trusting to his for he got me with child, and then forsook me. That very person you all know; he is now become a magistrate of this county; and I had hopes that he would have appeared this day on the bench and endeavored to moderate the court in my favor. Then I should have scorned to mention it; but I must now complain of it as unjust and unequal that my betrayer and undoer, the first cause of all my faults and miscarriages (if they must be deemed such), should be advanced to honor and power in that government which punishes my misfortunes with stripes and infamy!

I shall be told, 'tis like, that were there no assembly in this case, the precepts of religion are violated by my transgressions. If mine was a religious offense, leave it to religious punishments. You have already excluded me from the comforts of your Church Communion; is not that sufficient? You believe I have offended Heaven, and must suffer eternal fire; will that not be sufficient? What need is there, then, of your additional fines and whipping? I own, I do not think as you do; for if I thought what you call a sin was really such, I would not presumptuously commit it. But how can it be believed that Heaven is angry at my having children, when to the little done by me towards it, God has been pleased to add his Divine skill and admirable workmanship in the formation of their bodies and crowned it by furnishing them with rational and immortal souls?

Forgive me gentlemen, if I talk a little extravagantly on those matters. I am no divine; but, if you, gentlemen, must be making laws, do not turn natural and useful actions into crimes, by your prohibitions. But take into your wise consideration the great and growing number of bachelors in the country; many of whom, from the mean fear of the expenses of a family, have never sincerely and honorably courted a woman in their lives; and by their manner of living, leave unproduced (which is little better than murder) hundreds of their posterity to the thousandth generation. Is not this a greater offense against the public good than mine? Compel them, then by law either to marry or to pay double the fine of fornication every year. What shall poor young women do, whom custom hath forbid to solicit the men, and who cannot force themselves upon husbands, when the laws take no pains to provide them any—and yet severely punish them, if they do their duty without them;—the duty of the first great command of Nature, and of Nature's God—increase and multiply!—a duty from the steady performance of which nothing has been able to deter me; but for its sake I have hazarded the loss of the public esteem, and have frequently endured public disgrace; and therefore ought in my humble opinion, instead of a whipping, to have a statue erected to my memory.

XVIII. Some Problems of Social Freedom

Lillian Harman

This essay typifies the sort of pamphlet published by the circle surrounding Lucifer the Light Bearer. *This pamphlet was printed from a lecture originally delivered before the Legitimation League, a British organization, whose purpose was to eliminate the cultural and legal stigma attached to illegitimacy. The organization was directly inspired by the work of Moses Harman and prompted Lillian Harman's 1898 visit to England as an attempt to further combine efforts toward free love in America and Britain. Originally published through the "Office of the Adult" (The Adult: A Journal for the Advancement of Freedom in Sexual Relationships), this essay argues that "free life must be the outcome of free thought.*

For further information on Lillian Harman, please refer to her article on "Age of Consent" under Women and Sex.

In beginning my address I must make the startling confession that I do not know all about all the problems of Social Freedom. Perhaps there are some among my hearers who are in a similar predicament, and yet are striving to bring about better and higher conditions.

Sometimes I am asked, "What is your creed?" "What would you substitute for the conditions which you think restrict normal development?" Yankee-like, I answer with other questions: "What does the hygienist give you in place of the poisonous drugs he asks you to throw away? What does the Freethinker give in place of the hell-fire and avenging-God religion which he asks you to discard? Is it not true that "what is one man's meat is another man's poison," that the food which would be thoroughly assimilated by the organism of one man would cause another man to suffer all the tortures of dyspepsia? The hygienist will tell you to eat simple food, and reject that which experience teaches you disturbs the normal action of your stomach. In other words: regulate your diet by reason. So the Freethinker says: "You need reason only to tell you that the doctrine of hell-fire is a fiction of ignorance. Your God is only fossilized Ignorance. Phenomena which your ancestors could not understand they attributed to the working of a supernatural being with human passions and weaknesses whom they called God. The increase of knowledge must necessarily dethrone the God of Ignorance; hence the continued antagonism of theology to science.

God is called the Great Unknown; a confession that he is the personification of Ignorance."

I believe in freedom of thought and of action as long as free acts are not invasive. But Freedom is necessarily like space—without limit. For that reason I have been criticised for devoting my efforts toward the arousing of public sentiment to the importance of Liberty in one particular line. In justification of my action I have only to say that this is the age of the specialist. People have learned that force to be effectual must be concentrated. A pound of powder laid upon the ground and fired goes up in smoke without producing any apparent useful effect. Confined in the narrow bore of a cannon a few ounces will suffice to make a breach in the ranks of the enemy. So I have directed my force—however much or little I may possess—toward one division of the enemy's forces which I think should be disrupted in order to give humanity the chance to develop along the lines of Freedom.

The first object of this Society, and one with which I am in hearty sympathy, is the promotion of freedom in sexual relationships. To my mind, however, the greatest good attained by our work for this object is the enlargement of freedom in *social* relationships, of which the distinctly *sexual* is but one phase. That is to say, the narrow conventional creeds concerning sex manifestations, which are current at the present day, render all social intercourse between men and women strained and artificial. Thoughts of sex are given undue prominence through the very fact that sexual desire must be avoided or suppressed. Two men or two women may be good friends, and be their natural selves; but let a man and woman meet, and their friendship is interfered with by the necessity which they feel resting upon them, if they are conscientious, of avoiding sexual desire. The woman must not be as friendly as she feels, for her interest in the man may be construed into an invitation to flirtation, or she may be accused of "misleading" him. Every expression of friendship which she gives is practically held to be an implied contract to further steps. A coldness and reserve in the attitude of men and women toward each other is the natural result of this condition—a reserve which is broken through only by the impelling force of strong and unreasoning passion. This passion compels people to do that which they believe to be wrong, and so long as they believe it to be wrong it *is* wrong for them. The result is that when the imperious passion is satisfied, remorse takes its place, and shame and misery ensue. "The ideal must precede the real." This is why the common rebellions against marriage are failures. If a man believes that he is sinning against God when he works on Sunday he sins against *himself* if he works on that day. Hence the need of enlightened ideals in morals and religion, as well as elsewhere.

In a recent lecture this society was told by Mr. W. M. Thompson that freedom in love is impracticable, because no man can love and respect a woman who is the "common property of the herd," the inference being that a woman who is not the property of only *one* man must inevitably be the property of *all* men; that she can never by any possibility be the property of *herself*. And this is the natural and logical outcome of the acceptance of Christian morality. A woman is immature, an infant, the property of her father, until he gives her in marriage to another man who becomes her husband. She is then the property of her husband until his death, when she is his "relict." In other countries and ages this relict was so useless that it was burned just as the man's worn out garments might be, for why cumber the earth with a man's valueless possessions when the owner is gone?

In civilisation we permit the widow to live, though if she is *very* virtuous and desires the commendation of Madam Grundy, she refrains from marriage and wears mourning for the remainder of her days. She may, however, give herself in marriage to another man, but however great the mistake she may have made in doing so, she cannot rectify it. For her the choice is made. She belongs to her husband. Her person can never belong to herself.

And the law holds that not even the woman who sells or gives herself for the night instead of for a lifetime has the right to dispose of herself as she chooses. It has decided that when a prostitute is the complainant there can be no such thing as rape. "Once consent, always consent," has been its edict.

So I admit that Mr. Thompson has the authority of the customs and laws of past and present days, in support of his statement that a woman who does not believe in marriage must be the "common property of the herd." What then? Must we admit that what has been must always continue? It is not at all difficult to prove that in England a man may not marry his deceased wife's sister. But does this fact prove that such a relation is wrong, and that we should not protest against that law as absurd and unjust?

There are a few though constantly increasing number of women who are quietly but firmly taking the matter into their own hands, and deciding it for themselves. They ignore the dictates of law and custom, and refuse to belong to one or many men. If one such loves her deceased sister's husband, she does not take the trouble to ask the House of Lords for its permission to express that love. She considers that the consent or disapprobation of that body of men has nothing whatever to do with the case.

Said a man to one of these free women: "It would be very unpleasant for almost any other woman in your position, surrounded by people who do not agree with your views. Yet all seem to respect *you*."

"Why should they not respect me?" she asked. "I respect *myself*. I do and say nothing of which I am ashamed. I respect their opinions and lives regardless of the difference in our ideals. Why should you accuse them of being more unjust to any woman in my position than I am to them?"

Fortunately most men are better than their laws. I have become acquainted with a great many conservative men, and I can assure Mr. Thompson that I have found very few of them who believed that a free woman was necessarily the "common property of the herd," and even those who seemed to agree with him were not wholly impervious to reason.

"But what would you have?" I am asked. "Where would you draw the line?" "What would become of the family?" "What about the children?" These are questions constantly hurled at all who antagonise enforced legal marriage, or advocate free motherhood.

"What would I have?" In the first place, I would have people think. Age should make no custom exempt from criticism. Do not accept a thing as worthy of credence or support merely because your fathers or grandfathers gave it credence and support. Such a method is unprogressive. Nothing is too good, too holy, too pure for careful inspection. If marriage is a good thing its fruits are good. Let no foolish reverence for the opinions of others hinder you from examining the fruits of this custom which has such a vital effect on the happiness of millions of persons living, as well as of that of countless millions more yet unborn. If a lifelong union of one man and one woman is the condition of the greatest happiness, of the highest development of the individual and of the race, it will survive and become perfected in freedom. We need freedom to learn what *is* best for us. We need freedom to profit by our failures, as well as by our successes. We have had polygamy, polyandry, and monogamy and prostitution; we have experienced slavery in all its forms; but never yet have we had freedom of choice.

"Where would I draw the line?" Where common sense and sound reason dictate. We are not all gifted with equal reasoning powers, nor is any one person gifted with the same reasoning power at one time as at some other time. The line set to-day may be set further ahead tomorrow, and so the tendency is toward absolute freedom. We may never attain absolute freedom, but we can push forward in that direction by removing every obstacle which our reason tells us is detrimental to the best interests of humanity, and a barrier in the pathway of freedom. Of the past it has been well said:—

> "What is liberty now were license then;
> Their freedom our yoke would be."

And because we are hampered and crippled by the laws and restrictions inherited from our ancestors, we should realise the folly and injustice of hampering our descendants in a like manner. We have no right to draw the line for others. We *have* a right to draw the line for ourselves. In Grant Allen's great novel, "The Woman Who Did," Hermina fell into this fatal error. She felt that she had the right to differ from her father in any way, and to live her own life, even though by so doing she broke his heart. Yet she could not realise that her own child might differ from her just as radically as she had differed from her father, and quite as rightfully; and when the sudden realisation of that fact came to her, her own heart was broken.

I am often asked what I would have in place of the present marriage system if I had the power to change the laws. It would be quite as reasonable to ask me what size I would make the shoes if I had a monopoly of shoe-making for the entire human race. I do not understand that it is desirable to make the great majority wear shoes too large or too small, too light or too heavy for their comfort, merely that there may be apparent uniformity in size of feet. Such an arrangement would undoubtedly entail a great deal of inconvenience and suffering, and would cause people to awkwardly stumble and fall. I consider uniformity in mode of sexual relations as undesirable and impracticable as enforced uniformity in anything else. For myself, I want the right to profit by my mistakes. If I inadvertently place my hand in the fire, I shall take the liberty to withdraw it; and why should I be unwilling for others to enjoy the same liberty? If I should be able to bring the entire world to live exactly as I live at present, what would that avail me in ten years, when, as I hope, I shall have a broader knowledge of life, and my life therefore probably changed? I do not want to spend my life in converting the world to my method of existence. I want the world to have reason of its own, and use it.

"What would become of the family?" This is one of the most absurd objections urged against the opponents of legal marriage. The only happy marriages now are those which are happy in spite of the compulsory tie, and not because of it. Marriage does not prevent a man from abandoning his wife and children. The people who are happily married are those who are sexually mated, or intellectually mated, or both. The last instance is extremely rare.

We have a few natural desires and passions which have existed before all, independent of all, and will exist after all laws, if such time shall ever come. We would not lose the desire to eat if no articles of diet were prohibited, or if the manner of eating them were prescribed by law. And when we have outgrown barbarism in the sexual relations the love of man and woman for each other and for their children will live in a sweetness and purity now scarcely even dreamed of.

In the "Story of An African Farm," Olive Schreiner has Lyndall say:—

> "And then, when they have no other argument against us, they say, 'Go on, but when you have made woman what you wish, and her children inherit her culture, you will defeat yourself. Man will gradually become extinct . . . the passions which replenish the race will die.' Fools! A Hottentot sits by the roadside, and feeds on a rotten bone he has found there, and takes out his bottle of Cape-smoke, and swills at it, and grunts with satisfaction; and the cultured child of the nineteenth century sits in his arm chair, and sips choice wines with the lip of a connoisseur, and tastes delicate dishes with a delicate palate, and with a satisfaction of which the Hottentot knows nothing. Heavy jaw and sloping forehead—all have gone with increasing intellect; but the animal appetites are there still—refined, discriminative, but immeasurably intensified. . . . When all the later additions to humanity have vanished, will not the foundation on which they are built remain?"

It is claimed by its defenders that marriage is the friend of woman and of the children, and insures paternal responsibility. Someone has said that marriage is a lottery in which we have all to gain and nothing to lose. I deny it. It is a lottery in which we have *nothing* to gain and *all* to lose. It is an insurance scheme which does not and cannot pay its liabilities. It is what is called in America, a "confidence game," in which, under the pretence of giving much for practically nothing, the unsuspecting innocents are fleeced of all they have.

Ingersoll feels quite sure that he is opposed to freedom in love, yet he asks: "Do the believers in indissoluble marriage treat their wives better than others?" And this is his answer—

"A little while ago, a woman said to a man who had raised his hand to strike her, 'Do not touch me; you have no right to beat me; I am not your wife!' "

Colonel Ingersoll is a lawyer, and while his prejudices are in favour of marriage, he must admit the injustice of the system. It is true that men are, as a rule, better than the laws, but what a terrible power the law places in the hands of men who are willing to take advantage of it! As an instance, take this case which was decided in court in Scranton, Pennsylvania, last December.

Mary E. Hover was so cruelly treated by her husband that the neighbours had him arrested. On trial, he admitted the truth of her statement that he had abused her so that she had felt the effects for more than a week, and that she had been subjected to similar treatment for years. But he claimed that he had attempted to caress her, and in struggling to escape his caresses she had been hurt. In his charge to the jury the judge laid down the law that a man is entitled to a show of his wife's affections; that if the statement of the husband was correct the jury should acquit him, and this it proceeded to do.

If the man who attempted to win the affections of Mrs. Hover had not been married to her, he might have considered himself fortunate if his life had been spared by the indignant neighbours. But as he had purchased the *right* to a show of her affections, no one, not even she herself, could rightfully object. And this is the way in which marriage protects woman.

In Topeka, Kansas, a few years ago, a woman was sent to the insane asylum. In reporting the case, a local daily said:—"The evidence showed that her husband abused her body worse than a Satyr could be capable of, resulting in the loss of her mind."

But such cases as these do not very often find their way into the public prints. Their existence is ignored. It is dangerous to even mention them. The woman who has drawn a blank in the marriage lottery must conceal her disappointment, and pretend that she has a prize. And when an editor is found brave enough to denounce marital outrage, he is an enemy of society, a disrupter of the home, and he is placed behind prison bars. Physical outrage of a woman by a man is a crime—*provided* that man is not the woman's husband.

And in the face of all this we are asked, "What of the children? What will become of them when their mothers are not *protected* by marriage?"

What of the children, truly! Society has guaranteed to woman support of her children, in exchange for the surrender of her liberty in the bonds of marriage. And how does it fulfill its contract? Does it take the children of the men who are unable or unwilling to provide for them, and tenderly nurture them? Illustrations of the efficacy of its guarantees are to be seen on every hand by those who have eyes and use them.

In New York, for example, in 1896, 366 infants were sent to the institution on Randall's Island. Of these 366 *twelve* survived the beneficent care of the state. We are told that we must not bear children outside of marriage, because the state will have to provide for them. And this is the result! Three hundred and fifty-four dead, and twelve living! This is a specimen of the institutions which our critics tell us free women are to crowd with their offspring.

And how does protection protect in England? Does the wedding ring ever provide bread, except when left at the pawnbroker's? A few days ago I visited Wormwood Scrubs Prison. My guide told me that very many women were imprisoned for neglecting their children. "And I presume there are many men in for the same cause?" I said. "O, no," she replied; "not very many; but then you know it is the woman's place to take care of the children." Think of it! An ignorant young woman marries. She becomes the mother of babies that she does not want; no matter how she may dread the pain and danger and care involved in their birth, she must perform her marital duty; then when she "neglects" them, she is sent to prison, and her children go to the workhouse. Her husband is not sent to prison, because it is "the business of the woman to take care of the children." Many babies are born in that prison, I am told; but no matter how intensely the mother may desire to keep her babe, it is taken from her when nine months' old, and, if there are no friends to receive it, it is sent to the workhouse. And in this way Society provides for the children.

Rarely indeed are free men born of slave mothers. Just so long as we have legally enforced prostitution and rape, so long as the majority of homes are the abiding places of inharmony, degradation, and cruelty, as now, there can be little progress. Marriage is woman's worst enemy, and is therefore the enemy of the race. Marriage gave a Christian preacher the power to rob Annie Besant of her children. He could not have touched them if she had not been married to him. She was his property; therefore her children belonged to him.

Under freedom undesired children will not be born. For why should a woman pay the great price which must be paid, if she does not want the child for which she pays it? When a woman wishes to become a mother she may if she chooses make terms concerning the custody of the child to be begotten, before permitting herself to be impregnated.

Whether the homes to be established will be individual or cooperative or communistic will depend on the tastes, the desires, of the persons concerned. Under liberty there will inevitably be many varied modes of living.

The right of protest is vitally essential in morals as it was, and is, in religion. And free life must be the logical outcome of free thought.

Suggested Readings

Fisher, J. Greevz. *Illegitimate Children: An Inquiry into Their Personal Rights and a Plea for Abolition of Illegitimacy*. London: Reeves, 1893.

Humboldt, Wilhelm von. *The Limits of State Action*. Edited and translated by J. W. Burrow. Cambridge: Cambridge University Press, 1969.

Spencer, Herbert. *Social Statics*. London: John Chapman, 1851, pp. 172–192.

WOMEN AND WORK

The one area in which modern individualist feminism differs radically from the 19th-century movement is economics. During the 19th century, most libertarians, along with the majority of contemporary radicals, subscribed to the labor theory of value, which states that all wealth is created by labor and justly belongs to the laborers who produce it. If the fair value of an hour's labor is $100, then the laborer who receives this sum is fully and justly recompensed. If the laborer then lends this $100 at 10 percent interest and receives back $110, there is some difficulty in accounting for the extra $10. Since wealth can only be produced by labor and since the lender already has received the full value of his labor, the $10 must represent the labor of another human being which the lender is claiming as his own. The lender is thus usurping the labor of another. As Benjamin Tucker expressed it, the interest was "payment for a day's work a second time." This analysis led libertarians to condemn the practice of charging interest and rent as usury, a form of theft.

Although the 19th-century libertarians were staunch advocates of the free market, they opposed capitalism as a distortion of the market process and as a system of monopoly sustained by the state. For example, Tucker maintained that rent, a perceived mainstay of capitalism, "exists only because the state stands by to collect it and to protect land titles rooted in force or fraud. Otherwise the land would be free to all, and no one could control more than he used." The way to eliminate capitalism was to eliminate the state, for capitalism was the result of state intervention into the marketplace.

Critics of this position were quick to point out a flaw in the libertarian logic. If interest and rent were a form of theft, yet entered into voluntarily, would libertarians intrude themselves into a contractual situation or would they permit the theft to proceed? Sovereignty of the individual, the cornerstone of libertarian thought, demanded that all peaceful interactions be respected. Accordingly, contracts which violated the labor theory of value would have to be tolerated as voluntary interactions, although they were condemned morally. Tucker resolved this conflict of theory by stating that everyone had the right to make a "foolish" contract.

Current individualist feminism, which is still best understood as a subset of libertarianism, has adopted a more sophistocated view of the free market and capitalism. Capitalism, as the private ownership of the means of production, is simply an expression of self-ownership extended into the economic realm. Wealth can originate from a number of sources, only one of which is labor. A diamond lying on the road may embody no labor whatsoever and yet represent great wealth. Individualist feminism has incorporated Austrian economics as expounded by Mises, Hayek, and Rothbard into its theoretical framework.

The one point of continued agreement is that government interference in the economic realm, as in all other realms, is disastrous. It constitutes a violation of the personal freedom of one segment of society in order to benefit another segment. Thus, protective labor laws which restrict the hours and type of job a woman legally may work actually violate her right to freely contract to the benefit of male workers—especially white, male unions—who automatically have an advantage over women in the labor market. It is only through government that women can be discriminated against, not randomly, but as a policy. Only government can establish womanhood as a separate category under law.

The following essays reflect this change within the tradition of individualist feminism in regard to economic theory.

XIX. Are Feminist Businesses Capitalistic?

Rosalie Nichols

Contemporary feminism is laden with economic value judgments. The language of feminism, which speaks of "exploitation" and "class oppression," directly reflects the socialist economics and philosophy upon which it leans so heavily. It is axiomatically assumed that capitalism is the enemy, and any feminist who questions this axiom is ridiculed or ignored. Although women are enjoined to explore new possibilities, to dream new dreams, there is little discussion on the subject of capitalism. Apparently, some feminists fear a free forum in which competing economic theories are presented. It is this dogmatic rejection of free market economics which lends credence to the assertion that modern feminism is a subset of modern socialism.

Rosalie Nichols is the editor of Lesbian Voices *from which the following article is reprinted. A cogent advocate of capitalism, Nichols identifies it as the only system which leaves the individual, the woman, "free to pursue her own goals and purposes, to engage in voluntary transactions with others, and to reap the benefits of her own efforts." Capitalism is merely the extension of self-ownership to the economic realm.*

Are feminist businesses capitalistic? In order to answer this question, it is necessary to define our terms—not only the terms "feminism" and "business," but *also* the term "capitalism." So, let us define *all* our terms!

Definitions of feminism (as given in dictionaries, encyclopediae, and the press) generally fall into two categories.

The first category contains those definitions which emphasize *social, political, and economic equality with men*. I reject this definition of feminism because it makes the status of women *dependent* on the status of men and because it does not contain any reference to the *rights* of either sex. By this egalitarian definition, a Slave State could be "feminist," provided only that women and men were treated equally and were equally ranked in status and power up and down the levels of society. As long as a queen ruled with equal power beside every king—as long as there were a female general beside every male general—as long as there were equal numbers of female and male bureaucrats—as long as there were equal numbers of female and male overseers supervising the female and male slaves dragging their blocks side by side up the escalating

Great Pyramid of Statism, then all would be right with "feminists" in the glorious "feminist" world, according to the socio-economic-equality definition. This egalitarian definition of feminism says nothing about freedom or justice; it says nothing about the rights of the individual; and—incidentally—it says nothing about the "classless society" which its exponents so ardently desire.

The second category of definitions contains those which emphasize *equal rights with men*. Within this category, the term "rights" may be construed differently.

One construction is that the goal of feminism is to achieve equal *legal* rights with men (legal rights are those granted *by law*, i.e., by the *government* of a society). I reject this definition for several reasons: Again, this definition makes the status of women *dependent* on the status of men; women could claim those legal rights—and **only** those legal rights—which were enjoyed by men. This would lead to such obscenities as the proposal to *draft* women into the military in the name of "equality for women." Again, by this definition, we could have **equal slavery**, with no philosophical ground for complaint about our ideally "feminist" world. Further, this definition of feminism as a movement for equal *legal* rights places in the hands of the government (the State) our own voluntary *sanction* of their power to grant or deny recognition of our individual human rights. In a government *dominated by men*—notoriously corrupt, unprincipled, pragmatic, power-hungry, violence-prone men—that is a particularly dangerous power for us to invest in them; it amounts to cooperating in our own oppression. But even in a sexually egalitarian democracy, responsive to the voice of "the people" and eager to do the "greatest good for the greatest number," it is a dangerous proposition for the individual citizen to trust the government to define her rights—for the individual woman and *her* good may well be in conflict with the views of the "greatest number." . . . It is always the unpopular minority—right down to the minority of *one*—whose rights are violated through the "tyranny of the *majority*," who see as their "good" the supression or annihilation of "dissident elements." It has been said that it is never the right to *agree* that needs protection—only the right to *disagree*. (This is why, when the Statists accomplished their coup of imposing a powerful central government in the United States through the Constitution a group of civil libertarians insisted on appending a Bill of Rights to protect the individual and limit the powers of government—an effort which, in the long run, has failed in many areas.)

The only definition of feminism which I accept, therefore, is one which places my rights outside the authority of men, power, and society; **feminism is a political philosophy which recognizes and upholds the human rights of the individual woman.** Human rights are those objective natural rights which belong to a woman by virtue of her status as a rational being. The rights of a rational being are the rights to her own life, liberty, property, and pursuit of happiness.

The rights of a woman **do not depend** in any way on the rights of men. A woman exists *independently* of the existence of men. A woman is a human being *independently* of whether men are human (i.e., rational) beings or not. **My** existence and **my** identity as a human being—and therefore my objective natural **rights—do not depend** on any other person.

As a movement, then, **the goal of feminism is to gain and secure recognition of the rights of woman—and to guarantee to each and every individual woman that she may pursue her life and her happiness with the knowledge that her dreams, ambitions, goals, and purposes will not be hindered or impaired or limited by denial of her human rights.**

In a feminist society, a woman would be free to do *absolutely anything* which did not interfere with a similar exercise by others of their rights. She would be free to work or play, study or loaf, create or stagnate, be married or stay single, have children or remain childess, have a career or keep house, make love or be celibate, have one relationship or have many, be sober or use chemicals, join groups or stay aloof, travel or stay put, have luxuries or live ascetically, live in the city or work on a farm—or *any* other choices she would care to make. She would be free to do whatever she wanted with her *own* time, energy, and resources—alone or with the voluntary cooperation of others. But she would *not* be allowed to *impose her will* on others or to use the time, energy, or resources of others *against their will.* She would be free to enjoy the rewards of her *own* effort, but she would *not* be allowed to demand that others use *their* efforts to secure rewards *for* her or to save her from the consequences of her own self-destructive actions. She would be responsible for her own life, and she would reap its benefits or bear its penalties.

Such a society would be egalitarian only in the sense that every individual would enjoy the same human rights. It would not be egalitarian in the sense of forcing everyone down to the lowest common denominator. There would be no *privileges*—the word "privilege" means literally "one's own law" and denotes a special right or favor granted to a person or group by the State. Those who wanted rewards would have to earn them. But neither would individuals be prevented from improving themselves and their conditions. Each woman would be **free to rise**—intellectually, spiritually, professionally, socially, *and* economically.

Among the things which a woman would be free to do in a feminist society is to engage in *business*. She could be a manufacturer, producing goods for distribution; she could be a distributor, buying goods from manufacturers and selling to retailers; she could be a retailer, buying goods from manufacturers and distributors and selling to consumers; or she could combine all three operations. She could sell a product because she believed in its worth and wanted to find consumers who saw its value; or she could sell a product because there was a market for it and she was willing to sell her services to satisfy the consumers' demand for goods. In either case, her success would depend partly on her own ability and partly on the wisdom of foolishness (as the case may be) of the consumers. She would have no power to *force* people to buy her product, and they would have no power to *force* her to produce or sell it. The price she charged for her goods or services would be mutually agreed upon with the consumer; otherwise, the sale couldn't take place. She would have no power to *force* anyone to pay more than agreable, and the consumer would have no power to *force* her to accept less than she was willing. Her business would depend on voluntary transactions among free individuals. She could run her business alone, as a sole proprietor; she could have partners or form a collective; she could form a corporation and sell stock. She could hire workers if they were willing to be employed by her, and she could run her business operation hierarchically or non-hierarchically, according to her philosophy. Whatever form of business she chose to run, it would depend on voluntary transactions between her and her partners or employees. She would not be able to *force* people to work for her or to invest in her business, and they would not be able to *force* her to hire them or to share her business resources or management with them. In a free society, every individual may do anything which does not violate the rights of others; this is what freedom means.

Now—what is the name of the *economic system* which leaves the individual free to pursue her own goals and purposes, to engage in voluntary transactions with others, and to reap the benefits of her own efforts?

There is only *one* economic system which is based on total individual freedom. It has been called Free Trade, Free Enterprise, or Laissez-Faire **Capitalism**. There is no other economic system which would leave the individual entrepreneur, worker, and consumer free from restraint, regulation, and exploitation (I say "would" because total Laissez-Faire Capitalism has never been attained in the modern world). Under all other economic systems—under the ancient totalitarian systems, the feudal system of the Middle Ages, the monarchic mercantilist/colonialist system, modern fascism (which is what we have in the present U.S.A.), national socialism, or Communism—the economic choices and activities of the individual citizen are regulated, controlled, and manipulated by the State for the benefit of one group at the expense of the others. This is known as Statism, and it has been responsible for some of the worst ills suffered by womankind.

Historically, the State has denied women's property rights (consider the law of primogeniture which existed throughout the late Middle Ages and, in England, until 1926; consider also Blackstone's law which made husband and wife "one," with the husband "the one" with regard to property rights). The State has limited women's occupations (consider the guild system of the Middle Ages which monopolized crafts and trade for males; consider modern "protective" labor laws, which have protected women from getting jobs; consider such laws as the one in California which until recently prohibited women from employment as bartenders). The State has taxed women to pay for men's ventures, until this century denying women a voice in government. The State has, by a number of devices (tariffs, import quotas, monetary inflation, State-created monopolies, hidden taxes), artificially inflated prices above the free market level and thereby exploited women as consumers. The State has created tax-supported educational institutions which women are forced to help pay for while largely being denied access to their services, thereby hampering and limiting women's efforts at improving their condition. The State has created wars and military establishments which have worked untold hardships upon women in more ways than economic; and so on and so on. How any woman . . . can advocate any form of Statism is beyond my comprehension.

There are only *two* economic systems for us to choose between: Free Trade (Capitalism) or Regulated Trade (Statism). Trade cannot be regulated without *violating the right* of women to engage in voluntary transactions. *Feminism* is a political philosophy which recognizes and *upholds the human rights* of the individual woman. Therefore, feminism and a regulated economy (Statism) are mutually exclusive and antagonistic. A Statist society cannot be feminist. Only a free society can be feminist. And the economic system of a free society is Laissez-Faire Capitalism.

Are feminist businesses capitalistic? You bet they are! By definition, they can't be anything else.

XX. The Economic Position of Women

Suzanne La Follette

Concerning Women *by Suzanne La Follette (1893-) is perhaps the only book-length treatment of individualist feminism produced by an American. Her mentor and friend, Albert Jay Nock, wrote of the book, "[A]t every turn, throughout the future, until freedom is attained, this book will be dug up and drawn upon . . . as saying the final thing." (Unfortunately, his prediction was wrong; the book received little notice.) La Follette met Nock while working on the staff of* The Nation. *She worked with him again as one of the editors of* The Freeman, *a libertarian periodical.*

As an opponent of state interference into women's lives, La Follette attacked protective labor laws and minimum wage laws which "lessen the chances of women to compete with men in the labor market." To her, economic choice underlay all other freedoms for women. Her greatest significance, however, was in transmitting the individualist-feminist tradition from its golden age of the late 19th century through its decline during the 20th.

The following essay is extracted from Concerning Women *(1926).*

It is to the industrial revolution more than anything else, perhaps, that women owe such freedom as they now enjoy; yet if proof were wanting of the distance they have still to cover in order to attain, not freedom, but mere equality with men, their position in the industrial world would amply supply it. Men in industry suffer from injustices and hardships due to the overcrowding of the labour-market. Women suffer from these same injustices and hardships; and they have an additional handicap in their sex. The world of work, embracing industry, business, the professions, is primarily a man's world. Women are admitted, but not yet on an equal footing. Their opportunities for employment are restricted, sometimes by law, but more often by lack of training; and their remuneration as wage-earners and salaried workers is generally less than that of men. They have to contend with traditional notions of what occupations are fitting for their sex; with the jealousy of male workers; with the prejudices of employers; and finally with their own inertia and their own addiction to traditional concepts. All these difficulties are immensely aggravated by the keenness of the competition for work. If the opportunity to work were, as it should be, an unimpeded right instead of a privilege doled out by an employer, these handicaps of women would be easily overridden by the demand for their labour. I shall discuss this point more fully later on. It is sufficient here to note that when the war created a temporary shortage of labour, women were not only employed in, but were urged in the name of patriotism to enter, occupations in which until then only men had been employed. The effect of this temporary shortage on their industrial opportunities affords a hint of what their position would be if the glutting of the labour-market were permanently relieved. A shortage of labour means opportunity for the worker, male or female.

Women have always been industrial workers. Otis T. Mason even went so far as to declare that "All the peaceful arts of today were once woman's peculiar province. Along the lines of industrialism she was pioneer, inventor, author, originator." This view is in rather striking contrast with the contemptuous derogaton which has been for a long time current in European civilization, and has found expression in such cutting remarks as that of Proudhon, that woman "could not even invent her own distaff." It is no doubt a fairer view, although it is probably somewhat exaggerated. There is certainly no valid reason to suppose that sex is a barrier to the invention and improvement of industrial processes. Be this as it may, it is undeniable that women have always been producers. Among some primitive tribes, indeed, they are the only industrialists, the men occupying themselves with war and the chase or, among maritime peoples, with fishing. The modern invasion of the industrial field by women does not, then, represent an attempt to do something that women have never done before. It does represent an attempt to adapt themselves to the new conditions created by the industrial revolution.

The range of their opportunities has been considerably restricted by prejudices arising from the traditional sexual division of labour in European society. "In the developed barbarism of Europe, only a few simple household industries were on the whole left to women."[1] It was natural, then, when women followed industry into the larger field of machine-production, that it should be assumed that the industries in which they might fittingly engage would be those most nearly akin to the occupations which European society has regarded as peculiarly feminine. Before the World War, according to the Women's Bureau, "over seventy-five per cent of all women engaged in manufacture were concentrated in the textile and garment-making industries"; and we have the same authority for the statement that "except for certain branches of food-manufacture—such as flour making . . . women constitute from a third to two-thirds of the working forces in the industries concerned

[1]Ellis: Man and Woman. 5th ed. p. 14.

with the business of clothing and feeding both the fighting and the civilian population." The new opportunities opened up by the exigency of the war-period widened considerably the scope of women's activity; they were employed in machine-shops and tool-rooms, in steel- and rolling-mills, in instrument-factories, in factories manufacturing sewing machines and typewriters, in utensil-factories, in plants working in rubber and leather, in wood-working industries.

In some of these industries women continue to be employed. In others they were discharged to make room for men when the emergency was over. But even where they continue to be employed their opportunities for training are not equal to those of men. The Women's Bureau in 1922 issued a valuable bulletin on "Industrial Opportunities and Training for Women and Girls." According to this bulletin, the war-experience of women in new employments made it apparent that the most promising future for craftswomen in these fields lies in (a) machine-shops where light parts are made, (b) wood-product factories where assembling and finishing are important processes, (c) optical- and instrument-factories, (d) sheet-metal shops. The survey made by the Bureau to discover how many of the country's industrial training schools were fitting women for these trades disclosed the fact that in nine States where women, because of industrial conditions, are most in need of training for machine-shop, sheet-metal, furniture, or optical work, they are either excluded by public vocational schools from the courses in such works, or they are not encouraged, as men are, to enter those courses. In Ohio, for example, women were enrolled in only five of the fifty-three public vocational schools reporting, and in these five schools they were taught dressmaking, costume-design, dress-pattern making, embroidery, power-machine sewing, and pottery making. Men on the other hand, received instruction in the following courses which women needed: machine-shop practice, tool-making, shop mathematics, mechanical drafting, blue-print reading, metallurgy, pattern-making, sheet-metal work, welding, auto-mechanics and repair, motorcycle mechanics, gas engineering, cabinet-making and wood-working. Women were not debarred by rule or law from entering these courses, but they were not encouraged to do so. The courses, as one superintendent wrote, were "designed for men." The situation in Ohio is more or less the same as that in the other eight States. Women are either not admitted to vocational courses designed to prepare workers for the industries cited, or they are not encouraged to enroll. Yet, as the Bureau points out, these institutions are operated at the expense of the taxpayers, women as well as men, and their equipment should be used to serve women as well as men. "It is obvious," says the Bureau, "that the public vocational school authorities, with few exceptions, think of trade for women only in terms of dress-making and millinery, and are as yet quite oblivious to the fact that these trades, except in certain clothing centers, are not the big employers of woman labour, nor are they always the best trades at which to earn a livelihood. it is the semi-public school that is beginning first to recognize the new position which woman occupies in industry as a result of the war and is opening to her its doors and guiding her into courses leading to efficiency in the new occupations."

This blindness of the school authorities to the vocational needs of women goes to prove how strong is the force of traditional prejudices. The making of clothing has been largely in the hands of women for so long that even in cities where the only industries employing women are mechanical or wood-working, the public schools offer them courses in sewing and millinery. Prepossession does not yield all at once to established fact. If women can make a permanent place for themselves in their new occupations, public officials will eventually come to associate them with these occupations and follow the lead of the semi-public schools in fitting girls to engage in them on an equal footing with boys. But it will take time; and meanwhile women will continue to be a disadvantage in entering these occupations. So will they be at a disadvantage in entering any occupation where they have not before been employed, or where they are employed only in insignificant numbers, so long as prejudice or conservatism continues to debar them, and the necessary training is not as freely available to them as it is to men.

Above all, so long as their industrial status continues to be, as the Women's Bureau expresses it, "subsidiary to their home status," they can never be on a really secure footing in the industrial world. While employers assume that all male workers have families to support and that all female workers are in industry rather through choice than necessity and may, in periods when work is slack, fall back on the support of male relatives, so long will women be the first workers to suffer from any slowing down of industry. This was strikingly illustrated during the period of unemployment which succeeded the intense industrial activity made necessary by the war, when women were discharged in great numbers to make room for men, and much resentment was voiced against their retention in places which might be filled by men. "Back to the home," says the Women's Bureau, "was a slogan all too easily and indiscriminately flung at the wage-earning woman by those who had little conception of the causes which forced her into wage-earning pursuits." In periods of industrial depression it appears to be the regular practice to lay off the married women workers first, then the single women, and the men last.

How unjust to the woman worker, and how little justified by actual facts, is this survival of the idea that woman's place is the home, has been shown through investigations undertaken by the Women's Bureau and other agencies. The results of these investigations, published in Bulletin No. 30 of the Women's Bureau, show that the woman in industry is not merely working for pin-money, as thoughtless people assume, but that she is more often not only supporting herself on her inadequate wage, but contributing materially to the support of dependents. "Contributing all earnings to the family fund," says the Bureau, "is a very general practice among wage-earning women." This of course means, as the Bureau remarks, that however much or little her contribution may mean to the family, for the woman herself it means a surrender of economic independence. The contrast between single men and single women in this respect is significant. In an investigation conducted among workers in the shoe-making industry of Manchester, New Hampshire, the Bureau found that "comparing single men and women, the women contributed (to the family income) more extensively, both actually and relatively." The percentage of earnings contributed by sons and daughters is particularly interesting. The Bureau found that "in the families with per capita earnings of less than $500, 49.3 per cent of the sons and 71.6 per cent of the daughters contributed all their earnings, while in families with per capita earnings of $500 or more, 36.8 per cent of the sons and 53.4 per cent of the daughters contributed all earnings." When one remembers that the wage paid to women was so much lower than that paid to men that the Bureau pronounced them to be scarcely comparable, the fact that "the daughters contributed a somewhat larger proportion of the family earnings than did the sons" takes on added significance. The sons contributed almost as much in actual money as the daughters, but out of their higher wages they retained something for themselves, "thus assuring themselves of a degree of independence and an opportunity to strike out for themselves which is denied the daughters.

It is evident, then, that women, even in the "emancipation" of the industrial world, are continuing their immemorial self-sacrifice to the family, and that it is not the married woman alone, but the single woman as well, who makes this sacrifice. The conditions of the sacrifice have changed with the changes in industry, but the sacrifice continues.

The productive labour of women appears to be quite as indispensable to their families as it was in the days when they spun and wove and sewed and baked at home. This being the case, there is obviously no other ground than prejudice for the assumption that men, as the natural providers, should have preference in the labour-market. According to the census of 1920, thirty-five per cent of the men in the country are single; therefore it is fair to assume that thirty-five per cent of the men in industry are single. Two-thirds of the women in industry are single, but the available figures show that a much larger percentage of these women than of single men are contributing all or most of their earnings to their families, while married women workers are contributing all of their earnings. In view of these figures, there is patent injustice in the assumption that all men and no women have dependents to support.

So is there injustice in the assumption that women are naturally at least partly dependent on male workers, and therefore may fairly be forced to accept a smaller wage than men. This assumption is not only grossly unfair to the woman worker, but it does not tally with fact. A fine example of the kind of defence for the practice of sweating women workers that can be based on this assumption is quoted by the Women's Bureau from an unnamed commercial magazine. "Eighty-six per cent of women workers," runs this masterpiece of sophistry, "live at home or with relatives. [So, in all likelihood, do eighty-six per cent of male workers.] It is immaterial in these cases whether the earnings of each measure up to the cost of living scheduled for a single woman living alone, so that the theory of the need of a sufficient wage to support a single woman living alone does not apply to eighty-six per cent of the entire population [*sic*]." This quotation, says the Bureau, is typical of the attitude of the employer who pays his women employees less than a living wage on the plea that they live at home and therefore have few expenses. It is equally remarkable in its ruthless disregard of the just claim of the woman worker to the same share in the product of her toil that the male worker is allowed; and in its disregard of the fact that so long as eighty-six per cent of women workers are forced to accept a starvation-wage because they live at home, the other fourteen per cent who do not live at home will be forced by the pressure of competition to accept the same starvation-wage. The question how this fourteen per cent will eke out a living—whether through overwork, begging or prostitution—does not of course concern the employer; for it is one of the striking differences between chattle-slavery and wage-slavery that the owner of the wage-slave is under no obligation to keep his workers from starving. That is, presumably, their own lookout.

If employers are not given to concerning themselves with this question, however, communities are. Thirteen States have enacted laws fixing a minimum wage for women, three have fixed minimum wages in specified occupations, one has fixed a minimum wage which its industrial welfare commission has power to change, and nine have created boards or commissions with power to fix minimum wage-rates. It may be noted that in those States where the rate is fixed by law, it has not responded to the rising cost of living. In Utah and Arkansas, for example, the minimum wage for an experienced women is $7.50 a week. There is constant effort by interested individuals and organizations to get similar laws enacted in other States, in spite of the fact that in 1923 the Supreme Court of the United States declared unconstitutional the minimum wage-law of the District of Columbia. Such efforts, of course, are in reality efforts to secure class-legislation, as are all attempts to secure special enactments designed to benefit or protect women.

Of such enactments there is an ever increasing number. So rapidly do they increase, indeed, that women may be said to be in a fair way to exchange the tyranny of men for that of organized uplift. They are sponsored by those well-meaning individuals who deplore social injustice enough to yearn to mitigate its evil results, but do not understand it well enough to attack its causes; by women's organizations whose intelligence is hardly commensurate with their zeal to uplift their sex; and by men's labour-organizations which are quite frankly in favour of any legislation that will lessen the chances of women to compete with men in the labour-market.[2] Given the combined suasion of these forces, and the inveterate sentimentalism which makes it hard for legislators to resist any plea on behalf of "the women and children," almost anything in the way of rash and ill-considered legislation is possible, and even probable. There is on the statute-books of the various States

[2]Katharine Anthony found the workmen of Germany frankly in favour of any "protective" legislation that would hamper German working women ("Feminism in Germany and Scandinavia"); and the Woman's Party has met with the same attitude among unions in this country. Among the resolutions passed at the twenty-fifth convention of the International Moulders' Union of North America was the following: "*Resolved*, that the decision of this convention be the restriction of the further employment of child and woman labour in union core rooms and foundries, and eventually the elimination of such labour in all foundries by the example set by union foundries in the uplifting of humanity. . . . *Resolved*, that the incoming officers be directed to, either by themselves or in co-operation with others in the labour movement, give their best thought and effort in opposing the employment of female and child labour in jobs recognized as men's employment.

an imposing array of laws designed to "protect" women workers. There are only four States which do not in some way limit the hours of work for women; there are eleven which limit the number of successive days that they may work; fourteen have fixed the amount of time that shall be allowed them for their midday meal; twelve have ruled that a woman may work only a given number of hours without a rest-period. Sixteen States prohibit night-work in certain industries or occupations; two limit her hours of night-work to eight. There is also a tendency to extend to women special protection against the hazards of industry. In seventeen States the employment of women in mines is prohibited. Two States prohibit their employment in any industry using abrasives. In four States they are not allowed to oil moving machinery. Three regulate their employment in core-making; and four regulate the amount of the weight that they may be required to lift—the maximum ranging, oddly enough, from fifteen pounds in Ohio and Pennsylvania to seventy-four pounds in Massachusetts. In addition to those regulations which prohibit women from working in certain occupations or under certain conditions, "each State," says the Women's Bureau, "has many laws and rulings which prescribe the conditions under which women should work, covering such matters as the lifting of weights, provision of seats, and proper provision for sanitation and comfort." In six States, industrial commissions have power to have regulations for the health and welfare of workers. In three, the commissions have power to make regulations for women and minors only, and in one, for women, minors, learners, and apprentices.

Perhaps the most striking thing about all these multiform regulations governing the employment of women is the amount of misplaced zeal that they denote. "In most cases," says the Women's Bureau, "the laws which prohibit their employment have little bearing on the real hazards to which they are exposed. . . . Prohibiting the employment of women on certain dusty processes does not solve the problem of any industrial disease in a community. Men are also liable to contract pulmonary diseases from exposure to dusts. . . . It is very possible that under the guise of 'protection' women may be shut out from occupations which are really less harmful to them than much of the tedious, heavy work both in the home and in the factory which has long been considered their special province. *Safe standards of work for women must come to be safe standards for men also if women are to have an equal chance in industry.*" The italics are mine. It is worth mentioning here that only two States prohibit the employment of women in the lead-industry, which so far is the only one that has been proved more harmful to women than to men. The mass of legislation and regulation designed to protect women from the fatigues and hazards of industry would seem, then, to have been animated more by chivalry than by scientific knowledge; and while chivalry may be all very well in its place, it can hardly be expected to solve the industrial problem of women.

In connexion with so-called welfare-legislation, it is interesting to observe that women and children are customarily grouped together as classes requiring protection; and that various laws affecting their position in industry have been sanctioned by the courts as being for the good of the race and therefore not to be regarded as class-legislation. Such decisions certainly would appear to be reasonable in so far as they apply to children, who are the rising generation of men and women, and should be protected during their immaturity. But they can be held valid as they affect women only if woman is regarded as primarily a reproductive function. This view, apparently, is held by most legislators, courts, and uplifters; and they have an unquestionable right to hold it. Whether, however, they are just in attempting to add to the burdens of the working woman by imposing it upon her in the form of rules that restrict her opportunities, is another question. One thing is certain: if discriminative laws and customs are to continue to restrict the opportunities of women and hamper them in their undertakings, it makes little difference for whose benefit those laws and customs are supposed to operate, whether for the benefit of men, of the home, of the race, or of women themselves; their effect on the mind of woman and her opportunities, will be the same. While society discriminates against her sex, for whatever reason, she can not be free as an individual.

Should nothing, then, be done to protect women from the disabilities and hazards to which they are subject in the industrial world? Better nothing, perhaps, than protection which creates new disabilities. Laws which fix fewer hours of work for women than for men may result in shortening men's hours also in factories where many women are employed; but they may result in the substitution of men—or children—for women in factories where but few have been employed. Laws prohibiting night-work may reduce the chances of women to get much-needed employment, and may sometimes shut them out of work which would offer higher returns on their labour than anything they might get to do during the day—as, for example, night-work in restaurants, where the generous tips of after-theatre patrons add considerably to the earnings of waiters. Moreover, it is hard to see on what ground night-work could be held to be more harmful for women than for men.

Minimum-wage laws may fix a legal limit to the greed of employers, but they can not prevent the underpayment of women workers, for they are based on theoretical notions of a living wage, and have no relation to the actual value of the individual's labour. Where they are fixed by law, as I have remarked, a rise in the cost of living may render them ineffectual. As for those laws which undertake to protect women against the hazards of industry, they have usually, as the Women's Bureau has shown, very little relation to the hazards to which women are actually exposed; but they constitute a real barrier to industrial opportunity. On the whole, the vast and unwieldy array of laws and rules designed either to protect the woman worker, or to safeguard the future of the race at her expense, are a pretty lame result of a great deal of humanitarian sound and fury. *Parturiunt montes.*

It is quite natural that the result should be lame; for these protections and safeguards represent so many attempts to mind some one else's business; and the great difficulty about minding some one else's business is that however good one's intentions may be, one can never really know just where that some one's real interests lie, or perfectly understand the circumstances under which he may be most advantageously placed in the way to advance them, for the circumstances are too intimately bound up with his peculiar temperament and situation. As Mill has remarked in a passage which I have already quoted, the world has learned by long experience that affairs in which the individual is the person directly interested go right only when they are left to his own discretion, and that any interference by authority, save to protect the rights of others, is mischievous. The tendency of modern welfare-legislation is to make a complete sacrifice of individual rights not to the rights but to the hypothetical interests of others; and for every individual who happens to benefit by the sacrifice, there is another who suffers by it. If it is hard to regulate one human being for his own good, it is impossible to regulate people *en masse* for their good; for there is no way of making a general rule affect all individuals in the same say, since no two individuals are to be found who are of precisely the same temperament and in precisely the same situation.

There is in all this bungling effort to ameliorate the ills of working women and to safeguard through them the future of the race, a tacit recognition of economic injustice and a strange incuriousness about its causes. One would naturally expect that the conditions which move people to seek protective legislation would move them to question the nature of an economic system which permits such rapacity that any class of employees requires to be protected from it. Surely the forces of righteousness must know that there are reasons for the existence of the conditions which move them to pity and alarm; yet they seem quite willing to go on indefinitely battling against the conditions, and winning with great effort legislative victories which are constantly being rendered ineffectual through lax administration of laws, through the reluctance of employees to jeopardize their positions by testifying against employers or through unforeseen changes in economic conditions. During all this waste of time and effort, this building and crumbling and rebuilding of protective walls around the labourer, the causes of economic injustice continue their incessant operation, producing continuously a new crop of effects which are like so many windmills inviting attack by the Don Quixotes of reform.

Let us consider the effects of economic injustice on women, side by side with the reformer's work upon those effects. Women in industry suffer, as I have shown, the injustice of inequality with men as regards wages, opportunities, training, and tenure of employment. The reformer attacks the problem of wages, and secures minimum-wage laws based on some one's theory of what constitutes a living wage. No allowance is made for dependents because women, theoretically, have none. The amount allowed may from the first be inadequate, even for one person, or it may be rendered inadequate by a rise in the cost of living. In either case, it is purely arbitrary, and bears no relation whatever to the value of the worker's services. Still, such legislation might be better than nothing if there were nothing better to be done. The reformer is less zealous in his attempt to provide women with opportunities; his showing in this field is less impressive than in that of wages. Still, he has done something. If he has not been entirely responsible for the opening to women of many positions in government service, he has at least greatly assisted in securing them these opportunities. Farther than this, it must be admitted, it is difficult for him to go. He might, indeed, exert himself to see that women are provided by one means or another with equal opportunities to get training, but he can do little to affect the policies of private employers of labour, who can hardly be dictated to concerning whom they shall hire and whom they shall retain. Nor can he prevent employers from laying off women workers first when there is a slowing down in production. In three, then, out of four of the disadvantages which bear more heavily on women in industry than on men, the reformer, with all his excellent intentions, is unable to be very helpful; while in his zeal to safeguard the race, whose future appears to him to depend entirely on the health of the female sex, he has multiplied their disadvantages in the manner I have already described, without, however, having made any noteworthy advance toward the accomplishment of his purpose.

Now, had he chosen to inquire into the causes of the artificial disabilities by which women workers are handicapped, he might have discovered that these and the industrial hazards which cause him such grave concern may be traced to the same fundamental source; and that the just and only effective way of removing these disabilities and hazards is to eradicate the source. Women in industry are the victims of traditional prejudices: I have shown what those prejudices are—the idea that woman's place is the home, that women workers have no dependents, that they work for pin-money and therefore do not need a living wage, that upon them alone depends the future health of the race. But as I remarked at the beginning of this chapter, these prejudices could not be turned to the disadvantage of the woman worker if it were not for the over-crowding of the labour-market. So long as there are more people looking for work than there are jobs to be had, the advantage in fixing terms and conditions of labour is on the side of the employer. If men are obliged by their need to put up with underpayment, women will be forced to accept an even worse rate; if the tenure of men is uncertain, that of women will be even more so. If the conditions of industry are hazardous, the alternative of starvation will force the workers to risk injury or death unless the employer be required by law to maintain the proper safeguards. Suppose, however, that labour were scarce, that for every worker looking for employment there were a dozen employers looking for workers. Under such circumstances, the employer would be glad enough to hire the worker who could fill his particular requirements, without regard to sex, as employers did during the war when labour was scarce; and he would pay the worker a wage determined not by theory or prejudice, but by the amount of competition for the worker's services. If the employment he offered were hazardous, he would be obliged to maintain proper safeguards in order to retain his employees, and in addition would probably be forced to pay them a higher wage than they could earn in some safer employment. If he did not do these things, his workers would simply leave him for more satisfactory positions. Nor would he be able to overwork his employees, for if he attempted to do so, some rival employer would outbid him for their services by offering better hours and easier conditions of labour. Thus the peculiar disabilities of women workers would disappear with the disabilities of labourers in general, and not a stroke of legislation would be required to make industry both safe and profitable for the woman worker.

This condition is not unnatural or impossible. It is the present condition of chronic unemployment, of expensive and ineffectual "welfare" legislation, of wasteful and futile struggles between organized capital and organized labour—it is this condition that is entirely unnatural. Upon its removal, and not upon regulations which hamper the woman worker and reduce her to the status of a function, the future of the race depends. The ancestors of coming generations are men as well as women, and posterity will derive its heritage of health from its ancestors of both sexes. Its prospect of health will not be improved by legislation calculated to safeguard the health of women workers, so long as the children they bear continue to be exposed to an involuntary poverty which breeds ignorance, imbecility, disease and crime. The happiness as well as the health of future generations will depend in great measure upon the extent to which both men and women can release themselves from the deteriorating conditions of economic exploitation.

It is in business and in professional pursuits that the occupational progress of women, and their emancipation from traditional prejudices, are most marked. Although in the lower ranks of labour in these pursuits there is a mass of women who, impelled by necessity, work for low wages at mechanical tasks which offer no chance of advancement, there is, nearer the top, a large group of women who have been more fortunate in worldly position and education, and who are spurred as much either by interest in their work or a desire to be self-supporting, as by actual need to earn; who share, in other words, the attitude that leads young men to strike out for themselves even though their fathers may be able to support them. It is the woman animated by these motives who is doing most for the advancement of her sex; for it is she, and not the woman who works through necessity, who really challenges the traditional prejudices concerning the proper place of women. The woman labourer proves the *need* of women to earn; the business woman or professional woman who works because she wants to work, is establishing the *right* of women to earn. More than this, as she makes her way into one after another of the occupations that have been held to belong to men by prescriptive right, she is establishing her claim, as a human being, to choose her work from the whole wide field of human activity. It is owing to the attitude towards life adopted by such women, to their preference of independence and action over the dependence and passivity in vogue not so many years ago, that it is coming to be quite the expected thing that young women of the well-to-do classes shall set out to earn their living, as young men do, instead of stopping under the parental roof, with a watchful eye out for men who will marry and support them. Need I remark that nothing is more likely than this new attitude to bring about the substitution of the "union by affection" for the union by interest? The woman who is economically independent is under much less temptation to marry from economic motives than the woman for whom marriage represents the only prospect of security.

There is still a goodly number of prejudices and discriminations to be overcome before women in business and the professions shall stand on an equal footing with men as regards opportunity and remuneration. Except where she is in business for herself, the woman in these pursuits must generally be content with a lower rate of pay than men; and if observation may be taken to count for anything, she is expected to work somewhat harder for what she gets—less loafing on the job is tolerated in her than in the male employee. She is also more likely to find herself pocketed; that is to say, in a position from which, because of her sex, there is no possibility of further advance because the higher positions are reserved for men. It is so universally the rule that women must content themselves with reaching the lower rungs of the occupational ladder, that the instances where they manage to attain to places of responsibility and authority are still rare enough to be found worthy of remark in the press. The same thing is true of political positions; women are not yet represented in politics in anything like a just proportion to their numbers, nor are they often able to get themselves either elected or apppointed to responsible positions. None the less, considering the comparatively short time since their emergence into the business world and the world of public affairs, they are already making an excellent showing.

The world of business and the professions, like the world of industry, has its occupations which are considered peculiarly suitable for women. Strictly subordinate positions are thought to suit them very well; hence there is quite an army of women stenographers, bookkeepers, clerks and secretaries to be found in the business section of any modern city. The personnel of the nursing profession is made up almost exclusively of women; and the work of teaching in our public schools, especially where it is most conspicuously underpaid, is largely in their hands. There is, to be sure, an impression current amoung members of school boards that marriage disqualifies a woman for the teaching profession; but the single woman is fairly secure in her position, possibly because it does not pay well enough to be very attractive to men. Occupations connected with the arts are also held, in this country, to be particularly well adapted for women, although it must be noted that the prejudice of male musicians is effective enough to exclude them from the personnel of our important orchestras. It is in the creative arts that their work is most welcomed; more especially in the field of literature; and this may seem strange, in view of the fact that so many eminent authorities believe that their sex renders them incapable of attaining any significance in creative work. It is, I apprehend, rather to the low opinion in which aesthetic pursuits are held in this country than to a high opinion of female ability, that this peculiar condition must be ascribed.

But if certain occupations are considered peculiarly appropriate for women, there is none the less a great deal of prejudice against them in others. The idea that woman's place is the home has no more disappeared from the world of business and the professions than it has disappeared from the world of industry, even though it is the business woman and the professional woman who are doing most to dislodge it. And here it may be well to remark a fact that has already been noted, with some pointed comment, by Ethel Snowden, namely: that woman's invasion of the gainful occupations appears to be found unwomanly in proportion to the importance of the position to which she aspires.

It is the married woman in business or in professional work, as it is in industry, who suffers most from the surviving prejudices concerning her sex. When there are economies to be effected through the discharge of workers, the idea that the married woman is normally a dependent comes immediately to the fore, and she is the first employee to be discharged. For example, *Equal Rights* of 8 August, 1925, noted in an editorial that the city of St. Louis had begun a campaign for economy by discharging twelve married women; that there was a movement on in Germany to reduce governmental expenses by a wholesale discharge of women employees; and that, according to rumour; Mr. Coolidge's campaign of economy was being made to bear most heavily on married women. The comment of *Equal Rights* on the action of the city of St. Louis is worth quoting.

St. Louis employed twenty-seven married women. It investigated the economic condition of all these, retained nine, discharged twelve, and was, at last report, still considering the case of the other six. St. Louis did not investigate the economic condition of the men employees, to see whether or not these might continue to live if they were discharged. St. Louis did not try to find out whether or not these men had fathers, brothers, mothers, or wives who might support them while they were looking for other jobs. St. Louis assumed that men have a right to economic independence and the increased happiness and opportunity that it brings. St. Louis assumed that women have no such right.

In other words, St. Louis assumed, as the German and American Governments apparently assume, and as most private employers assume, that women are employed on sufferance; especially married women. Of course it should be remembered that the position of the married woman in this respect is only worse than that of single women, and that the position of women is only worse than that of men; for, as I have already remarked, under a monopolistic economic system the opportunity to earn a living by one's labour comes to be regarded as a privilege instead of a natural right. Women are simply held to be less entitled to this privilege than men.

That marriage should so often assume the nature of a disability for the woman who either wishes or is obliged to earn, whereas it often operates in favour of the male worker, may be attributed to the traditional assumption that married women are dependent on, and subject to, their husbands. I remarked in the preceding chapter that the married woman who wishes to engage in business finds herself, in many communities, hampered by legal disabilities arising from her marital status, whereas her husband is under no corresponding disabilities. Her position as an industrial and salaried worker is rendered insecure if not by law, at least by the same psychology that keeps legal disabilities in force. This psychology may be defined as the expectation that a woman when she marries shall surrender a much greater degree of personal freedom than the man she marries. The man who does not object to his wife's having a career is considered generous and long-suffering. His insistence on her abandoning it and contenting herself with looking out for his domestic comfort is thought to be quite natural. On the other hand, the woman who interferes in any way with a husband's career is regarded as an extremely selfish person; while any sacrifice of herself and her ambitions to her husband and his, is thought of merely as a matter of wifely duty. How often does one hear that such and such a woman has given up her position because "her husband didn't want her to work." There is, too, a very general assumption that every

[3]There are, of course, exceptions to this rule; as when a woman has, before her marriage, already made a great reputation. In such a case the husband would be thought selfish who demanded the sacrifice of her career. But the husband who demands the sacrifice of a potential career is generally thought to be well within his rights.

married woman has children and should stay at home and take care of them. Now, perhaps every married woman should have children; perhaps in a future state of society men and women will marry only when they wish to bring up a family. But at present it is not so; therefore at present the assumption that a married woman should stay at home and take care of her children leaves out of account the fact that large and increasing number of married women are childless. It may be contended that these women should stay at home and take care of their husband; but even if we assume that the unremitting personal attention of his wife is essential to the comfort and happiness of a married man, there would still remain the question of his title to this attention at the cost of her own interests.

We are dealing here with an attitude which, general though it be, has been outmoded by the conditions of modern life. The sexual division of interests and labour which has been insisted upon so long amoung European peoples does not very well fit in with the organization of industrial and social life in the twentieth century. Our social ideology, like our political ideology, is of the eighteenth century; and its especial effectiveness at present is by way of obscuring our vision of the changed world that has emerged from the great economic revolution of the last century. A division of interests and labour which was convenient if not just under the conditions of economic and social life which preceded the industrial revolution, is neither convenient nor just under the conditions which prevail today. The care of young children and the management of a household may result in an unequal division of labour in families where the husband's inability to provide for the needs of his family forces the wife to assume the burdens of a breadwinner. When one reads through the literature on the question of hours of labour for women in industry, one is struck by the persistent stressing of the married woman's double burden of breadwinning and housekeeping. These women, it seems, must not only earn money to contribute to their families' support, but they must, before setting out for work and after returning from it, prepare the family meals, get the children ready for school or the day-nursery, take them there and call for them, wash, sew, and perform a hundred other household tasks. This double burden is often made an argument for establishing shorter hours of work for women in industry, but never for expecting the husband to share the wife's traditional burden as she has been forced to share his. I have no doubt that innumerable husbands are doing this; but there is no expectation put upon them to do it, and those who do not are in no wise thought to shirk their duty to their families, as their wives would be thought to do if they neglected to perform the labour of the household.

Quite analogous to this attitude of the advocates of special legislation for working women is that of the people who concern themselves with the so-called problem of the educated woman, which is supposed to be that of reconciling domesticity with intellectual pursuits. A timely illustration of this attitude is the establishment by Smith College of an institute for the "co-ordination of women's interests." The purpose of this institute, in the words of President Neilson, is "to find a solution of the problem which confronts almost every educated woman today——how to reconcile a normal life of marriage and motherhood with a life of intellectual activity, professional or otherwise," Here again is the tacit assumption that marriage is the special concern of woman, and one whose claims must take precedence over her other interests, whatever they may be; that marriage and motherhood constitute her normal life, and her other interests something extra-normal which must somehow be made to fit in if possible. I have heard of no institute intended to find a way to reconcile the normal life of marriage and fatherhood with a life of intellectual activity, professional or otherwise; although when one considers how many educated men of today are obliged to compromise with their consciences in order to secure themselves in positions which will enable them to provide for their families, one is persuaded that some such institute might be at least equally appropriate and equally helpful with that which Smith College has established.

Let us forget for a moment the sophisticated traditional attitude toward this question of marriage and parenthood, and go back, as it were, to the beginning—to a fact recognized in the animal world and not entirely overlooked by primitive man, namely: that every offspring has two parents who are equally responsible for its care and protection. In the animal kingdom one finds a widely varied division of the labour connected with the care of the young. For example, the male of certain species is found to perform functions which our own usage has led us to regard as maternal. Among the viviparous animals the heavier share of responsibility rests with the female during the gestation, birth and extreme youth of the offspring; and among primitive human beings the actual physical dependence of the offspring on the mother is likely to be prolonged over a period of several years. It was, perhaps, this necessity of a close physical association between mother and child that led to a sexual division of labour under which the mother undertook the physical care of children while the father undertook the task of providing food. It must be remarked, however, that this division of labour by no means excludes productive labour on the part of the woman. Among most tribes she augments the food-supply through agriculture, grubbing, or sometimes through fishing or hunting; and there are tribes, notably in Africa, where she is the sole provider for the family. The Vaertings have remarked that the drudgery connected with the care of children is invariably imposed by the dominant upon the subject sex; a view which is in perfect consonance with what we know of the general human willingness to transfer to other shoulders the burden of uninteresting though necessary labour. Since women have most often been subject, they have most often been forced to undertake this drudgery, either in lieu of or in addition to the labour of providing food and shelter for their families.

This is to say that their subject position has added considerably to what newspaper editors and other commentators are fond of calling the burden of Eve. Since woman is the childbearing sex, it has seemed natural to a great many peoples to increase the disadvantage at which her share in reproduction naturally places her, by making her confinement at home permanent instead of occasional, and by permitting her few, if any, interests save those connected with reproduction; in short, by prolonging and enhancing her subjection to the demands of the race. This is why the term married woman is still taken to imply the term housekeeper; an implication which, as the *Freeman* remarked editorially some years ago, modern civilization must renounce "if it wants such of its women as are editors and bank-presidents to be mothers as well."

Civilization shortens the period of the child's physical dependence on the mother by shortening the period of lactation. On the other hand, it increases fecundity to such an extent that where religious superstition or ignorance prevents the use of contraceptives, the burden of childbearing is greatly increased. This result of civilization is not, however, commonly found among the educated classes; and even among those classes where children are most numerous, I have already shown that women are not restrained by motherhood from engaging in gainful occupations outside the home. On the contrary, the number of their offspring is more often their chief incentive to this course. Among well-to-do families, prepared foods and wet-nursing have for a long time been rather generally employed to relieve mothers even of the responsibility of lactation, while the custom of assigning the physical care of children to hired substitutes has reduced their actual work to that of bringing the child into the world. That this mode of caring for children is approved by all classes is evident from their readiness to adopt it when fortune favours them with an opportunity. It is occasionally inveighed against by moralists, but on the whole it is coveted and approved, especially while women devote to frivolous pursuits the leisure that it leaves them. When a woman adopts this mode in order to reconcile motherhood with a serious interest outside the home, it is a different matter, and lays her open to the charge of neglecting her family, though in fact she may spend no more hours away from home than the woman who gives her morning to shopping and her afternoon to playing bridge. Why this should be the case I am at a loss to know, unless it be that a serious interest outside the home appears to smack too much of an assertion of her right to live her life for her own sake rather than for the sake of the race or that of her husband—a self-assertion not readily to be accepted without such reservations as find expression in institutes designed to "co-ordinate women's interests."

It appears, then, that the care of the young is the concern of both sexes, and is so recognized in the animal world and among human beings; and that among the latter such differences in usage as exist touching this matter are differences in the apportioning of the burden. Even in our own day, when there is observable a tendency to forget that the child has more than one parent—that parent being the mother—the father's claim to his children is still recognized in law, often to the prejudice of the mother's; and so, likewise, is his obligation to provide for them. Indeed, the child may be said to be regarded as exclusively the mother's only while it is young; for it is a general custom among us to speak of Mrs. So-and-So's baby, but of Mr. So-and-So's son or daughter. Let us, then, recognize the claim and interest of both parents. Let us also remember that the economic organization has so extensively altered that the traditional division of labour—this division is always profoundly affected by consideration of the young—has been outmoded as far as thousands of families are concerned. Let us also assume that woman has established her right to be considered as a human being rather than a function or a chattel. Then it must seem reasonable to assume that the co-ordination of interests to be brought about concerns both sexes equally; that the problem to be confronted is that of reconciling a normal life of marriage and parenthood not only with the freest possible development of intellectual interest but with the utmost devotion to any chosen profession.

I can not pretend to foretell how this problem will be settled; for its solution will depend upon the general solution of the labour-problem. It may be that the necessary collectivism of modern industry will result in a collectivist system of caring for children. Such a system would by no means be an innovation; it would simply constitute an extension and adaptation of means which already exist—of nurseries for very small children and schools for older ones. Whatever its demerits might be, such a system would certainly represent an enormous economy of effort. The average home is adapted less to the needs of children than to those of adults; hence a mother of young children must spend a great deal of her time in preventing her young charges from injuring themselves with dangerous household implements, from falling downstairs or off of furniture too high for them, and from touching objects which would not be safe in their hands. In a properly equipped nursery, on the other hand, the furniture and all the objects are adapted to the size and intelligence of the children. Children have the advantage of numerous playmates; and one person can supervise the play of a dozen of them with less fatigue than the mother of one is likely to feel at the end of a day in the average home.

The Russians have already taken some steps in this direction by establishing both nurseries and schools in connexion with certain factories. From what I can gather of their policy, it would seem that they regard the care and education of children as being very much the concern of the whole community. They look upon childbearing as a service to the community, but they do not appear to take the view that women should be required to perform this service at the expense of their independence, for they have instituted a system of subsidies for pregnant and nursing working mothers, with rest-periods before and after confinement, and subsidy during confinement amounting to the daily subsidy multiplied by fifteen.[4]

I have already indicated in the preceding chapter what it seems to me would be the course of free people in this matter of reconciling the care of children with the greatest possible freedom for both parents. It seems hardly necessary to call attention to the obvious fact that the question is simply that of placing the care of the young in the hands of those who are interested in it and fitted for it, instead of forcing it willy-nilly upon either sex through a traditional expectation and a traditional division of labour. In a free society, those parents who wished to pursue careers incompatible with the actual care of young children would avail themselves of the services of substitutes, as the well-to-do classes do at present; and they might do so with even greater confidence because, as I have remarked, those engaged in caring for and teaching the young

[4]From the Laws and Decrees of the Soviet Government on medical questions, sanitation, etc., published in Moscow, 1922.

would do so as a matter of interest primarily and only secondarily as a means of livelihood. There is another important consideration to be taken into account, and that is, that in a free society the problem of reconciling the occupations of the parents with their personal supervision of their children would be much easier to solve; for their hours of labour would be greatly decreased. It is only where production must support an enormous amount of idleness and waste that it is necessary to overwork producers.

It is possible, of course, that the institution of economic freedom might check the present tendency of women to engage in gainful occupations outside the home. It most certainly would if the vast increase of opportunity which it offered were reserved exclusively for men; but to bring about this result it would be necessary for traditional anti-feminist prejudices to survive much more strongly than they do today. The position of women has too radically changed to admit of their exclusion from direct participation in the benefits of economic freedom; therefore if they resigned the increased economic opportunities that it offered them, and withdrew to the sphere of domesticity, they would do so as a matter of choice. Why should we not expect them to choose the exclusive domesticity which might be rendered possible through the increased earning power of men? They probably would, where it suited their taste to do so; but one of the most powerful incentives to do so would no longer exist, namely: the desire for economic security. Women, to be sure, are not exempt from the characteristic willingness of humankind to live by the exertions of others; but I would remark that there is this difference between the person who does this indirectly, through legalized privilege, and the person who depends directly on the bounty of another: that the former is independent and the latter is dependent. Women are not strangers to the human desire for freedom; and when the fear of want is allayed they are quite likely to prefer an easy and secure self-support to the alternative of economic dependence. Moreover, economic freedom would set domesticity in competition with the interests of women rather than their needs; for it would set all people free to engage in occupations that interested them, whereas at present the vast majority do whatever offers them a living. Under these circumstances it might reasonably be expected that the number of women who would continue in business and in industrial and professional pursuits, even after marriage and the birth of children, would greatly increase.

Indeed, if we postulate an economic system under which every human being would be free to choose his occupation in accordance with his interests, I see no more reason to suppose that women would invariably choose domesticity than to suppose that all men would choose blacksmithing. Under such a régime I doubt that even the power of the expected which affects them so strongly at present, would long continue in an effectiveness which it has already begun to lose. Women, I think, might be expected to choose their occupations with the same freedom as men, and to look for no serious interruption from marriage and the birth of children. There are a good many women at present who very ably reconcile motherhood with a chosen career. I think we might expect to find more of them rather than fewer, in a free society. One thing is certain, and it is the important thing: they would be free to choose. If it be woman's nature, as some people still believe, to wish to live at second hand, then in a free society they will freely make that choice, and no one can complain of it—unless it be the men on whom they elect to depend. However, to assume from past experience that they do want to live at second hand is to assume that all the social and legal injustices which have been employed to force them to do so, were unnecessary; and when have Governments and communities wasted their power in exercising compulsion where no compulsion was needed?

XXI. Trade Unionism and Women's Work

Susan Anthony

The following essay, extracted from Susan Anthony's Women's Place in Industry and Home *(1932), analyzes the relationship between women and trade unions. Anthony states: "It became obvious to the workers that if men's wages were to be raised and maintained at a level corresponding to the obligations of many of them, the competition of women must be prevented." Trade unions and the legislation they engendered served to limit that competition by placing women at a disadvantage in the labor market. Although it deals with British unions, the high quality of her essay and its relevance to American unions dictated its inclusion in this collection.*

The restrictions which had been suspended by the Trade Unions during the European War, 1914–1918, had a long history; a history, in fact, longer than that of the Unions themselves. In medieval times, girls generally had not practised craft work under the same conditions as boys; they had much less often been regularly apprenticed. Consequently when adult they had less often worked as independent Guild members, since membership was normally reached through the gate of apprenticeship. But in Guild work, craft or commercial, women commonly helped the men of their family, and widows frequently succeeded to their husband's Guild status. It was possible, therefore, for women to acquire high Guild status, both in their own right if, as did sometimes occur, they had been apprenticed as children, or if the Guild right of the husband descended to his widow; but it was more usual for their labour to be subordinate to that of men, and it was normally regarded as casual labour, being in fact particularly important in that respect, since it was the *only* casual labour permitted a Guildsman to employ. A rush of trade orders could not be met by engaging another skilled worker at short notice, since apprenticeships were of long term, and the number allowed to each master was commonly limited. Wives and daughters therefore had a definite labour value even though their labour was usually subordinate in kind.[1]

[1]See *English Apprenticeship and Child Labour*, by O. J. Dunlop; also *Working Life of Women in the Seventeenth Century*, and *Growth of English Industry and Commerce*, p. 352.

The principles and organization of medieval Guilds and of modern Trade Unions differ, however, in many material respects, and to understand the latter, a study of the soil from which the Trade Union movement sprang is probably more valuable than research into the practice of the Guilds.[2] That soil was the new economic organization of society produced by the industrial revolution of the eighteenth century.

English society at this time experienced three simultaneous revolutions: in manufacturing industry, in agriculture and land tenure, and in political philosophy. The manufacturer began to use more complicated machines, and more capital. The possession of capital sufficient for effective use for manufacturing became restricted to a smaller proportion of the population, and industry became centralized and specialized. Farming developed in a similar way; more scientific methods demanded larger units under centralized control, and the remaining available common lands were gradually enclosed. Parliament, instead of setting itself to organize the industrial life of the nation with regard for the welfare of the individual and society, as had formerly been considered the function of government, was persuaded that national wealth could be most effectively promoted by the abdication of any such directing power.

One of the manifold effects of this economic revolution was to alter the basis and source of the worker's family income. The greater part of the industry of the country had been located in the worker's home, and in these circumstances even babies in petticoats joined in the work.[3] The proceeds were legally the father's, but it was obvious that the "breadwinning" was not exclusively his province, and that each member of the family above the merest infancy took its share in earning the bread it ate. In industry so conducted, there was no competition between stronger and weaker individuals, between legally-maintained and legal supporter, man or woman as such. Their gains increased progressively with their numbers, or in proportion to their combined strength and industry.

But under the new conditions which arose in the eighteenth century

[2]In respect of women's labour, however, the problems of Guilds and Unions were in some respects similar, and might provide an interesting comparative study.

[3]In Yorkshire "there was hardly anything above four Years old but its Hands are sufficient to itself" (Defoe, *Tour through the whole Island of Great Britain, 1724*). In a *Report to the Board of Trade, in 1697,* John Locke urged that children of poor and improvident parents, above the age of *three* should be sent to working schools to learn and practise spinning and knitting. See *English Social Life in the Eighteenth Century,* M. D. George, p.9 Textile work was the most usual method of employing poor people's children.

this was changed. With the new centralization of industry, and its departure from the home to the factory, each individual in the family had to seek, compete for, or forfeit, profitable employment.

The effect of this change on family life did not become everywhere immediately apparent. The change occurred at different rates in different industries. Hand labour and individual home capital sometimes competed with factory labour for a considerable period.[4] Consequently, although one or more members of a family might go to the factory, those who could not or would not go, could still earn money while staying at home. Also, during the earlier industrial period, there were still in many places opportunities for independent rural livelihood, not only for the agricultural worker, but even for the factory-hand, and occasionally for the coal-miner. The Yorkshire weaver had been used to keep his cow on his own plot of ground; the new factories were often placed in rural surroundings, and for a time old customs survived side by side with new.

In the payment of the family wage there was also for some time mutual aid between capitalized agriculture and manufacture. The agricultural labourer's family now sometimes had the chance of supplementing his inadequate individual earnings by doing factory work instead of domestic industrial work, and the capitalist manufacturer was relieved of the necessity to pay each employee a family-subsistence wage, because the rural situation of "the works" provided their families with rural employment, if not independence. Both farming and the manufacturing employer were thus aided in offering wages reckoned on an individual subsistence basis. Until the reform of the Poor Law in 1834, they derived further encouragement for this procedure (which, it must be remembered, tradition, founded on the earlier economic circumstances of labourers' families, seemed to justify) by the Poor Law practice of assisting from the rates those families in which the earned income was insufficient for the support of the family. This assistance was in certain cases given on a scale in proportion to the number of children in the family.[5] The withdrawal of Poor Law assistance after

[4]Cotton-weaving, for instance, was carried on by hand-looms to a great extent until the 1830's. See Hammond, *Skilled Labourer*, Chap. IX; Pinchbeck, *Women Workers and the Industrial Revolution*, Chap. VIII.

[5]The practice of systematically subsidizing wages from rates, so as to raise them to a constant figure according to the size of the family; and of assuring the labourer of the receipt of this sum whether he could find work or no; and of sending each worker out to auction his labour under these circumstances to the highest bidder—was the result in certain parishes of an Act passed in 1782. It kept wages from rising above the level of

1834 did not always result in the raising of the agricultural labourer's wage, but in the more purposeful provision by the farmer of work for the women and children.[6]

The survival of the old system side by side with the new thus concealed for a time the problems which arose from the centralization of labour, and the change from a family-earned to an individually-earned income. But as profitable domestic industries, and the opportunities for independent rural livelihood, were driven out of existence, and after the system of subsidizing wages from rates was abandoned, there seemed to be no way of proportioning the income to the family except for all the members of it to work for the capitalist employer in farm or factory, as they had previously worked independently at home. If they did do this, however, the last state of the workers was usually worse than the first. That factory work could not readily be combined with domestic cares, as domestic work could, was only one of the difficulties. Equally fatal, in its effect on the family's standard of life, was the fact that the members of it were not now co-operating but competing for livelihood. Unless they could effectively combine (and until 1824 the law forbade them to combine at all), their very numbers tended to lower the wages of each; and besides this, the wage or employment of the man was undercut by the competition of a form of labour customarily supposed to require only a lower reward.

The accepted convention of the lesser need of women was chiefly based on the obligation of the husband to maintain his wife and young children, but it was strengthened by the fact that in the days of family (i.e. domestic) industry, working-class women who did not belong to a family had been at a disadvantage. Spinsters had usually suffered

---

individual subsistence. The practice of assisting from the rates workers whose families were too large for subsistence on their wages did not begin with this (Speenhamland) system. Locke, in the Report already quoted, wrote: "A great number of children giving a poor man a title to an allowance from the parish, this allowance is given once a week or once a month . . . to the father in money, which he not infrequently spends at the alehouse. . . . " Lecky states that "with the warm approbation of Pitt (in 1796) parochial relief was made proportionate to the number of children in a family" (*History of England in the Eighteenth Century*, Vol. VI, p. 206, ed. 1887).

[6]"In the districts where (after the Poor Law Amendment Act) scales (of rate-allowances supplementary to wages) were abolished, farmers had higher wages to pay. . . . Even so, earnings were still insufficient to maintain a family. There were, therefore, definite attempts to provide regular employment for wives and children, and farmers made it a rule to employ the families of their labourers before taking on extra hands. At Glynde, in Sussex . . . work was found for women . . . and for children . . . throughout the year when the allowance system was abolished" (*Women Workers and the Industrial Revolution*, p. 77).

such a straitened, hand-to-mouth existence that their ilk were unlikely to expect more than a mere subsistence wage in capitalist, centralized industry.[7]

If it was possible for an employer to secure his labour at a comparatively low wage, current industrial ethics, in the eighteenth and early nineteenth century, instructed him to do so. The sex of the employee made no difference to this general rule. Consequently the convention that women needed less favoured the offer of work to women rather than men, as the new methods of industrial organization gained ground. Examples of such "undercutting" of men's employment and wages by women may be found both in connection with agriculture and with manufacturing industry.

> "As capitalistic farming developed and with it the desire to lower the cost of production, women's labour was increasingly in demand. Such advocates of new methods as Marshall and Arthur Young frequently pointed out the advantages to be gained from their employment. After pointing out the cost of transplanting, for example, Arthur Young added naïvely: 'This is doing it very cheap . . . from whence it is evident, that transplanting should always be done by women!' "[8]
>
> "The cheapness of women's work caused a general depression of wages over the whole country—a result which was observable from the earliest days of their employment as labourers. In 1788 Marshall had pointed out that the employment of women to hoe corn was 'beneficial' to the farmer, since by it 'the wages for Men are lowered'. As time went on and the employment of women increased the effects were more noticeable, and after 1834 the earnings of women and children allowed married men to be employed for wages on which they could not otherwise have lived, and made it difficult for single and old men to secure employment at all."[9]

Nearly seventy years after Arthur Young wrote, an investigator of the West of England textile industry reported:

> "When it becomes needful to lower wages, women are employed, who will readily undertake it at a lower rate than men receive . . . indeed, it appears to be a custom in every trade to pay women at a

[7]This seems to be the deduction to be drawn from such evidence as is available. Wages obtainable in the domestic textile processes varied very much from time to time and from place to place, but in general appear to have been barely sufficient to support a single person living alone.

[8]Pinchbeck, *op. cit.*, p. 100, quoting Young, *Eastern Tour* (1771 ed.).

[9]*Ibid.*, p. 102, quoting Marshall, *Rural Economy of Gloucestershire*, 1789.

lower rate than men receive for the same article. I have found it in the broadcloth trade, in the blanket trade, and in the silk-velvet trade."[10]

Factory Inspectors reported in 1843:—

> "The small amount of wages paid to women, acts as a strong inducement to employ them instead of men, and in power-loom shops this has been the case to a great extent."[11]

In some cases the practice was carried one degree further; the married women undercut the single women. In a speech in 1844 Lord Ashley (afterwards Shaftesbury) quoted a letter giving an instance of this:—

> "Mr. E. . . . a manufacturer, informed me that he employs females exclusively at his power looms; . . . gives a decided preference to married females especially those who have families at home dependent on them for support; they are attentive, docile, more so than unmarried females, and are compelled to use their utmost exertions to procure the necessities of life."[12]

It became obvious to the workers that if men's wages were to be raised and maintained at a level corresponding to the obligations of many of them, the competition of women must be prevented.

In branches of work too heavy, or in any way considered unsuitable for the employment of women, men had less need to fear their competition, and it was found that wages were not reduced to the same extent as in the trades where they competed. For instance it is recorded that

> "in the woollen trade the width of the loom and the corresponding strength required excluded all but a few muscular women from such branches as broad-cloths, blankets and carpets."[13]

In the general reduction of wages which afflicted the trade from 1815 onwards, the cloth-weavers suffered less than others. In the cotton trade, on the other hand, the observed sequence of cause and effect was reversed:—

> "Disastrous effects were especially noticeable after the power loom was employed for the heavier work in which up to that time men had had the monopoly. Girls as well as boys were put to the trade at an

[10]Pinchbeck, *op. cit.*, p. 178, quoting *Report on Handloom Weavers*, 1840.

[11]*Ibid.*, p. 188 n., quoting *Factory Inspector's Reports*, 1843.

[12]*Ibid.*, p. 194.

[13]Pinchbeck, *op. cit.*, p. 166. Axminster carpets were an exception.

> early age, and constant reductions of wages in the nineteenth century made it essential for most women to continue at work after marriage."[14]

Theoretically, therefore, one might expect that in many branches of work which were particularly heavy, wages would be maintained because women were not employed. But in the early industrial period, instances of this were probably very rare, the reason being that it is only in quite modern times that the question whether some kinds of work were too hard for women has been raised at all. Women worked in the mine, at the forge, at the quarry, as well as in factories and fields. In the mines they were chained to trucks weighing as much as 250 lb., which they dragged along the rough, uneven passages. Sometimes these passages were only two to three feet high. Nor was the collier woman the only heavy worker, though she received, later, the most attention. The idyllic occupation of the dairymaid included the handling of cheeses weighing upwards of 140 lb., and labour from summer dawn to dark. Women, and children of both sexes, shared the heaviest work of the farm, driving the three- or four-horsed plough and loading the dung-cart. Women had worked as smith-wives from medieval times, and as late as the 1840's many women were working at domestic forges in the Midlands. In the early days of the Industrial Revolution there was scarcely any industry in which women were not employed, or in which, when individual earnings superseded family earnings, they did not compete with men to the detriment of wages.

Though the male wage-earners could not, therefore, in the earlier days of capitalist industrialism, secure a higher wage in most trades owing to exclusive demands for male labour, nevertheless they came to realize that if they *could* exclude women, or segregate them in certain branches they might more effectively unite to put forward a uniform demand based on their own recognized needs, and so secure higher payment than a woman would customarily ask, or be likely to receive. Early instances of such action occurred among a group of Western wool-weavers, and among the London silk-weavers. Mr. and Mrs. Hammond record that in the West Country during the eighteenth and early nineteenth century, light woollen weaving "was done almost entirely by women, 'those who do the work being the wives or daughters of agricultural labourers, of mechanics or others.' " But

> "There was one curious exception in the case of this trade, at Cul-

[14]*Ibid.*, p. 167.

lompton, where the men had bound themselves not to allow any woman to learn the trade. This prohibition lasted for nearly a century, till 1825, when the advantages of obtaining help from their own wives and daughters broke down resistance. Nearly fifteen years later there were still 250 men to 62 women, and the prices paid were higher than in other parts of the district."[15]

In the London silk-weaving industry, carried on in Spitalfields, an attempt was made in 1769 to exclude women from the better-paid classes of work. Silk-weaving had been primarily a women's industry as early as the fifteenth century,[16] but now, in the Book of Prices set out as the basis of agreement, the following statement was included:—

> "No woman or girl to be employed in making any kind of work except such works as are herein fixed and settled at 5½*d.* per ell . . . or . . . per yard or under for the making. . . . And no woman or girl is to be employed in making any sort of handkerchief of above the usual or settled price of 4*s.* 6*d.* per dozen for the making thereof PROVIDED always . . . that in case it shall hereafter happen that the Kingdom of Great Britain shall engage in war . . . that then every manufacturer shall be at liberty to employ women or girls in the making of any sort of works as they shall think most fit and convenient without any restraint whatsoever. . . . [17]

This attempt at stabilizing wages in the silk industry was not permanently successful, but the silk-weavers were peculiarly fortunate in the alternative event. After strikes and rioting, they managed to procure legislation (in 1773, only three years before the outlook of politicians was influenced in the contrary direction by the publication of Adam Smith's *Wealth of Nations*) by which the local magistrates were empowered to fix their wage-rates. Equal pay for men and women was secured, presumably at a satisfactory rate. Until this legislation was repealed, the silk workers' attitude to the questions which agitated their contemporary Trade Unionists were peculiar to themselves; they were content with labour conditions, and refused to support a petition for the repeal of the Combination Laws, because they looked upon the law not as an enemy but a friend. "The law, cling to the law, it will protect us!" they exclaimed; but the law did not cling to them, and the Spitalfields Acts

[15]*Skilled Labourer*, p. 162.

[16]See Clark, *op. cit.*, pp. 139–42, and Pinchbeck, p. 169 n.

[17]*London Life in the Eighteenth Century*, by M. D. George, quoting *A List of Prices in . . Branches of the Weaving Manufactory. . .* 1769.

by which their wages were regulated were repealed at about the same date as the Combination Acts.[18]

The Luddite riots, which came to a head in 1811–1812 among the Framework Knitters of Leicester, appear to have been caused "by the use of a new machine which enabled the manufacturers to employ women in work in which men had been before employed."[19] "The repeated reductions of wages, the rapid alterations of processes, and the substitution of women and children for adult male workers, had gradually reduced the workers to a condition of miserable poverty."[20] Much of the discontent seems to have centred round the employment of women, and the low payment they in particular received. Attempts were made to prevent them from working. On Christmas Day, 1811, a steward wrote to his master describing the activities of Luddites at Pentridge, Derby:—

> ". . . two men came to this place who called themselves inspectors from the Committee, they went to every stockinger's (i.e. operative's) house and discharged them from working under such prices as they gave them a list of . . . Where they found a frame worked by a person who had not served a regular apprenticeship, or by a Woman, they discharged them from working, and if they promised to do so (i.e. to desist) they stuck a paper upon the frame with these words written upon it: 'Let this frame stand, the colts removed.' Colt is the name given to all those who have not served a regular apprenticeship."[21]

Even among the coal-miners the view began to prevail that the employment of women prevented the man receiving a family subsistence wage. This was the more remarkable because among colliers the old system of family work (though in their case for a capitalist proprietor) survived into the nineteenth century. The men employed their

[18] *History of Trade Unionism*, p. 98 and n. See also pp. 54–5, and Pinchbeck, *op. cit.*, p. 176 n.

[19] *Skilled Labourer*, p. 257, quoting from the *Annual Register* of 1812 an account of a Report of the Secret Committee of the House of Lords on the disturbances.

[20] *History of Trade Unionism*, p. 86.

[21] *Skilled Labourer*, p. 263. It is interesting that the only personal violence said to have been done by the Notts Luddites was offered to an employer who had previously received a threatening letter about women's wages. It was represented that a middlewoman in his employ "gives her Girls but half a Crown a week . . . for which they work a great number of Hours. You must be sensible, Sir," the writer continues, "that these unfortunate girls are under very strong temptations to turn prostitutes, from their extreme Poverty. The Captain (of the Luddites) . . . these People being defenceless he conceives them to be more immediately under his protection as he believes their Wages are the lowest in England. . . ."

own wives and children as helpers, and in some cases personally received, and personally spent, their wages.[22] Yet even so

> "There were colliers in the West Riding who strongly objected to their (i.e. women's) employment, because 'they prevent lads and men getting their proper wages.' In parts of Scotland also it was opposed 'not so much from the soreness of the work as from a notion they have that it cheapens their own labour'; and in accordance with the policy pursued by the Unions to force up wages after 1825, the men themselves had in 1836–1837, excluded women from both coal and ironstone pits. For a time it remained a rule of the Unions that no woman should be allowed underground, but the temptation to employ them proved too strong, and they found their way back again. It is possible that a similar notion of self-interest had its influence in prompting the resolution of 350 Barnsley miners—some of them employers of women—who, in 1841, declared, with only five dissentients, 'that the employment of girls in pits is highly injurious to their morals, that it is not proper work for females, and that it is a scandalous practice'."[23]

All these efforts were limited in extent to the particular industry in which the men in question were employed. But in 1842, a deputation from the Short-Time Committee of the West Riding, representing the male operatives, waited on Peel and Gladstone, and included in their demands "the gradual withdrawal of all females from the factories." Peel, as a manufacturer, interested in the supply of cheap labour, disapproved of the proposal. Gladstone was more sympathetic, and

> "thought the object might be achieved by the following regulations: 'First by fixing a higher age for the commencement of infant female labour, than . . . of infant male labour in factories. Secondly, by limiting the number of females in proportion to the number of males in any one factory. Thirdly, by forbidding a female to work in a factory after her marriage, and during the lifetime of her husband' "[24]

Gladstone's proposals cause one to reflect on the strange limitations consistent with a Victorian Liberal's idea of individual liberty.

A proposal similar to that of the Short-Time Committee had been put forward ten years before in the pages of Leigh Hunt's journal, *The Examiner*[25] All children under fourteen and "females of any age," it was

[22]"Until the end of the eighteenth century, colliers frequently borrowed money which was repaid out of the labour of their children" (Pinchbeck, *op. cit.*, pp. 257–8).

[23]Pinchbeck, *op. cit.*, pp. 264–5.

[24]*Ibid.*, p. 200 n.

[25]Pinchbeck, *op. cit.*, p. 199, quoting *The Examiner*, January 29, 1832.

suggested, should gradually be excluded from manufactories. This suggestion actually called forth a reply from "The Female Operatives of Todmorden." It is so unusual to find wage-earning women of that time (1832) speaking for themselves, and they put their case so admirably, that this letter must be quoted as it is given by Miss Pinchbeck:—[26]

"SIR,

Living as we do, in the densely populated manufacturing districts of Lancashire, and most of us belonging to that class of females who earn their bread either directly or indirectly by manufactories, we have looked with no little anxiety for your opinion on the Factory Bill. . . . Your are for doing away with our services in manufactories altogether. So much the better, if you had pointed out any other more eligible and practical employment for the surplus female labour, that will want other channels for a subsistence. If our competition were withdrawn, and short hours substituted, we have no doubt but the effects would be as you have stated, 'not to lower wages, as the male branch of the family would be enabled to earn as much as the whole had done', but for the thousands of females who are employed in manufactories, who have no legitimate claim on any male relative for employment or support, and who have, through a variety of circumstances, been early thrown on their own resources for a livelihood, what is to become of them?

In this neighbourhood, hand-loom has been almost totally superseded by power-loom weaving, and no inconsiderable number of females, who must depend on their own exertions, or their parishes for support, have been forced, of necessity, into the manufactories, from their total inability to earn a livelihood at home.

It is a lamentable fact, that, in these parts of the country, there is scarcely any other mode of employment for female industry, if we except servitude and dressmaking. Of the former of these, there is no chance of employment for one-twentieth of the candidates that would rush into the field, to say nothing of lowering the wages of our sisters of the same craft; and of the latter, galling as some of the hardships of manufactories are (of which the indelicacy of mixing with the men is not the least), yet there are few women who have been so employed, that would change conditions with the ill-used genteel little slaves, who have to lose sleep and health, in catering to the whims and frivolities of the butter-flies of fashion.

We see no way of escape from starvation, but to accept the very tempting offers of the newspapers, held out as baits to us, fairly ship ourselves off to Van Diemen's Land, on the very delicate errand of husband-hunting; and, having safely arrived at the 'Land of Goshen',

[26] *Ibid.*, p. 199.

> jump ashore, with a 'Who wants me?' Now, then, as we are a class of society who will be materially affected by any alteration of the present laws, we put it seriously to you, whether, as you have deprived us of our means of earning our bread, you are not bound to point out a more eligible and suitable employment for us?
>
> Waiting with all humility, for your answer to our request, we have the honour to subscribe ourselves, the constant readers of *The Examiner*,
>
> THE FEMALE OPERATIVES OF TODMORDEN."

"In reply," writes Miss Pinchbeck, "the editor of *The Examiner* admitted the cogency of these arguments and as a compromise naïvely suggested that 'the interdiction might be confined to *married* females, and those whose parents are alive, and not in receipt of parish relief!' But at the same time, in all seriousness, he advocated emigration as offering the greatest advantages for that large class of young women whose 'parents or other near relatives' were unable 'to support and protect them'."

Neither the proposals of *The Examiner* nor those of the Short-Time Committee were translated into legislative action at the time, but similar, if less drastic, suggestions continue to be made in the twentieth century. The employment of married women is restricted in certain occupations; and to the question circulated by the War Cabinet Committee *Is it considered desirable to regulate the employment of married women?* a number of replies were received in the affirmative.

The policy of exclusion of women's labour, urged by male Trade Unionists in the interests of their own wage-rates, was reinforced by another current in the stream of public opinion. During the nineteenth century the theory became prevalent that certain kinds and conditions of work suitable or inevitable for men, were not suitable or inevitable for women. This view spread rapidly during the reign of Queen Victoria, and found concrete expression in the suggestion that women should not work under sweated conditions in factories, or at all in mines.

There was, indeed, ground for supposing that the conditions of industrial work might lead to rapid race deterioration, and might be more detrimental to the health of women and children than of men. Probably these evils were not new certainly in the mines, and possibly in many cottage-homes and town tenements where domestic industry had previously been carried on, conditions had been as bad as in early nineteenth-century factories. But there was probably a greater proportion of healthy outdoor work in earlier times, and it may have been easier to adjust burdens to individual strength, under a domestical system of industry; and even if that were actually seldom done, the pre-existence of evils could hardly justify acquiescence in their continuance, when the concentration of work brought them to public notice.

When proposals for protective legislation first arose, current political philosophy held sacrosanct the freedom of the labourer to contract with his employer untrammelled by legal regulation. This was held to be essential to the economic welfare of both parties. There was, however, so great a tendency to think of "economic man" as an adult male, that to legislate for women and children did not seem so heretical as, according to the orthodox doctrine of *laissez-faire,* it actually was, nor so inimical to their interests as, if that doctrine were true, it certainly would be. Early industrial legislation therefore concerned itself particularly with women and young persons, either being directed exclusively towards amelioration of the conditions of one or both these groups, or differentiating its application in respect of them, or being based on their needs more particularly.

Differential industrial legislation, and the problems arising from it, will be discussed more fully in the next chapter. We are here concerned with it, and the sentiments which gave rise to it, only as factors influential in determining the actions and attitude of the male Trade Unionist *vis-à-vis* the female worker.

The theory that certain kinds and conditions of work permissible for men, were unsuitable for women, does not seem to have been resented by the men. It would appear that they generally welcomed this point of view, not so much because they shared it—they were probably too conservative for that—but because they desired to limit the competition of women with men on economic grounds. In one trade after another we find the men expressing apprehension for the health, happiness, or morals of women who might have the misfortune to compete with them, and each historian of industry notes that these sentiments do not quite ring true. Thus Miss Pinchbeck surmises that "a notion of self-interest" may have prompted the Barnsley miners in their decision that the employment of girls in pits was highly injurious to their morals, not proper work for females, and a scandalous practice. Mrs. Drake discovers the same motive in the expostulation addresssed by the Potters' Unions, in 1845, "to maidens, mothers and wives" newly brought into competition with them owing to the introduction of a new machine.[27] In the Metal Trades many attempts were made to secure

[27]*Women in Trade Unions,* p. 6.

the exclusion of women, ostensibly on the grounds of their own welfare. But they followed on previous efforts in which the low wages accepted by the women were the admitted motive, so that their sincerity was suspect.

> "In 1866, a single pen factory in Birmingham engages, according to good authority, no less than 2,000 women . . . the competition of 'cheap female labour' causes the despair of the men's trade unions. Through the 'seventies and 'eighties, the Birmingham Brass Workers, the Nut and Bolt Makers, the Chain Makers, the Nail Makers, raise their voices in protest against the female invasion."[28]

The men would not support the women's Trade Union movement in its early days, because by so doing they would be recognizing "those presumptuous females who 'turn at the lathe and file at the vice' in Birmingham, cutting out their own men-folk." When the representative of the Midlands Trades Federation moved, in the Trade Union Congress of 1887, "to introduce such amendments to the Factory and Workshops Act as shall prevent the employment of females in the making of chains, nails, rivets, bolts, etc., *such work not being adapted to their constitution*"[29]—the benevolent motive—the kiss, one might call it, or perhaps more aptly, the wag—in the tail of the resolution, could impress only the uninitiated.

When the Journeymen Tailors' Society sought to prevent the competition of women, they had a more difficult case to make out. In the light of history and tradition, it was almost impossible to describe sewing or cutting as work not proper for females, highly injurious to their morals, or ill-adapted to their constitution. If a benevolent motive were required for the exclusion of women from this industry it must be discovered in some hardship of quite general application.

> "Have not women," said the Journeymen Tailors, "been unfairly driven from their proper sphere in the social scale, unfeelingly torn from the maternal duties of a parent and unjustly encouraged to compete with men in ruining the money value of labour? *The Times* lies when it says that the Tailors of the Metropolis have struck against these poor creatures, with whose sufferings and privations the Committee deeply sympathize, and the terms under which they obtain employment are too gross for the public ear."[30]

When organization enabled, or initiative or extreme need impelled

[28]*Women in the Engineering Trades*, p. 7.

[29]*Women in Trade Unions*, p. 20.

[30]*Ibid.*, p. 4.

the women workers to give public expression to their own views, it is common to find them strongly objecting to such proposals to exclude them from industry, or from particular industries; and they objected none the less because these proposals were made under a semblance of regard for their welfare. In the Owenite movement of the 1830's, when the women were swept into Trade Unionism on the general wave of enthusiasm, "the 'Grand Lodge of Operative Bonnet Makers' vies in activity with the miscellaneous 'Grand Lodge of the Women of Great Britain and Ireland'; and the 'Lodge of Female Tailors' asks indignantly whether the 'Tailors' Order' is really going to prohibit women from making waistcoats."[31] The Women's Trade Union League, formed in 1874, constantly opposed the attempts of the men's Metal Unions to exclude women from the Midland trades, and from other industrial work. They were suspicious of every form of restriction, and strongly opposed protection which took the form of prohibiting the employment of the person protected, "even when that person was a mother with young children."[32]

The most extreme and exclusive form of protection of women, passed into law in 1842, was the complete prohibition of their work underground in mines; the culmination of the benevolent agitation led by Lord Shaftesbury. It does not seem that the views of either the men or women workers had much influence in bringing this about; the motives were altruistic, on the part of a group of benevolent philanthropists and the public they aroused. It was strange that the benevolence which prohibited the employment of women underground, did not extend to relieve their sufferings on expulsion. The fear of unemployment—unemployment forced upon them in the name of their own welfare, and social progress—which had aroused the genial but determined opposition of the Lancashire factory women to *The Examiner's* proposals, was brought to realization ten years later among the mining women.

> "The greatest pressure occurred in East Scotland, where 2,400 had been employed, and where the isolation of the mining districts made it exceedingly difficult to get other employment. . . . Numbers of women . . . unable to procure a living any other way, continued to go down the pits by stealth, sometimes disguised as men. And since in Scotland, the law gave them no claim to parish relief, the plight of many, especially those who had parents or children dependent on them, was pitiable in the extreme."[33]

[31] *History of Trade Unionism*, p. 136.

[32] *Women in Trade Unions*, p. 21.

[33] Pinchbeck, *op. cit.*, p. 269.

It is perhaps one of the most pathetic episodes in industrial history, though not unique in kind, that after the labour of women was prohibited in mines, the higher wages which owners had to pay the men enforced the introduction of improvements which, if they had been brought in earlier, would have saved the women "frae toil an' pain ayont conceevin' ".

The benevolent objections to the industrial work of women tended to fall under three distinct heads: that the work in question was "not adapted to their constitution," by which it was usually inferred that it was by its nature beyond the physical strength of a female, or dangerous to them as potential mothers; that the conditions under which the work was carried on were specially detrimental to women (night work, long hours, etc.); or that it was unkind to women to permit them to work anywhere except in their own or someone else's home.

The last position, taken up by *The Examiner*, the Journeymen Tailors, the Short-Time Committee of the West Riding in 1842, and by others from time to time, was so obviously untenable as a policy for industry, the sex, and the nation as a whole, that it requires no serious discussion. It was but a last-ditch argument of those who wished to exclude women for ulterior motives; or a kite flown by masculine theorists unacquainted with the economic realities of the situation.

Those who opposed the employment of women on work requiring much physical strength, stood on firmer ground; but their advocacy of exclusion was less needed. The keener appreciation of economy which naturally accompanies division of labour and modern industrial method, would bring about the preferential, if not the exclusive, employment of men rather than women in heavy work requiring a high degree of strength or allied skill, quite apart from any consideration of special benefit to either sex. This might fail to occur if the unit of labour were divisible, and if the women's wage were disproportionately lower than the men's, so as to make it possible to employ a greater number of them to do the same amount of work at lower cost in wages. But that course had countervailing economic disadvantages; the overhead charges would be higher. It would seem, on the whole, that little pressure from the men, or expression of benevolence on either side, was required to ensure the monopoly by men of heavy manual labour in most industries, after industry had become centralized.

When the monopoloy of "heavy" work by men had become more or less a general rule, a certain amount of further ground was consolidated by the men, on the plea that they should not be employed *only* on arduous work; each worker should have an opportunity to take the rough with the smooth. Thus the evidence given before the War Cabinet Committee shows how the men objected, except for the special purposes of the war, to being given a complete monopoly of the heavier or more difficult work, unless they were also allowed to monopolize some of the easier.

> "The Amalgamated Society of Engineers were of opinion that (women's) employment tended to concentrate men on work which was either highly skilled, arduous or physically disagreeable. 'That is one of the reasons why men on highly-skilled work . . . are not complaining.' "
>
> "In the Boot and Shoe trade (during the war) . . . some 11,000 (women) were employed in the men's departments, clicking, pressing, lasting, finishing and stitching. Of these processes, however, 'clicking' was generally held by witnesses to be too dangerous for women, and other processes, except stitching, too heavy. The cutting of the linings, upon which the women were largely employed, was not unsuitable, but the women had not sufficient experience, and the employers preferred the men. Nor were the men prepared to give over, after the war, all the light jobs to women, and had further a sentimental objection to 'mixed' departments."[34]

In these later attempts at consolidating an existing exclusion, there was, of course, no expression of benevolence. For although those who benevolently sought to exclude women from particularly heavy work stood on firmer ground than those who sought to exclude them from industrial work altogether, their foothold was ever shrinking, amid the flood of progress and mechanization. Physical strength was less and less needed in industry; comparison of industrial with domestic work became less and less to the advantage of the latter, and it was difficult to suggest that women had been unfeelingly torn from the home. The invention of new machines became the Union man's nightmare, as we find graphically described in the Webbs' account of a typical Trade Unionist's life:—

> "The club is . . . a centre for obtaining the latest trade news. Here . . . are to be heard reports of reductions or advance of wages . . . or the first rumour of that bug-bear to the men: the invention of new machines, with its probable displacement of their labour; or even worse, the introduction of women and boys at reduced prices."[35]

The man's natural monopoly of greater strength had failed to give

[34] *Report of War Cabinet Committee*, p. 85, par. 93, and p. 92, par. 97.
[35] *History of Trade Unionism*, p. 445.

him its full advantage before the industrial revolution, because, for one thing, the more primitive division of labour prevented the advantage being fully appreciated, and for another, the man and woman cooperated, rather than competed, in many branches of industry. Industrial developments had discovered man's advantage, only again to deprive him of much of it by mechanical inventions which superseded human physical strength altogether, or took little account of the comparatively slight difference between the natural force of male and female.

At the same time as it became more and more difficult to secure the exclusion of women on the grounds of the strength, endurance, or length of training and skill required, in the majority of manufacturing processes, it also became more and more difficult to suggest the same policy on the ground of unhealthy conditions of work. In this connection, indeed, the men's Trade Unions had, by the end of the nineteenth century, already eaten a large slice of their cake: they had used the special sympathy felt by the Victorian philanthropists for women and children, to improve conditions of work for all. The welfare of the weaklings was the thin end of the wedge driven deep into the trunk of *laissez-faire*. The Trade Unions used it as such, while disregarding with instinctive common sense (as a general rule) the proprietary interest in industrial amenities which philanthropists seemed to claim for the female sex. Thus the special sympathy felt for women and children who had to work long hours, was made full use of by the Cotton Workers' Unions, when they were seeking support for the Eight Hours Bill, in 1872. They even demurred to working openly with the Parliamentary Committee of the Trades Union Congress for the Bill, because they were afraid that by so doing they would lose the support of those who were sympathetic to the women and children, but not to Trade Unions.

> "So far as the public and the House of Commons were concerned, the Bill was accordingly . . . 'based upon quite other grounds'. Its provisions were ostensibly restricted, like those of the Ten Hours' Act, to women and children; and to the support of Trade Union champions . . . was added that of such philanthropists as Lord Shaftesbury and Samuel Morley. But it is scarcely necessary to say that it was not entirely . . . for the sake of the women and children that the skilled leaders of the Lancashire cotton operatives had diverted their 'Short-Time Movement' from aggressive strikes to Parliamentary agitation. The private minutes of the Factory Acts Reform Association contain no mention of the woes of the women and the children, but reflect throughout the demand of the adult male spinners for a shorter day. And in the circular 'to the factory operatives' . . . we find the

spinners' Secretary combating the fallacy that 'any legislative interference with male adult labour is an economic error' and demanding 'a legislative enactment largely curtailing the hours of factory labour' in order that his constituents, who were exclusively adult males, might enjoy . . . 'nine hours per day . . .' It was, however, neither necessary nor expedient to take this line in public."[36]

The Bill in question provided one of the earliest instances (if not the earliest) of opposition from the leaders of the Suffrage movement, or those in sympathy with them, to industrial legislation differentiating between men and women. In this particular case the cloven hoof was particularly well hidden, because the legislation differentiated in the litter, without any differentiation being intended by its promoters in the eventual practice of the law. But Mr. Fawcett scented brimstone, and danger to women, in the limitation of legislation to one sex, even though the limitation was hypocritical.

The Short-Time battle was fought and won in the Cotton Industry, where women had been entrenched from the infancy of the trade, where they were comparatively well organized, and where, in at least one important branch, they received equal rates of pay. In many industries equal pay and the improvement of conditions for all workers together only became the men's Union policy after the hope of exclusion or segregation of women had been, if not successful, abandoned. The sympathy which was a source of benefit to the women when they shared its effects with men, seldom proved as welcome when directed exclusively towards themselves.

The exclusion of women from certain branches of work by the action of men's organizations has continued to be effective, to a considerable extent, and legislative prohibition of their employment in particular trades or processes has been recently extended, in accordance with the Washington (International Labour Organization) Convention of 1919. Such exclusion has undoubtedly had some effect in stabilizing men's wage-rates in monopolized trades or processes; but the practicability and success of the policy are limited. The constant changes of industrial processes, the introduction of new machines, and the increasing stringency of supervision and regulation of industry by the State in the interests of all workers, without distinction of sex, make it increasingly difficult for the Trade Unionist to put up a reasoned defence against the introduction, or even substitution of men by women, where the employer wishes to effect this change.

[36]*History of Trade Unionism*, pp.310–11.

From the earliest days of Trade Unionism it was recognized that an alternative policy existed, to prevent women undercutting men's employment, namely, to organize, and urge women to organize, to secure equal pay. We have seen that the London silk-weavers were among the first to attempt the exclusion of women from the better-paid classes of work, but when their attempts were not successful they secured from Parliament the famous Spitalfields Acts, by which magistrates were empowered to regulate their wages. The wage-regulations which followed were made without regard for sex.[37] Until the Acts were repealed half a century later, the London silk-weavers were comparatively prosperous, in spite of general depression of trade towards the close of the period. After the repeal of the Acts, a very great reduction of wages took place. In 1834 nearly 900 men, women and children of the district (Bethnal Green) were in the workhouse ("chiefly operatives in the silk business"), while over 6,000 persons (mostly weavers and their dependents) were receiving out-door relief.[38]

Among the Lancashire cotton weavers, equal pay between men and women has had a longer trial. In this trade the men for a long time refused to go into the factories, but competed with the manufacturers by working on hand-looms at home. By the time they were forced into centralized industry, the women's right to employment could not be denied, wages had been standardized at the women's level, and competition with the besieged domestic workers had forced the manufacturers to cut even these wages as low as possible. But strong organization of the two sexes combined, working on a basis of piece-work rates without distinction of sex, served to raise the cotton-weavers' wage-level until, by the early twentieth century it was, for women, on the average a high one, and probably a fair average for the men employed, as compared with that of men of corresponding skill in other industries.

For the last half-century, however, it is probably the Engineering trades which have been the most important in determining the official Trade Union attitude to women's labour. During the 'eighties, the men's Metal Unions of the Midlands made great efforts to prevent the employment of women altogether, which efforts met with determined opposition from the women's representatives at the Trade Union Con-

[37]See Pinchbeck, *op. cit.*, pp. 177–8, quoting Sholl, *Short History of the Silk Manufacture.* It would seem that until 1811 it was taken for granted that wages as regulated would be paid without distinction of sex, but that on a master refusing then to pay a journeywoman the regular wage, an Amending Act was passed, "enabling women to obtain their price under the same pains and penalties as the men."

[38]*Ibid.*, pp. 176–7 n.

gress. As a compromise, a resolution was passed in 1888, to the effect that "where women do the same work as men, they should receive equal pay." This remains the official policy of Trade Unionism, and similar resolutions were passed by a number of individual Unions, though constantly rejected by others to the present day.

In supporting the resolution a certain Juggins, secretary of the Nut and Bolt Makers, who had been the leader of the party which opposed "the iniquitous system of female labour," explained "that he had come to the conclusion that nothing but better pay for women could cure the evil, and they had therefore resolved to organize women as soon as possible."[39]

The resolution was somewhat ambiguous. Trade Unionism is based on the application of the standard rate and the common rule; its principles demand equal pay according to the job, the time worked, or by uniform piece-rates, irrespective of the capacity or bargaining power of the individual worker. Unless the same principles were intended to be applied to the work of women, the formula could have no useful meaning. But on whatever lines the phrase "the same work" was to be interpreted, it was obvious that any attempt to put it into practice would depend for success on the women being organized on the same lines, and in co-operation with men. The Trade Union organization of women, which compared with that of men was little more than embryonic, received a great impetus. The meteoric and successful strike of the previously unorganized girl Matchmakers, unexpectedly brought about by the journalism of Mrs. Annie Besant in the same year as the Trade Union Congress registered the resolution on equal pay, added to the impulse. The movement to bring women into the Trade Union world merged into the new wave of activity and the new Union outlook which was sweeping in great numbers of unskilled workers who had before been (intentionally) untouched by the gospel of organization.

> "The plumber vied with the engineer, the carpenter with the shipwright, in helping to form Unions among the labourers who work with or under them. And the struggling Unions of women workers, which had originally some difficulty in gaining admittance to Trades Councils and the Trade Union Congress, gratefully acknowledged a complete change in the attitude of their male fellow-workers. Not only was every assistance now given to the formation of special Unions among women workers, but women were, in some cases, even welcomed as members by Unions of skilled artisans."[40]

[39]*Women in Trade Unions*, p. 20.

[40]*History of Trade Unionism*, p. 421.

But sometimes the new enthusiasm did not reach as far as the women, and the old antagonism to their competition remained.

> "The whole constitution of the Amalgamated Society of Engineers was, in 1892, revised for the express purpose of opening the ranks of this most aristocratic of Unions to practically all the mechanics in the innumerable branches of the engineering trade."[41]

But the women remained unrecognized by the Society, and other Metal Unions took the same line as the A.S.E. A campaign to enlist women workers in separate craft Unions, or in a general women's Union (the National Federation of Women Workers) proved a difficult task.

The organization of women in Trade Unions is, in fact, very much more difficult than that of men. The lower average age of the workers; their attitude to their work (the view that it is not likely to be their permanent source of livelihood); the domestic duties they almost all accept as having prior claims to those of public life, and the greater diffidence in public affairs which convention has long imposed, and still to some extent occasions—all these conditions act as a special bar to the enlistment and the strength of women in Trade Unions. Until the establishment of Trade Boards, and still to a great extent afterwards, the extremely low pay received by many women was a further bar to organization, because it prevented the expenditure of the most meagre amount on contributions.

Substantial results have followed unremitting efforts of the last half-century to organized women workers. The Trade Union movement has been served in this field by some of its most able, sympathetic and forceful leaders—Miss Mary Macarthur, Mrs. Margaret MacDonald, Miss Margaret Bondfield, Miss Susan Lawrence, Miss Gertrude Tuckwell, and others who are following in their footsteps. The establishment of Trade Boards in the worst "sweated" industries has raised many women's wages sufficiently to permit them to contribute a few pence a week without the difficulties of earlier times. There was a great increase of enthusiasm and numbers of women Trade Unionists during the war period. Nevertheless, the proportion of women organized in Trade Unions remains low compared with the proportion of men.

Many of the important Unions, including the Metal Unions whose opposition to the labour of women led to the Congress resolution, remained exclusively men's organizations, and the attempts to organize women so as to secure equal pay when on "the same work," had to be

[40] *History of Trade Unionism,* p. 421.

[41] *Ibid.,* p. 420.

directed to the formation of separate Unions, or recruitment to a general Women's Union. The Union of Women Chain-makers at Cradley Heath was one of the separate Unions in the Metal Industry. But the wages of women chain-makers remained scandalously low despite their organization, until they were covered by the 1909 Trade Boards Act.

The wages of unskilled or semi-skilled workers in general have risen compared with those of skilled men, during the last half-century; and women, who are mostly semi-skilled workers in industry, have benefited in the general lift. But the Congress resolution on equal pay has been little more than a dead letter. If no other policy had been possible—if there had been no tradition or alternative of attempted exclusion—the men might have invited the women workers into joint Unions throughout industry, organized them in the manner of the large amalgamated Textile Unions, and secured equal pay with their co-operation. But where the demand for equal pay was to depend on the organization of the women, acting separately though in co-operation with the men, it had rarely a hope of success, for the organized strength of the women, proportionately to their numbers, was much less.

Even in those industries where the men and women are jointly organized, it frequently occurs that lip-service only is paid to the ideal of Equal Pay, and in practice little attempt is made to secure it. The Trade Union negotiator who represents his members is out for the best he can get for them. He is not prepared to sacrifice pounds to principles; he may *reculer pour mieux sauter*, but only when he can see where the last leap is likely to land him. The aggregate cash benefit of equal pay, to the workers, seems highly problematical; whereas the average employer, even if he employs men, recognizes a social obligation to pay a man more than a woman, of the same grade of life, or doing the same work. What, in terms of cash, is the workers' representative to demand: that the employer should pay all his employees the amount he is (perhaps reluctantly) willing to pay the men, or that he should scale the men down and the women up to an intermediate level—a level less than that on which the men have been saying they can fulfill their minimum (standard) obligations?

The National Union of Shop Assistants, Clerks and Warehousemen offers a case in point. Large numbers of men and women are organized in this Union. The difficulties, such as undercutting of wages, which would be obviated by the payment of equal rates for similar work, are recognized by the Union, which has adopted in its programme the policy of Equal Pay; but in practice the officers find they can but accept a minimum weekly wage, for Shop Assistants, which differentiates between adult men and women to the extent of about £1 a week. Reserves of unorganized labour, male and female, willing to accept lower rates respectively, make it sufficiently hard work for the Union to secure the standards set, and they see little hope of general advantage for their members in objecting to sex-differentiation.

It would be easy, but futile, to condemn such action as hypocritical; to point to the Equal Pay resolution on the Union's programme, and compare the demands actually put forward in negotiation. Before taking this line, however, let us consider the action of the Trade Boards when faced with this same problem of the relation between men's and women's rates. Each Board is a body consisting of representatives of employers, workers (who before the establishment of the Board have been only poorly, if at all, organized) and impartial members, appointed by the Minister of Labour. Though the members of the Board have little reason to take account of the Trade Union Congress resolution in favour of Equal Pay, they may be supposed to hold in respect the similar principle laid down in the International Labour Convention of Versailles, 1919.

> "One of the fundamental problems which issues from attempts at rate fixing," writes Miss Sells, in her book on *The British Trade Boards System*, "is the relation between the prescribed rates of wages for men and women. *No underlying principle is evident in the determinations of the Boards as a whole.* Although it cannot be said that in either case wages have always been prescribed which actually meet the money requirements of a living wage for a man with a family to support, or of a single woman living alone, it is these two ideas which Trade Boards, since 1918, seem to have had in mind as a foundation upon which to fix men's and women's wages, respectively. However, the compromise which is incident to collective bargaining in the Board Meetings, the economic conditions of a particular trade or other circumstances, may so alter the original wage scheme that some of the rates are thrown entirely out of plumb with these ideas. In several trades where men's and women's work is clearly differentiated, for instance, it appears that the men workers have compromised by allowing the women's rates to be set at a low figure in order to keep their own wages up.[42] Employers in a number of trades where women workers are predominant are willing to agree to such an arrangement, because it reduces their total wages bill.
>
> The principles of equal pay for the job and equal pay for equal work have been brought up again and again, but for the most part it has

[42]A woman Trade Union officer comments on this, that the women's representatives may have made similar suggestions to maintain the women's wage-levels at the expense of the men's.

seemed an impractical basis for wage adjustment for the reason that women seldom do exactly the same work as men. In the case of four trades, viz. Boot and Shoe Repairing, Brush and Broom-making, Furdressing, and Sugar Confectionery manufacture, the same time rates of wages have been prescribed for both men and women who are engaged upon certain jobs where the work is the same. In two of these trades the object in fixing the same rates for both men and women is generally believed to have been to protect the male workers, and thus far the operation of the rates in one trade, at least, appears to have led to a readjustment of the work in the trade as between men and women. The object of the Sugar Confectionery Board in prescribing the same rates of wages for women as for men who are engaged in . . . occupations . . . which are ordinarily known as men's occupations . . . was honestly to apply the principle of equal pay for the job.

The principle of equal pay for equal output is recognized by those Boards . . . which have fixed the same piece rates for women as for men. Relatively speaking, there are fewer men than women engaged upon a piece basis, and even piece tasks are usually different for the two sexes, so that it is not often feasible even to prescribe like piece prices for men and women.

Equal pay for equal value, which is the principle incorporated in the recommendations regarding International Labour Standards of the Treaty of Versailles, is sometimes stated by persons connected with Trade Boards to be the general principle upon which Trade Boards endeavour to work. If this general principle is to be applied in fixing time-rates, presuming that it means equal value in quality and quantity, it should be preceded by job analysis and tests for the purpose of discovering just what are the relative values of male and female workers on a given job. In no case known to the writer has such a scientific inquiry been undertaken by a Trade Board.[43]

When the application of any one of these principles has seemed inexpedient or has failed, it is customary for the workers' side to demand four-fifths . . . or five-sixths . . . of the male time-rate for female workers upon the basis of the cost of living for a woman living alone, but this has not often been granted.

An analysis of the relation between the male and female general minimum time-rates shows that female rates most nearly approximate to male rates in Boot and Shoe Repairing, e.g. 70 per cent. . . . the lowest of all being Coffin Furniture, at 49.1 percent. The average of these percentages is 57.6 per cent, and the average weekly wage of women is 29*s.* as opposed to 52*s.* for men. . . . If we compare these results with the average for all trades in 1914, given by the War Cabinet

[43]Nor are instances reported of men's wage-rates being fixed, or there being any suggestion that they should be fixed, lower than women's in industries where the woman's output is suspected to be higher.

Committee on Women in Industry as rather less than 50 per cent., some progress seems to have been made over pre-War days, though the percentage is not so high . . . as in 1918, when the women's wage stood at rather more than 66.3 per cent. of the men's."[44]

So one finds that the relation between men's and women's wages under Trade Board regulation is very similar to their relation under conditions of collective bargaining. Equal Pay for men and women is recognized, in a somewhat hazy, ambiguous way, as an ideal; there are exceptional instances of its practice; but the pressure of other economic interests in most cases prevents its realization.

It has already been noted that in the Cotton-weaving branch of the Lancashire textile industry, an important exception is found to the general rule; men and women are employed on similar work, and remunerated according to identical piece-work rates. It is significant that in this district, and especially in this industry, it is customary for women to remain at or return to work after marriage.

The more commonly accepted convention that women retire from work after marriage, to be maintained on their husband's wages, is among the most important factors preventing the application of the widely accepted ideal of equal pay, or its substitution as a practical policy alternative to restriction of admission or training of women for well-paid work. Those who desire equal pay have a very direct concern in the customs and laws of marriage. The possibility of some practical reconciliation between the conflicting ideals of Equal Pay and the Wife's Personal Care of her Home is considered in later chapters.

It is significant that in spite of considerable strain, the Trade Union movement maintains its solidarity, and does not irrevocably split along the line of sex. The women workers, as daughters often partially dependent, and prospectively dependent wives, sympathize with the men's demand for preferential employment and/or higher pay. The division of their sympathies is an important element in mitigating the shock of conflict. It increases the difficulty of securing representation of the point of view of the woman worker *qua* worker, and so tends to make women's wage-rates and opportunities dependent on the men's demand or permission, rather than on the women's organization.

The conventions of civil marriage are thus in yet another way an important factor within the Trade Union movement in standardizing low wages for women. Professor Sargent Florence, in a recent article in the *Economic Journal* (March 1931) has developed the view that they

[44]*The British Trade Boards System*, by D. Sells, pp. 153–5.

are the most important factor, and that the importance of Trade Union or other "artificial" limitations on the occupational field open to women has been over-estimated.

Briefly, his argument is as follows: the generally accepted theory that the low wages of women are due to the restricted occupational field open to them, offers an insufficient explanation. The restrictions imposed by men's Trade Unions on women's employment would soon be overridden by employers, at least to a much greater extent than they now are, if there were not other influences at work. For the cheapness of women's work (the lowness of their "efficiency wage") is in many instances real enough, and appreciated as such by employers. The main class of work in which both men and women are employed is, broadly speaking, semi-skilled work, for which the period of training is short, so that a comparatively quick labour-turnover, such as occurs especially with women workers, is not of very great importance. In the general wages system ruling in most industrial countries, semi-skilled women's wages are, in fact, below unskilled men's wages, and probably only 50–70 per cent. of the wages of similarly skilled men.

But the women's "supply-price curve" is peculiar. There are a considerable number of women readily available for industrial employment at this comparatively low wage, but the supply is definitely limited, and when the limit is reached, women are only obtainable at a price higher than any "likely to be thought reasonable in business circles." The women willing to accept low wages are (in general) the unmarried women; the latter are (in general) the married women. There is a wide gulf fixed between the price which each of these groups set upon their labour, and in consequence only the former group is actually called into the labour market under anything like normal conditions.

The conflict between the economic interests of the man and woman worker in industry certainly exists, and may be severe, but is limited in extent by the limited effective supply of female labour, and may therefore be much exaggerated by observers who note the comparative cheapness of the women's wages, and the restrictions imposed by men's Trade Unions.

> "It is usually assumed that the economic forces of supply and demand act antagonistically to the male Trade Unionist position; that the demand for women's labour, based on women's apparently superior efficiency in relation to wage, will inevitably undermine the attempt to restrict women's employment. Within limits this assumption is, I think, valid. A certain supply of women can be obtained cheap, and the men's Trade Union wage will be undercut—but only up to a point.

> And if this point were not soon reached I do not think Trade Union restrictions on the employment of women would avail. In fact, however, once a certain number of women is absorbed by industry, the remainder do not clamour to overcome Trade Union barriers.
>
> For the supply of women available for employment cheap in any one area is strictly limited by certain institutional factors. This . . . in the last resort is perhaps the most important factor in the situation."

With this explanation of the economic situation, in its general outline, I find myself in agreement. But I think any analysis of the problem which treats it as though the psychological element were essentially static, leads to an underestimate of the effect of Trade Union and other "artificial" restrictions on women's work. Professor Sargent Florence infers a comparison between the influence of such restrictions and the influence of "institutional factors" (such as the working-class convention of marriage-retirement for women) on the low wages of women, and concludes that the former are of less importance than the latter. But these forces do not act independently. Marriage, for natural, sentimental, and conventional reasons, raises the value of a woman's domestic work. Restrictions on women's industrial employment prevent them from fitting themselves for, or having any expectation of securing, the better-paid industrial jobs. Women cannot therefore expect to secure work at what would be, from *their* point of view, and that of their family, a reasonable wage, after marriage. This fact has considerable influence on the orientation of their life, and on their upbringing. They prepare their minds for a non-industrial adult life, take less interest in industrial employment while they are engaged in it, and are inclined to demand less from it, individually and collectively, than they would if they were presented with more opportunities for rising to well-paid work, and if retirement were consequently less taken for granted.

Thus the gulf which inevitably separates the supply price of the unmarried woman from that of the wife is artificially widened as a result of the restrictions placed upon the latter's opportunity to qualify for good wages, and these restrictions have a certain indirect effect on women's wage-rates over and above the very limited direct effect Professor Sargent Florence seems to attribute to them.

The conflict between the interests of men and women in industry, in its modern form, arose in consequence of the centralization and capitalization of industry which was part of the Industrial Revolution. The Trade Union movement, which until about 1870 was almost exclusively a male activity, arose as a result of the same developments. Since the earliest days of the movement the undercutting of men's wages and employment by women has been recognized as one of the chief menaces to the working-class standard of life. Attempts have been made to counteract it in various ways. Many of the Unions have, at one time or another, sought to prevent the employment of women in their particular industry altogether, and the suggestion has been made that they should be prohibited all industrial employment. Or the Unions have sought to exclude women from the better-paid branches of work; or they have sought to secure, through joint or co-operating organizations, equal wages for men and women so that the women should have no preference in employment. At the least, higher wages, if still unequal, have been sought for the women. In all these methods some successes can be registered. With the aid of other social forces, women have been entirely excluded from some branches of industry in which they were formerly occupied; in many industries or factories the better-paid work is not considered "women's work"; and instances exist of adult women's wages being fixed and maintained on an equal level with men's, and of the joint efforts of men and women securing a rise in the woman's wage-level.

The struggle has been a constant feature of the Trade Union movement. At no time has the menace ceased. The extent and severity of the conflict is at normal times limited, but it continues to exist as a drag on the workers' standard of life. Men's wages are maintained at the expense of the women's but the conventionally low wages of women are a danger to the men. They are an especial danger to the general standard of life in times of depression, when the lowness of a man's wages or unemployment pay may force domestic women into industry at equally low or lower wages, thus flooding the market with cheap labour over and above the normal supply, and further delaying wage-recovery.

The existence of this menace is not due to the Trade Unions. Although the effect of action taken by men's organizations for the past century and more has probably been, on the whole, to depress the price of women's work, the primary inequality of price between women's work and their own, which is the cause of the conflict, arises independently of their actions, through the survival of an older economic relationship between the sexes, into an era of industrial civilization.

XXII. Protective Labor Legislation

Joan Kennedy Taylor

Protective labor laws have a complex history within feminism. During the late 19th century, while mainstream feminists concentrated on the suffrage drive, many socialist feminists championed labor laws which "protected" women. Typically, these laws restricted the age at which girls could begin work, and the hours and conditions of labor. Some feminists considered protection labor laws to be so essential that they argued against the original ERA proposal on the grounds that it might render the laws obsolete. Individualist feminists were one of the few groups to oppose these laws as state interference with a woman's right to contract.

Contemporary feminism approaches protective labor laws in a contradictory manner. Although it is somewhat fashionable to criticize 19th-century laws as class legislation which restricted a woman's ability to compete in the labor market, thus benefiting men, 20th-century labor laws have become sacrosanct. Laws against sexual harassment and unequal pay are demanded, and the paternalistic state is requested to intervene in the marketplace once more to protect women.

The following article by Joan Kennedy Taylor was first issued as a discussion paper by the Association of Libertarian Feminists. Taylor is the publications director of the Manhattan Institute and a longtime officer of ALF—the only contemporary organization devoted to individualist feminism.

In the early nineteenth century, textile factories were established in New England, and for the first time American women (and children) had the opportunity to work outside their own homes and fields, and to work for pay, while leaving the men free to do the "real work" on the farm. Harsh as conditions in these early factories might seem to us today, the life they offered was immeasurably better for a woman than life on the farm, and factory work was quickly taken up. Robert W. Smuts tells us, in *Women and Work in America,* that "a factory had only to open its doors in any part of the rural United States to find itself besieged by girls and young women from miles around, all eager for work. . . . The average farm girl was accustomed to long hours of hard manual labor." Once factory work was available, it became customary in the U.S. for most children to go to work at twelve or fourteen, according to Smuts. By 1890, one million young women were factory workers.

During this period, cities were growing, and the United States was becoming transformed from an agricultural nation into an industrial one. And as industrialization advanced, factory work was no longer the province of women and children. More and more men entered the factories, too. The work became divided into men's work and women's work, although many "women's jobs" took physical strength. "Thus," Smuts tells us, " 'opening' tin plate sheets was women's or boy's but never men's work in the Pittsburgh area. The opener had to catch fifty-pound stacks of six to eight sheets, firmly stuck together as they emerged hot from the rollers, bang them on the floor to loosen the sheets, and then forcibly tear the sheets apart with gloved hands while kneeling on the stack to hold it down."

As men became a larger and larger part of the industrial force, reformers began to question the effect that factory work had on women's health. *Sex in Industry,* by Azel Ames, a report for the Massachusetts Bureau of Labor Statistics published in 1875, was devoted to the premise that industrial work for women upset the menstrual cycle and therefore damaged the health, sanity, and fertility of women.

Four years later, in 1879, the first enforceable law regulating women's working hours was passed in Massachusetts.

Two Supreme Court cases, one in 1905 and one in 1908, established the legal framework for protective legislation for women. In 1905, the Court held that it was unconstitutional for New York State to put a ten-hour limit on the working hours of bakery employees of both sexes, because it interfered with freedom of contract. But three years later, in the case of *Muller v. Oregon,* it upheld as constitutional Oregon's maximum-hours law for women. This decision established the right of states to set up protective legislation for women only, even though such legislation would be unconstitutional if applied to other groups. The Court held that "Woman is properly placed in a class by herself and legislation designed for her protection may be sustained when like legislation is not necessary for men and could not be sustained." And it went on to say, "Woman's physical structure and the performance of the maternal functions place her at a disadvantage . . . woman becomes an object of public interest and care in order to preserve the strength and vigor of the race."

In other words, the government has a right to interfere with women's lives because it is public policy to ensure the future of the race. This argument led to a large network of state laws regulating the working conditions of women, and is still used today to justify these laws.

Not all women believed that their best interests were represented by this argument. Many women saw nothing wrong with prevailing working conditions, for themselves or for their children. A memorandum by Anne Corinne Hill, submitted to the Senate Judiciary Committee in support of the ERA, points out that "reformers who pushed for government supervision of child labor came to include women in the legislation, because it was thought that control of women's working hours was essential to successful control of children's hours in the same factories. Without such a safeguard, young girls tended to lie about their age in order to work as long as their older sisters and mothers."

Perhaps one reason for the rise of protective legislation was that during the period when those laws were being passed, around the turn of the century, neither women nor children could vote on it. By 1890, men dominated factory employment. But a not-so-odd coincidence we find, according to Smuts, that as late as 1959, "Even though women are somewhat more widely distributed throughout manufacturing industry than they were in 1890, women's place in the factory has changed remarkably little. . . . Few have highly skilled or supervisory jobs."

Libertarians would suspect that this result, undoubtedly satisfactory to male workers and those who represent them, has been achieved, at least in part, by passing the legislation that limits the hours, rest periods, minimum wages, occupations, and weight-lifting of women. By the late 1960s many feminists were suspecting this, too. Unfortunately, instead of simply moving to strike down these laws, many of them chose to put their reliance in administrative law and legally-enforced "affirmative action," and began to bring successful cases against discriminatory protective laws under Title VII of the Civil Rights Act of 1964. Many proponents of such cases wished to pick and choose which "protections" they would consider discriminatory, and some spoke of extending certain protective legislation to men rather than ending it for women.

Other feminists put their major effort behind the Equal Rights Amendment. Washington attorney Marguerite Rawalt was one who felt that only the ERA would deal adequately with protective legislation, by simply invalidating it all. In her testimony for the ERA she said, "The counter-proposal advanced today that protective legislation be made equally applicable to men ignores the Court's opinion that like legislation for men 'could not be sustained.' You bet it could not—men workers would not tolerate any restrictions on their hours of work with premium pay and promotions, as witness union contracts. And if weight-lifting limitations became applicable to men workers, as they have been to females, *who would do the work?*" (Emphasis hers.)

Law professor Leo Kanowitz, an ERA supporter, agreed with Ms. Rawalt that extending protective legislation wouldn't be practical, because most men and many women want to work overtime. He deplored this, and suggested during the ERA hearings that it is due to "labor's failure to educate its membership." (Kanowitz had earlier opposed the ERA, contending that litigation on Fourteenth Amendment—equal protection—grounds would accomplish the same purposes.)

Not all feminists are supporters of the ERA. Those who are, without exception see that protective legislation for women actually diminishes the employment opportunities of women, and call such laws "not protective but restrictive." This fact is good news for libertarians, since it at least opens the door for a consideration of a free-enterprise approach to working conditions in general. This may already be happening. Ruth Miller, of the Amalgamated Clothing Workers of America, testified to the Senate Judiciary Committee in dismay, about an attempt to modify the California law forbidding women (but not men) to work more than eight hours in any one day:

"I cannot refrain from telling you that in the effort to achieve the ten-hour day in California, proponents of the equal rights amendment joined hands with employers in support of the extension of hours . . . They gave their support despite the fact that employers made it quite clear that the question of equality was not their concern but rather the elimination of regulations."

If libertarians can approach feminists by agreeing with their suspicion of protective legislation, perhaps we can gain a widespread recognition of the fact that "the question of equality" *is* the elimination of regulations.

Suggested Readings

Kraditor, Aileen S. *The Radical Persuasion, 1890–1917*. Baton Rouge: Louisiana University Press, 1981, pp. 154–204.

Rand, Ayn. *Capitalism: The Unknown Ideal*. New York: New American Library, 1966.

Sachs, Albie. "The Myth of Male Protectiveness and the Legal Subordination of Women: An Historical Analysis" in *Women, Sexuality and Social Control*. Edited by Carol Smart and Barry Smart. Boston: Routledge & Kegan Paul, 1978.

Schreiner, Olive. *Woman and Labor*. New York: F.A. Stokes, 1911.

WOMEN AND LICENSING

XXIII. State Aid to Science

Gertrude Kelly

As a medical doctor in the late 1800s, Gertrude Kelly saw her profession become gradually locked into the state through licensing laws, state aid, and regulation of medical schools. As an individualist anarchist contributing to Benjamin Tucker's Liberty *(1881–1908), she expressed her opposition to this trend by arguing that the state smothers the very essence of science—the love of knowledge and innovation. Kelly was equally aware of the role state involvement played in restricting the options of the worker, particularly of the immigrant. Perhaps her own experiences as an Irish immigrant had made her sensitive to the prejudice and suspicion with which aliens were viewed by many native Americans. Her articles in* Liberty *are united by the common themes of opposition to the state, concern for the laborer, and a demand for women's rights. The following essay, originally read before the Alumnae Association of the Woman's Medical College of the New York Infirmary, June 1, 1887, is indicative of the high quality of content and the clarity of style Gertrude Kelly achieved in her work.*

If what I say to you today should seem to you out of place, you must blame the chairman of your executive committee and not me; for, when she asked me to contribute something for this meeting, she assured me that anything which affected the relation of medical women to society, anything which related to the advancement of science, was a proper subject of discussion at the annual meeting of the Alumnae Association.

Herbert Spencer closes the second volume of his "Principles of Sociology" with these words:

> The acceptance which guides conduct will always be of such theories, no matter how logically indefensible, as are consistent with the average modes of action, public and private. All that can be done, by diffusing a doctrine much in advance of the time, is to facilitate the action of forces tending to cause advance. The forces themselves can be but in small degrees increased, but something may be done by preventing misdirection of them. Of the sentiment at any time enlisted on behalf of a higher social state there is always some (and at the present time a great deal) which, having the broad, vague form of sympathy with the masses, spends itself in efforts for their relief by multiplication of political agencies of one or other kind. Led by the hope of immediate beneficial results, those swayed by this sympathy

> are unconscious that they are helping further to elaborate a social organization at variance with that required for a higher form of social life, and are by so doing increasing the obstacles to attainment of that higher form. On a portion of such the foregoing chapters may have some effect by leading them to consider whether the arrangements they are advocating involve increase of that public regulation characterizing the militant type, or whether they tend to produce that greater individuality and more extended voluntary cooperation characterizing the industrial type. To deter here and there one from doing mischief by imprudent zeal is the chief proximate effect to be hoped for.

In these times of ours, when all classes in society, from the Bowery Socialists to the highest professors of science, seem to vie with one another in demanding State interference, State protection, and State regulation, when the ideal State to the workingman is that proposed by the authoritarian Marx, or the scarcely less authoritarian George, and the ideal State to the scientist is the Germany of today, where the scientists are under the government's special protection, it would seem idle to hope that the voices of those who prize liberty above all things, who would fain call attention to the false direction in which it is desired to make the world move, should be other than "voices crying in the wilderness." But, nevertheless, it is not by accident that we who hold the ideas that what is necessary to progress is not the increase, but the decrease, of governmental interference have come to be possessed of these ideas. We, too, are "heirs of all the ages," and it is our duty to that society of which we form a part to give our reasons for the "faith that is in us."

My endeavor today will be to prove to you two propositions: first, that progress in medical or any other science is lessened, and ultimately destroyed, by State interference; and, secondly, that even if, through State aid, progress in science could be promoted, the promotion would be at too great an expense, at the expense of the best interests of the race. That I shall succeed in convincing you of the truth of these propositions is too much to hope for, but at least I shall cause you to reëxamine the grounds for the contrary opinions that you entertain, and for this you should thank me, as it is always important that the position of devil's advocate should be well filled.

It seems strange that it should become necessary to urge upon Americans, with their country's traditions, that the first condition necessary to mental and moral growth is freedom. It seems strange in these times,—when all the unconscious movements of society are towards the diminution of restraint, whether it be that of men over women, of parents and teachers over children, of keepers over criminals and the insane; when it is being unconsciously felt and acted upon, on all sides, that responsibility is the parent of morality,—that all the conscious efforts of individuals and groups should be towards the increase of restraint.

A knowledge of the fact that all the ideas prevalent at a given time in a given society must have a certain congruity should make us very careful in accepting ideas, especially as regards politics, from such a despotic country as Germany, instead of receiving them with open arms as containing all the wisdom in the world, which now seems to be the fashion. As Spencer pointed out some time since, the reformers of Germany, while seeking a destruction of the old order, are really but rebuilding the old machine under a new name. They are so accustomed to seeing every thing done by the State that they can form no conception of its being done in any other way. All they propose is a State in which the people (that is, a *majority* of the people) shall hold the places now held by the usurping few. That English-speaking workmen should seek to wholly replace themselves under the yoke of a tyranny from which they have taken ages to partially escape, is only to be explained by the vagueness of the forms in which this paradise is usually pictured, and by that lack of power of bringing before the mind's eye word-painted pictures.

Again, in Germany—and it is that with which we are more nearly concerned today—it is said that scientific men under the protection of the government do better work than other men who are not under the protection of their governments. That this apparently flourishing condition of science under the patronage of the German government is no more real than was the condition of literature under Louis XIV., and that it cannot continue, I think a little examination will enable us to see. As Leslie Stephen has demonstrated, to suppress one truth is to suppress all truth, for truth is a coherent whole. You may by force suppress a falsehood, and prevent its ever again rising to the surface; but, when you attempt to suppress a truth, you can only do so by suppressing all truth, for, with investigation untrammelled, some one else is bound in time to come to the same point again. Do you think that a country, one of whose most distinguished professors, Virchow, is afraid of giving voice to the doctrine of evolution, because he sees that it inevitably leads to Socialism (and Socialism the government has decided is wrong, and must be crushed out), is in the way of long maintaining its supremacy as a scientific light, when the question which its scientific men are called upon to decide is not what is true, but what the government will allow to be said? I say nothing for or against the doctrine of evolution; I say nothing for or against its leading to Socialism; but I do say that the society whose scientific men owe devotion, not to truth, but to the Hohenzollerns, is not in a progressive state. As Buckle has shown, the patronage of Louis XIV. killed French literature. Not a single man rose to European fame under his patronage, and those whose fame was the cause of their obtaining the monarch's favor sank under its baneful influence to mere mediocrity.

It seems to be generally forgotten by those who favor State aid to science that aid so given is not and cannot be aid to science, but to particular doctrines or dogmas, and that, where this aid is given, it requires almost a revolution to introduce a new idea. With the ordinary conservatism of mankind, every new idea which comes forward meets with sufficient questioning as to its truth, utility, etc.; but, when we have added to this natural conservatism, which is sufficient to protect society against the introduction of new error, the whole force of an army of paid officials whose interest it is to resist any idea which would deprive, or tend to deprive, them of their salaries, you will readily see that, of the two forces which tend to keep society in equilibrium, the conservative and the progressive, the conservative will be very much strengthened at the expense of the progressive, and that the society is doomed to decay. Of the tendency which State-aided institutions have shown up to the present to resist progress, excellent evidence is furnished by one, at least, of those very men, Huxley, who now clamors so loudly for State aid to science. When we consider that we have now reached but the very outposts of science; that all our energies are required for storming its citadel; that human nature, if placed in the same conditions, is apt to be very much the same; that those persons who have the power and the positions will endeavor to maintain them,—do you think it wise to put into the hands of any set of men the power of staying our onward movements? That which we feel pretty sure of being true today may contain, and in all probability does contain, a great deal of error, and it is our duty to truth to cultivate the spirit which questions all things, which spirit would be destroyed by our having high-priests of science. Hear Huxley in testimony thereof in his article on the "Scientific Aspects of Positivism":

> All the great steps in the advancement of science have been made just by those men who have not hesitated to doubt the "principles established in the science by competent persons," and the great teaching of science, the great use of it as an instrument of mental discipline,

> is its constant inculcation of the maxim that the sole ground on which any statement has a right to be believed is the impossibility of refuting it.

Is the State, then, to reward all those who oppose a statement as well as all those who support it, or is it only to reward certain of the questioners, and, if so, which, and who is to decidee what statements have not been refuted? Are some persons to be aided in bringing their opinions, with their reasons for holding them, before the world, and others to be denied this priviliege? Are the scientific men to be placed in power so different in nature from all those who have preceded them that they will be willing to cede the places and the salaries to those who show more reason than they? Here is Huxley's testimony in regard to the manner in which the State-aided classical schools promoted the introduction of physical science into those schools:

> From the time that the first suggestion to introduce physical science was timidly whispered until now, the advocates of scientific education have met with opposition of two kinds. On the one hand they have been pooh-poohed by the men of business, who pride themselves on being the representatives of practicality; while on the other hand they have been excommunicated by the classical scholars, in their capacity of Levites in charge of the arts of culture and monopolists of liberal education.—*Science and Culture.*

And again, the State, or the State-aided institutions have never been able, even with the most Chinese system of civil-service examinations, to sift the worthy from the unworthy with half the efficiency which private individuals or corporations have done. But let us hear Huxley upon this subject:

> Great schemes for the endowment of research have been proposed. It has been suggested that laboratories for all branches of physical science, provided with every apparatus needed by the investigator, shall be established by the State; and shall be accessible under due conditions and regulations to all properly qualified persons. I see no objection to the principle of such a proposal. If it be legitimate to spend great sums of money upon public collections of painting and sculpture, in aid of the man of letters, or the artist, or for the mere sake of affording pleasure to the general public, I apprehend that it cannot be illegitimate to do as much for the promotion of scientific investigation. To take the lowest ground as a mere investment of money the latter is likely to be much more immediately profitable. To my mind the difficulty in the way of such a scheme is not theoretical, but practical. Given the laboratories, how are the investigators to be

> maintained? What career is open to those who have been encouraged to leave bread-winning pursuits? If they are to be provided for by endowment, we come back to the College Fellowship System, the results of which for literature have not been so brilliant that one would wish to see it extended to science, unless some much better securities than at present exist can be taken that it will foster real work. You know that among the bees it depends upon the kind of a cell in which the egg is deposited, and the quantity and quality of food which is supplied to the grub, whether it shall turn out a busy little worker or a big idle queen. And in the human hive the cells of the endowed larvae are always tending to enlarge, and their food to improve, until we get queens beautiful to behold, but which gather no honey and build no court.—*Universities, Actual and Ideal.*

One of my chief objections to State-aid to anything is that it tends to develop a great many big idle queens at the expense of the workers. There is no longer any direct responsibility on the part of those employed to those who employ them, as there is where private contract enters into play. In fact, the agents determine how and for what the principals shall spend their money, and they usually decide in favor of their own pockets. I cannot furnish you with a better illustration than that supplied by my own experience. Before I studied medicine I taught school for a couple of years in an almshouse. The waste there was perfectly enormous. The officials, when remonstrated with, made answer: "It was all on the county." The freeholders came once a week, and ate sumptuous dinners—at the expense of the county. At the close of my college course it was my good fortune to enter the Infirmary, where I saw everything ordered with the economy of a private household. No waste there! Those who furnished the funds were directly interested in seeing that they were used as economically as possible. I never heard of the trustees of the Infirmary proposing to have a dinner at the expense of the Infirmary.

Even were the government perfectly honest, which it is practically impossible for it ever to be (being divorced from all the conditions which promote honesty), not bearing the cost, it is always inclined to make experiments on too large a scale, even when those experiments are in the right direction. When we bear the expenses ourselves, we are apt to make our experiments slowly and cautiously, to invest very little until we see some hope of return (by return I do not mean necessarily a material return), but when we can draw upon an inexhaustible treasury—farewell to prudence!

Of course, I do not mean to deny that under any state of society, until men and women are perfect, there always will be persons who are inclined to become big idle queens, but what I do object to is that we ourselves should voluntarily make the conditions which favor the development of these queens "who gather no honey and build no court."

Of the tendency of governments to crystallize and fossilize any institutions or ideas upon which they lay their protecting hands no better example can be furnished than that of the effect of the English government on the village communities of India, as reported by Maine ("Village Communities"). Where the institutions were undergoing a natural decay, the English government stepped in and, by its official recognition of them in some quarters, gave them, says Maine, a fixedness which they never before possessed.

There is another point to which I wish to draw the attention of those of our brethren who clamor for State aid. Who is to decide what ideas are to be aided? The majority of the people? or a select few? The majority of the people have never in any age been the party of progress; and, if it were put to a popular vote tomorrow as to which should be aided,—Anna Kingsford in her anti-vivisection crusade, or Mary Putnam Jacobi in her physiological investigation,—I am perfectly sure that the populace would decide in favor of Anna Kingsford. Carlyle says:

> If, of ten men, nine are fools, which is a common calculation, how in the name of wonder will you ever get a ballot-box to grind you out a wisdom from the votes of these ten men? . . . . I tell you a million blockheads looking authoritatively into one man of what you call genius, or noble sense, will make nothing but nonsense out of him and his qualities, and his virtues and defects, if they look till the end of time.

If, of ten men, nine are believers in the old, I say, how can you in the name of wonder get a ballot-box to grind you out support of the new from the votes of these ten men? They will support the old and established, and the outcome of your aid to science is that you or I, who may be in favor of the new, and willing to contribute our mite towards its propagation, are forced by majority rule to give up that mite to support that which already has only too many supporters. But perhaps you will say that not the populace, but the select few, are to decide what scientific investigations are to be rewarded. Which select few, and how are *they* to be selected? Of all the minorities which separate themselves from the current of public opinion, who is to decide which minority has the truth? And, allowing that it is possible to determine which minority has the truth on a special occasion, have you any means by which to prove that this minority will be in favor of the next new truth? Is there not danger that, having accomplished its ends, it in turn will become conservative, and wish to prevent further advance? A priesthood of science would differ in no manner from any other priesthood the world has yet seen, and the evil effect which such a priesthood would have upon science no one has more clearly seen or more clearly demonstrated than Huxley in his "Scientific Aspects of Positivism." Again, admitting that great men endowed with supreme power could remain impartial, we still have no evidence on record to prove that great men are endowed with more than the ordinary share of common sense, which is so necessary in conducting the ordinary affairs of life. Indeed, if the gossip of history is to be in any way trusted, great men have usually obtained less than the ordinary share of this commodity. Frederick the Great is reported to have said that, if he wished to ruin one of his provinces, he would hand its government over to the philosophers. Is it into the hands of a Bacon, who had no more sense than to expose himself (for the sake of a little experiment which could have been made just as well without the exposure), a Newton, who ordered the grate to be removed when the fire became too hot for him, a Clifford, who worked himself to death, that the direction of the affairs of a people is to be given, with the assurance that they will be carried on better than now?

Without multiplying evidence further, I think I have given sufficient to prove to you that there is no means by which State aid can be given to science, without causing the death of science, that we can make no patent machine for selecting the worthiest and the wisest; and I now desire to show you that, even if it were possible to select the worthiest and the wisest, and to aid none but the deserving, still aid so given would be immoral, and opposed to the best interests of society at large.

Of course I take it for granted that I am appealing to a civilized people, who recognize that there are certain rights which we are bound to respect, and certain duties which we in society owe to one another. We have passed that stage, or, at least, we do not often wish to acknowledge to ourselves that we have not passed it, in which "he may take who has the power, and he may keep who can." Next to the right to life (and indeed as part of that same right) the most sacred right is the right to property, the right of each to hold inviolable all that he earns. Now, to tax a man to support something that he does not wish for is to invade his right to property, and to that extent to curtail his life, is to take away from him his power of obtaining what he desires, in order to supply him with something which he does not desire. If we once admit that the State, the majority, the minority (be it ever so wise), has a right to do this in the smallest degree, no limit can be set to its interference, and we may have every action, aye, every thought, of a man's arranged for him from on high. Where shall we draw the line as to how much the State is to spend for him, and how much he is to spend for himself? Are grown men to be again put into swaddling clothes? You may say that you desire to increase his happiness, his knowledge, etc., but I maintain that you have no right to decide what is happiness or knowledge for him, any more than you have to decide what religion he must give adherence to. You have no right to take away a single cent's worth of his property without his consent. Woe to the nation that would strive to increase knowledge or happiness at the expense of justice. It will end by not having morality, or happiness, or knowledge. Do you think that the citizens of a State, who constantly see their rights violated by that State, who constantly see their property confiscated without their ever being consulted, are very likely to entertain a very high respect for their neighbors' rights of property or of person, do you think that they are very likely to be very moral in any way, any more than children, whose rights are constantly invaded by their parents, are likely to show an appreciation of one another's rights? To suppose that public life may be conducted in one way, and private life in another, is to ignore all the teaching of history, which shows that these lives are always interlaced.

The first step in immorality taken, the State having confiscated the property of its citizens, preventing them from expending it in the way they desire, to spend it for them in a way they do not desire, ends by starving their bodies and cramping their minds. Witness the case of modern Germany. Again the testimony is not mine. I always wish the advocates of Statism to furnish the evidence that kills them. Some little time since,—probably our new alumnae will remember the circumstance,—one of our professors who never wearies of telling us of the glories of German science, while speaking of the sebaceous horns which appear on the faces of German peasants, and describing a case which once came to his clinic, incidentally remarked of this case: "You understand he had never seen the growth himself, as these peasants have no looking-glasses." The thought at once occurred to me: "Is this what Germany gives to its people, to the vast majority of its population, on whom it lays its enormous burden of taxation?" Is not the advance of science of great importance to the German peasant who never sees a looking-glass? Would it be any wonder that in wild rage he should sometimes seek to destroy this whole German science and culture which end only by crushing him still farther into the earth? Of what use is science unless it increase the happiness and the comfort of the people? Is it a new fetich upon whose altar millions must be sacrificed? No, the science which would seek to entrench itself upon class-domination is a false one, and inevitably doomed to perish. Have we, the outcome of English civilization, determined to lower the standard raised by Bacon, that the object of the "new philosophy is to increase human happiness and diminish human suffering"? Are we willing to assist in dividing the people of this country into two classes, one of which is to have all the luxuries which science and art can afford, and the other to have no looking-glasses? *Now* is the time for us to decide.

How then is science to be advanced, you may inquire, if the majority cannot decide that which is true, and the select few also cannot decide? In the way in which up to the present it has been advanced,—by individuals contributing their small shares; and with ever increasing force will it advance, as the general culture becomes greater and broader. It will advance by having no opinion protected from discussion and agitation, by having the greatest possible freedom of thought, of speech, and of the press. That the unaided efforts of a people are capable of causing advance belongs fortunately no longer to the domain of opinion, but of fact. They have already caused all the progress that has been made, not only without the aid of the State, but in opposition to the State and the Church, and all the other conservative and retrogressive forces in society. They have already, as Spencer says, evolved a language greater in complexity and beauty than could be conceived of in any other way. They have, as Whately says, succeeded in supplying large cities with food with scarcely any apparent waste or friction, while no government in the world, with all the machinery at its command, has ever yet succeeded in properly supplying an army.

Yes, freedom, hampered as it has been, has done and is doing all these things, and all that it is capable of doing in the future none but the prophets may see.

We have the morning star,
O foolish people! O kings!
With us the day-springs are,
Even all the fresh day-springs.
For us, and with us, all the multitudes of things.

XXIV. Women and the Rise of the American Medical Profession

Barbara Ehrenreich and Deirdre English

Although not individualist feminists, Barbara Ehrenreich and Deirdre English have produced three studies of the relationship between women and "men of science"—the experts who have had such dramatic impact on the daily lives of women—which add insight into the individualist-feminist tradition. Witches, Midwives and Nurses: A History of Women Healers *(1973),* Complaints and Disorders: The Sexual Politics of Sickness *(1973), and* For Her Own Good: 150 Years of the Experts' Advice to Women *(1978) have become classic source material for those who question the treatment of women by doctors, psychologists, and other social scientists.*

The following essay, extracted from Witches, Midwives and Nurses, *examines the rise of the American Medical Association as a legal monopoly designed to drive out the healthy competition of lay doctors, many of whom were women. The essay investigates how "one particular set of healers, who happened to be male, white and middle class, managed to oust all the competing folk healers, midwives and other practitioners who had dominated the American medical scene in the early 1800s." It demonstrates how state licensing is a discriminatory tool.*

In the US the male takeover of healing roles started later than in England or France, but ultimately went much further. There is probably no industrialized country with a lower percentage of women doctors than the US today: England has 24 percent; Russia has 75 percent; the US has only seven percent. And while midwifery—*female* midwifery—is still a thriving occupation in Scandinavia, the United Kingdom, the Netherlands, etc., it has been virtually outlawed here since the early twentieth century. By the turn of the century, medicine here was closed to all but a tiny minority of necessarily tough and well-heeled women. What was left was nursing, and this was in no way a substitute for the autonomous roles women had enjoyed as midwives and general healers.

The question is not so much how women got "left out" of medicine and left with nursing, but how did these categories arise at all? To put it another way: How did one particular set of healers, who happened to be male, white and middle class, manage to oust all the competing folk healers, midwives and other practitioners who had dominated the American medical scene in the early 1800's?

The conventional answer given by medical historians is, of course, that there always was one *true* American medical profession—a small band of men whose scientific and moral authority flowed in an unbroken stream from Hippocrates, Galen and the great European medical scholars. In frontier America these doctors had to combat, not only the routine problems of sickness and death, but the abuses of a host of lay practitioners—usually depicted as women, ex-slaves, Indians and drunken patent medicine salesmen. Fortunately for the medical profession, in the late 19th century the American public suddenly developed a healthy respect for the doctors' scientific knowledge, outgrew its earlier faith in quacks, and granted the true medical profession a lasting monopoly of the healing arts.

But the real answer is not in this made-up drama of science versus ignorance and superstition. It's part of the 19th century's long story of class and sex struggles for power in all areas of life. When women had a place in medicine, it was in a *people's* medicine. When that people's medicine was destroyed, there was no place for women—except in the subservient role of nurses. The set of healers who became *the* medical profession was distinguished not so much by its associations with modern science as by its associations with the emerging American business establishment. With all due respect to Pasteur, Koch and the other great European medical researchers of the 19th century, it was the Carnegies and Rockefellers who intervened to secure the final victory of the American medical profession.

The U.S. in 1800 could hardly have been a more unpromising environment for the development of a medical profession, or any profession, for that matter. Few formally trained physicians had emigrated here from Europe. There were very few schools of medicine in America and very few institutions of higher learniing altogether. The general public, fresh from a war of national liberation, was hostile to professionalism and "foreign" elitisms of any type.

In Western Europe, university-trained physicians already had a centuries' old monopoly over the right to heal. But in America, medical practice was traditionally open to anyone who could demonstrate healing skills—regardless of formal training, race or sex. Ann Hutchinson, the dissenting religious leader of the 1600's, was a practitioner of "general physik," as were many other ministers and their wives. The medical historian Joseph Kett reports that "one of the most respected medical men in late 18th century Windsor, Connecticut, for example, was a freed Negro called 'Dr. Primus.' In New Jersey, medical practice, except in extraordinary cases, was mainly in the hands of women as late as 1818. . ."

Women frequently went into joint practice with their husbands: The husband handling the surgery, the wife the midwifery and gynecology, and everything else shared. Or a woman might go into practice after developing skills through caring for family members or through an apprenticeship with a relative or other established healer. For example, Harriet Hunt, one of America's first trained female doctors, became interested in medicine during her sister's illness, worked for a while with a husband-wife "doctor" team, then simply hung out her own shingle. (Only later did she undertake formal training.)

Enter the Doctor

In the early 1800's there was also a growing number of formally trained doctors who took great pains to distinguish themselves from the host of lay practitioners. The most important real distinction was that the formally trained, or "regular" doctors as they called themselves, were male, usually middle class, and almost always more expensive than the lay competition. The "regulars' " practices were largely confined to middle and upper class people who could afford the prestige of being treated by a "gentleman" of their own class. By 1800, fashion even dictated that upper and middle class women employ male "regular" doctors for obstetrical care—a custom which plainer people regarded as grossly indecent.

In terms of medical skills and theory, the so-called "regulars" had nothing to recommend them over the lay practitioners. Their "formal training" meant little even by European standards of the time: Medical programs varied in length from a few months to two years; many medical schools had no clinical facilities; high school diplomas were not required for admission to medical schools. Not that serious academic training would have helped much anyway—there was no body of medical science to be trained in. Instead, the "regulars" were taught to treat most ills by "heroic" measures: massive bleeding, huge doses of laxatives, calomel (a laxative containing mercury) and, later, opium. (The European medical profession had little better to offer at this time either.) There is no doubt that these "cures" were often either fatal or more injurious than the original disease. In the judgement of Oliver Wendell Holmes, Sr., himself a distinguished physician, if all the medicines used by the "regular" doctors in the US were thrown into the ocean, it would be so much the better for mankind and so much the worse for the fishes.

The lay practitioners were undoubtedly safer and more effective than the "regulars." They preferred mild herbal medications, dietary changes and hand-holding to heroic interventions. Maybe they didn't know any more than the "regulars," but at least they were less likely to do the patient harm. Left alone, they might well have displaced the "regular" doctors with even middle class consumers in time. But they didn't know the right people. The "regulars," with their close ties to the upper class, had legislative clout. By 1830, 13 states had passed medical licensing laws outlawing "irregular" practice and establishing the "regulars" as the only legal healers.

It was a premature move. There was no popular support for the idea of medical professionalism, much less for the particular set of healers who claimed it. And there was no way to enforce the new laws: The trusted healers of the common people could not be just legislated out of practice. Worse still—for the "regulars"—this early grab for medical monopoly inspired mass indignation in the form of a radical, popular health movement which came close to smashing medical elitism in America once and for all.

The Popular Health Movement

The Popular Health Movement of the 1830's and 40's is usually dismissed in conventional medical histories as the high-tide of quackery and medical cultism. In reality it was the medical front of a general social upheaval stirred up by feminist and working class movements. Women were the backbone of the Popular Health Movement. "Ladies Physiological Societies," the equivalent of our know-your-body courses, sprang up everywhere, bring rapt audiences simple instruction in anatomy and personal hygiene. The emphasis was on preventive care, as opposed to the murderous "cures" practiced by the "regular" doctors. The Movement ran up the banner for frequent bathing (regarded as a vice by many "regular" doctors of the time), loose-fitting female clothing, whole grain cereals, temperance, and a host of other issues women could relate to. And, at about the time that Margaret Sanger's mother was a little girl, some elements of the Movement were already pushing birth control.

The Movement was a radical assault on medical elitism, and an affirmation of the traditional people's medicine. "Every man his own doctor," was the slogan of one wing of the Movement, and they made it very clear that they meant every woman too. The "regular," licensed, doctors were attacked as members of the "parasitic, non-producing classes," who survived only because of the upper class' "lurid taste" for calomel and bleeding. Universities (where the elite of the "regular" doctors were trained) were denounced as places where students "learn to look upon labor as servile and demeaning" and to identify with the upper class. Working class radicals rallied to the cause, linking "King-craft, Priest-craft, Lawyer-craft and Doctor-craft" as the four great evils of the time. In New York State, the Movement was represented in the legislature by a member of the Workingman's Party, who took every opportunity to assail the "privileged doctors."

The "regular" doctors quickly found themselves outnumbered and cornered. From the left-wing of the Popular Health Movement came a total rejection of "doctoring" as a paid occupation—much less as an overpaid "profession." From the moderate wing came a host of new medical philosophies, or sects, to compete with the "regulars" on their own terms: Eclecticism, Grahamism, Homeopathy, plus many minor ones. The new sects set up their own medical schools, (emphasizing preventive care and mild herbal cures), and started graduating their own doctors. In this context of medical ferment, the old "regulars" began to look like just another sect, a sect whose particular philosophy happened to lean towards calomel, bleeding and the other stand-by's of "heroic" medicine. It was impossible to tell who were the "real" doctors, and by the 1840's, medical licensing laws had been repealed in almost all of the states.

The peak of the Popular Health Movement coincided with the beginnings of an organized feminist movement, and the two were so closely linked that it's hard to tell where one began and the other left off. "This crusade for women's health [the Popular Health Movement] was related both in cause and effect to the demand for women's rights in general, and the health and feminist movements become indistinguishable at this point," according to Richard Shryock, the well-known medical historian. The health movement was concerned with women's rights in general, and the women's movement was particularly concerned with health and with women's access to medical training.

In fact, leaders of both groups used the prevailing sex stereotypes to argue that women were even better equipped to be doctors than men. "We cannot deny that women possess superior capacities for the science of medicine," wrote Samuel Thomson, a Health Movement leader, in 1834. (However, he felt surgery and the care of males should be reserved for male practitioners.) Feminists, like Sarah Hale, went further, exclaiming in 1852: "Talk about this [medicine] being the appropriate sphere for man and his alone! With tenfold more plausibility and reason we say it is the appropriate sphere for woman, and hers alone."

The new medical sects' schools did, in fact, open their doors to women at a time when "regular" medical training was all but closed to them. For example, Harriet Hunt was denied admission to Harvard Medical College, and instead went to a sectarian school for her formal training. (Actually, the Harvard faculty had voted to admit her—along with some black male students—but the students threatened to riot if they came.) The "regular"physicians could take the credit for training Elizabeth Blackwell, America's first female "regular," but her alma mater (a small school in upstate New York) quickly passed a resolution barring further female students. The first generally co-ed medical school was the "irregular" Eclectic Central Medical College of New York, in Syracuse. Finally, the first two all-female medical colleges, one in Boston and one in Philadelphia, were themselves "irregular."

Feminist researchers should really find out more about the Popular Health Movement. From the perspective of our movement today, it's probably more relevant than the women's suffrage struggle. To us, the most tantalizing aspects of the Movement are: (1) That it represented both class struggle and feminist struggle: Today, it's stylish in some quarters to write off purely feminist issues as middle class concerns. But in the Popular Health Movement we see a coming together of feminist and working class energies. Is this because the Popular Health Movement naturally attracted dissidents of all kinds, or was there some deeper identity of purpose? (2) The Popular Health Movement was not just a movement for more and better medical care, but for a radically different kind of health care: It was a substantive challenge to the prevailing medical dogma, practice and theory. Today we tend to confine our critiques to the organization of medical care, and assume that the scientific substratum of medicine is unassailable. We too should be developing the capability for the critical study of medical "science"—at least as it relates to women.

Doctors on the Offensive

At its height in the 1830's and 1840's, the Popular Health Movement had the "regular" doctors—the professional ancestors of today's physicians—running scared. Later in the 19th century, as the grassroots energy ebbed and the Movement degenerated into a set of competing sects, the "regulars" went back on the offensive. In 1848, they pulled together their first national organization, pretentiously named *the American* Medical Association (AMA). County and state medical societies, many of which had practically disbanded during the height of medical anarchy in the '30s and '40s, began to reform.

Throughout the latter part of the 19th century, the "regulars" relentlessly attacked lay pracitioners, sectarian doctors and women practitioners in general. The attacks were linked: Women practitioners could be attacked because of their sectarian learnings; sects could be attacked because of their openness to women. The arguments against women doctors ranged from paternalistic (how could a respectable woman travel at night to a medical emergency?) to the hardcore sexist. In his presidental address to the AMA in 1971 Dr. Alfred Still, said:

> Certain women seek to rival men in many manly sports . . . . and the strongminded ape them in all things, even in dress. In doing so they may command a sort of admiration such as all monstrous productions inspire, especially when they aim towards a higher type than their own.

The virulence of the American sexist opposition to women in medicine has no parallel in Europe. This is probably because: First, fewer European women were aspiring to medical careers at this time. Second, feminist movements were nowhere as strong as in the U S, and here the male doctors rightly associated the entrance of women into medicine with organized feminism. And, third, the European medical profession was already more firmly established and hence less afraid of competition.

The rare woman who did make it into a "regular" medical school faced one sexist hurdle after another. First there was the continuous harassment—often lewd—by the male students. There were professors who wouldn't discuss anatomy with a lady present. There were textbooks like a well-known 1848 obstetrical text which stated, "She [Woman] has a head almost too small for intellect but just big enough for love." There were respectable gynecological theories of the injurious effects of intellectual activity on the female reproductive organs.

Having completed her academic work, the would-be woman doctor usually found the next steps blocked. Hospitals were usually closed to women doctors, and even if they weren't, the internships were not open to women. If she did finally make it into practice, she found her brother "regulars" unwilling to refer patients to her and absolutely opposed to her membership in their medical societies.

And so it is all the stranger to us, and all the sadder, that what we might call the "women's health movement" began, in the late 19th century, to dissociate itself from its Popular Health Movement past and to strive for respectability. Members of irregular sects were purged from the faculties of the women's medical colleges. Female medical leaders such as Elizabeth Blackwell joined male "regulars" in demanding an end to lay midwifery and "a complete medical education" for all who practiced obstetrics. All this at a time when the "regulars" still had little or no "scientific" advantage over the sect doctors or lay healers.

The explanation, we suppose, was that the women who were likely to seek formal medical training at this time were middle class. They must have found it easier to identify with the middle class "regular" doctors than with lower class women healers or with the sectarian medical groups (which had earlier been identified with radical movements.) The shift in allegiance was probably made all the easier by the fact that, in the cities, female lay practitioners were increasingly likely to be immigrants. (At the same time, the possibilities for a cross-class women's movement on *any* issue were vanishing as working class women went into the factories and middle class settled into Victorian ladyhood.) Whatever the exact explanation, the result was that middle class women had given up the substantive attack on male medicine, and accepted the terms set by the emerging male medical profession.

Professional Victory

The "regulars" were still in no condition to make another bid for medical monopoly. For one thing, they still couldn't claim to have any uniquely effective methods or special body of knowledge. Besides, an occupational group doesn't gain a professional monopoly on the basis of technical superiority alone. A recognized profession is not just a group of self-proclaimed experts; it is a group which has authority *in the law* to select its own members and regulate their practice, i.e., to monopolize a certain field without outside interference. How does a particular group gain full professional status? In the words of sociologist Elliot Freidson:

> A profession attains and maintains its position by virtue of the protection and patronage of some elite segment of society which has been persuaded that there is some special value in its work.

In other words, professions are the creation of a ruling class. To become the medical profession, the "regular" doctors needed, above all, ruling class patronage.

By a lucky coincidence for the "regulars," both the science and the patronage became available around the same time, at the turn of the century. French and especially German scientists brought forth the germ theory of disease which provided, for the first time in human history, a rational basis for disease prevention and therapy. While the run-of-the-mill American doctor was still mumbling about "humors" and dosing people with calomel, a tiny medical elite was traveling to German universities to learn the new science. They returned to the US filled with reformist zeal. In 1893 German-trained doctors (funded by local philanthropists) set up the first American German-style medical school, Johns Hopkins.

As far as curriculum was concerned, the big innovation at Hopkins was integrating lab work in basic science with expanded clinical training. Other reforms included hiring full time faculty emphasizing research, and closely associating the medical school with a full university. Johns Hopkins also introduced the modern pattern of medical education—four years of medical school following four years of college—which of course barred most working class and poor people from the possibility of a medical education.

Meanwhile the US was emerging as the industrial leader of the world. Fortunes built on oil, coal and the ruthless exploitation of American workers were maturing into financial empires. For the first time in American history, there were sufficient concentrations of corporate wealth to alow for massive, organized philanthropy, i.e., organized ruling class intervention in the social, cultural and political life of the nation. Foundations were created as the lasting instruments of this intervention—the Rockefeller and Carnegie foundations appeared in the first decade of the 20th century. One of the earliest and highest items on their agenda was medical "reform," the creation of a respectable, scientific American medical profession.

The group of American medical practitioners that the foundations chose to put their money behind was, naturally enough, the scientific elite of the "regular" doctors. (Many of these men were themselves ruling class, and all were urban, university-trained gentlemen.) Starting in 1903, foundation money began to pour into medical schools by the millions. The conditions were clear: Conform to the Johns Hopkins model or close. To get the message across, the Carnegie Corporation sent a staff man, Abraham Flexner, out on a national tour of medical schools—from Harvard right down to the last third-rate commercial schools.

Flexner almost singlehandedly decided which schools would get the money—and hence survive. For the bigger and better schools (i.e., those which already had enough money to begin to institute the prescribed reforms), there was the promise of fat foundation grants. Harvard was one of the lucky winners, and its president could say smugly in 1907, "Gentlemen, the way to get endowments for medicine is to improve medical education." As the smaller, poorer schools, which included most of the sectarian schools and special schools for blacks and women—Flexner did not consider them worth saving. Their options were to close, or to remain open and face public denunciation in the report Flexner was preparing.

The Flexner Report, published in 1910, was the foundations' ultimatum to American medicine. In its wake, medical schools closed by the score, including six of America's eight black medical schools and the majority of the "irregular" schools which had been a haven for female students. Medicine was established once and for all as a branch of "higher" learning, accessible only through lengthy and expensive university training. It's certainly true that as medical knowledge grew, lengthier training did become necessary. But Flexner and the foundations had no intention of making such training available to the great mass of lay healers and "irregular" doctors. Instead, doors were slammed shut to blacks, to the majority of women and to poor white men (Flexner in his report bewailed the fact that any "crude boy or jaded clerk" had been able to seek medical training.) Medicine had become a white, male, middle class occupation.

But it was more than an occupation. It had become, at last, a profession. To be more precise, one particular group of healers, the "regular" doctors, was now the medical profession. Their victory was not based on any skills of their own: The run-of-the-mill "regular" doctor did not suddenly acquire a knowledge of medical science with the publication of the Flexner report. But he did acquire the *mystique* of science. So what if his own alma mater had been condemned in the Flexner report; wasn't he a member of the AMA, and wasn't it in the forefront of scientific reform? The doctor had become—thanks to some foreign scientists and eastern foundations—the "man of science": beyond criticism, beyond regulation, very nearly beyond competition

Outlawing the Midwives

In state, new, tough, licensing laws sealed the doctor's monopoly on medical practice. All that was left was to drive out the last holdouts of the old people's medicine—the midwives. In 1910, about 50 percent of all babies were delivered by mid-wives—most were blacks or working class immigrants. It was an intolerable situation to the newly emerging obstetrical specialty: For one thing, every poor woman who went to a midwife was one more case lost to academic teaching and research. America's vast lower class resources of obstetrical "teaching material" were being wasted on ignorant midwives. Besides which, poor women were spending an estimated $5 milion a year on midwives—$5 million which could have been going to "professionals."

Publicly, however, the obstetricians launched their attacks on midwives in the name of science and reform. Midwives were ridiculed as "hopelessly dirty, ignorant and incompetent." Specifically, they were held responsible for the prevalence of puerperal sepsis (uterine infections) and neonatal ophthalmia (blindness due to parental infection with gonorrhea). Both conditions were easily preventable by techniques well within the grasp of the least literate midwife (hand-washing for puerperal sepsis, and eye drops for the ophthalmia.) So the obvious solution for a truly public-spirited obstetrical profession would have been to make the appropriate preventive techniques known and available to the mass of midwives. This is in fact what happened in England, Germany and most other European nations: Midwifery was upgraded through training to become an established, independent occupation.

But the American obstetricians had no real commitment to improved obstetrical care. In fact, a study by Johns Hopkins professor in 1912 indicated that most American doctors were *less* competent than the midwives. Not only were the doctors themselves unreliable about preventing sepsis and ophthalmia but they also tended to be too ready to use surgical techniques which endangered mother or child. If anyone, then, deserved a legal monopoly on obstetrical care, it was the midwives, not the MD's. But the doctors had power, the midwives didn't. Under intense pressure from the medical profession, state after state passed laws outlawing midwifery and restricting the practice of obstetrics to doctors. For poor and working class women, this actually meant worse—or no—obstetrical care. (For instance, a study of infant mortality rates in Washington showed an increase in infant mortality in the years immediately following the passage of the law forbidding midwifery.) For the new, male medical profession, the ban on midwives meant one less source of competition. Women had been routed from their last foothold as independent practitioners.

The Lady with the Lamp

The only remaining occupation for women in health was nursing. Nursing had not always existed as a paid occupation—it had to be invented. In the early 19th century, a "nurse" was simply a woman who happened to be nursing someone—a sick child or an aging relative. There were hospitals, and they did employ nurses. But the hospitals of the time served largely as refuges for the dying poor, with only token care provided. Hospital nurses, history has it, were a disreputable lot, prone to drunkeness, prostitution and thievery. And conditions in the hospitals were often scandalous. In the late 1870's a committee investigating New York's Bellevue Hospital could not find a bar of soap on the premises.

If nursing was not exactly an attractive field to women workers, it was a wide open arena for women *reformers*. To reform hospital care, you had to reform nursing, and to make nursing acceptable to doctors and to women of "good character," it had to be given a completely new image. Florence Nightingale got her chance in the battle-front hospitals of the Crimean War, where she replaced the old camp-follower "nurses" with a bevy of disciplined, sober, middle-aged ladies. Dorothea Dix, an American hospital reformer, introduced the new breed of nurses in the Union hospitals of the Civil War.

The new nurse—"the lady with the lamp", selflessly tending the wounded—caught the popular imagination. Real nursing schools began to appear in England right after the Crimean War, and in the US right after the Civil War. At the same time, the number of hospitals began to increase to keep pace with the needs of medical education. Medical students needed hospitals to train in; good hospitals, as the doctors were learning, needed good nurses.

In fact, the first American nursing schools did their best to recruit actual upper class women as students. Miss Euphemia Van Rensselear, of an old aristocratic New York family, graced Bellevue's first class. And at Johns Hopkins, where Isabel Hampton trained nurses in the University Hospital, a leading doctor could only complain that:

> Miss Hampton has been most successful in getting probationers [students] of the upper class; but unfortunately, she selects them altogether for their good looks and the House staff is by this time in a sad state.

Let us look a little more closely at the women who invented nursing, because, in a very real sense, nursing as we know it today is the product of their oppression as upper class Victorian women. Dorothea Dix was an heiress of substantial means. Florence Nightingale and Louisa Schuyler (the moving force behind the creation of America's first Nightingale-style nursing school) were genuine aristocrats. They were refugees from the enforced leisure of Victorian ladyhood. Dix and Nightingale did not begin to carve out their reform careers until they were in their thirties, and faced with the prospect of a long, useless spinsterhood. They focused their energies on the care of the sick because this was a "natural and acceptable interest for ladies of their class."

Nightingale and her immediate disciples left nursing with the indelible stamp of their own class biases. Training emphasized character, not skills. The finished product, the Nightingale nurse, was simply the ideal Lady, transplanted from home to the hospital, and absolved of reproductive responsibilities. To the doctor, she brought the wifely virtue of absolute obedience. To the patient, she brought the selfless devotion of a mother. To the lower level hospital employees, she brought the firm but kindly discipline of a household manager accustomed to dealing with servants.

But, despite the glamorous "lady with the lamp" image, most of nursing work was just low-paid, heavy-duty housework. Before long, most nursing schools were attracting only women from working class and lower middle class homes, whose only other options were factory or clerical work. But the philosophy of nursing education did not change—after all, the educators were still middle and upper class women. If anything, they toughened their insistence on lady-like character development, had the socialization of nurses became what it has been for most of the 20th century: the imposition of upper class cultural values on working class women. (For example, until recently, most nursing students were taught such upper class graces as tea pouring, art appreciation, etc. Practical nurses are still taught to wear girdles, use make-up, and in general mimic the behavior of a "better" class of women.)

But the Nightingale nurse was not just the projection of upper class ladyhood onto the working world: She embodied the very spirit of feminity as defined by sexist Victorian society—she was Woman. The inventors of nursing saw it as a natural vocation for women, second only to motherhood. When a group of English nurses proposed that nursing model itself after the medical profession, with exams and licensing, Nightingale responded that ". . . nurses cannot be registered and examined *any more than mothers*." [Emphasis added.] Or, as one historian of nursing put it, nearly a century later, "Woman is an instinctive nurse, taught by Mother Nature." (Victor Robinson, MD. *White Caps, The Story of Nursing)* If women were instinctive nurses, they were not, in the Nightingale view, instinctive doctors. She wrote of the few female physicians of her time: "They have only tried to be men, and they have succeeded only in being third-rate men." Indeed as the number of nursing students rose in the late 19th century, the number of female medical students began to decline. Woman had found her place in the health system.

Just as the feminist movement had not opposed the rise of medical professionalism, it did not challenge nursing as an oppressive female role. In fact, feminists of the late 19th century were themselves beginning to celebrate the nurse/mother image of femininity. The American women's movement had given up the struggle for full sexual equality to focus exclusively on the vote, and to get it, they were ready to adopt the most sexist tenets of Victorian ideology: Women need the vote, they argued, not because they are human, but because they are Mothers. "Woman is the mother of the race," gushed Boston feminist Julia Ward Howe, "the guardian of its helpless infancy, its earliest teacher, its most zealous champion. Woman is also the homemaker, upon her devolve the details which bless and beautify family life." And so on in paeans too painful to quote.

The women's movement dropped its earlier emphasis on opening up the professions to women: Why foresake Motherhood for the petty pursuits of males? And of course the impetus to attack professionalism itself as inherently sexist and elitist was long since dead. Instead, they turned to professionalizing women's natural functions. Housework was glamorized in the new discipline of "domestic science." Motherhood was held out as a vocation requiring much the same preparation and skill as nursing or teaching.

So while some women were professionalizing women's domestic roles, others were "domesticizing" professional roles, like nursing, teaching and, later, social work. For the woman who chose to express her feminine drives outside of the home, these occupations were presented as simple extensions of women's "natural" domestic role. Conversely the woman who remained at home was encouraged to see herself as a kind of nurse, teacher and counsellor practicing within the limits of the family. And so the middle class feminists of the late 1800's dissolved away some of the harsher contradictions of sexism.

The Doctor Needs a Nurse

Of course, the women's movement was not in a position to decide on the future of nursing anyway. Only the medical profession was. At first, male doctors were a little skeptical about the new Nightingale nurses—perhaps suspecting that this was just one more feminine attempt to infiltrate medicine. But they were soon won over by the nurses' unflagging obedience. (Nightingale was a little obsessive on this point. When she arrived in the Crimea with her newly trained nurses, the doctors at first ignored them all. Nightingale refused to let her women lift a finger to help the thousands of sick and wounded soldiers until the doctors gave an order. Impressed, the doctors finally relented and set the nurses to cleaning up the hospital.) To the beleaguered doctors of the 19th century, nursing was a godsend: Here at last was a kind of health worker who did not want to compete with the "regulars," did not have a medical doctrine to push, and who seemed to have no other mission in life but to serve.

While the average regular doctor was making nurses welcome, the new scientific practitioners of the early 20th century were making them *necessary*. The new, post-Flexner physician, was even less likely than his predecessors to stand around and watch the progress of his "cures." He diagnosed, he prescribed, he moved on. He could not waste his talents, or his expensive academic training in the tedious details of bedside care. For this he needed a patient, obedient helper, someone who was not above the most menial tasks, in short, a nurse.

Healing, in its fullest sense, consists of both curing and caring, doctoring *and* nursing. The old lay healers of an earlier time had combined both functions, and were valued for both. (For example, midwives not only presided at the delivery, but lived in until the new mother was ready to resume care of her children.) But with the development of scientific medicine, and the modern medical profession, the two functions were split irrevocably. Curing became the exclusive province of the doctor; caring was relegated to the nurse. All credit for the patient's recovery went to the doctor and his "quick fix," for only the doctor participated in the mystique of Science. The nurse's activities, on the other hand, were barely distinguishable from those of a servant. She had no power, no magic and no claim to the credit.

Doctoring and nursing arose as complementary functions, and the society which defined nursing as feminine could readily see doctoring as intrinsically "masculine." If the nurse was idealized Woman, the doctor was idealized Man—combining intellect and action, abstract theory and hard-headed pragmatism. The very qualities which fitted Woman for nursing barred her from doctoring, and vice versa. Her tenderness and innate spirituality were out of place in the harsh, linear world of science. His decisiveness and curiosity made him unfit for long hours of patient nurturing.

These sterotypes have proved to be almost unbreakable. Today's leaders of the American Nursing Association may insist that nursing is no longer a feminine vocation but a neuter "profession." They may call for more male nurses to change the "image," insist that nursing requires almost as much academic preparation as medicine, and so on. But the drive to "professionalize" nursing is, at best, a flight from the reality of sexism in the health system. At worst, it is sexist itself, deepening the division among women health workers and bolstering a hierarchy controlled by men.

Suggested Readings

Davies, Emily. *Thoughts on some Questions Relating to Women, 1860–1908*. Cambridge: Bowes & Bowes, 1910.

Ehrenreich, Barbara and Deirdre English. *For Her Own Good: 150 Years of the Experts' Advice to Women*. Garden City, N.Y.: Anchor, 1978.

———. *Complaints and Disorders: The Sexual Politics of Sickness*. Old Westbury, N.Y.: The Feminist Press, 1973.

Szasz, Thomas S. *The Manufacture of Madness*. New York: Dell Publishing Co., 1970.

WOMEN AND CHURCH

XXV. Cardinal Gibbons's Ignorance

Ellen Battelle Dietrick

In the late 1800s, some proponents of free love and feminism subscribed to the theory that the allegedly excessive sexual drive of men was due to the suppression and attempted rejection of sexuality by Christian society. Although feminism was growing steadily more respectable and concerned with the status quo, more radical feminists pointed to the subservient role allotted to women by the Bible and religious figures such as St. Paul. The role of religion in the oppression of women was the theme of Stanton's controversial Woman's Bible (1895). *It is also the theme of the following article written by the feminist Ellen Battelle Dietrick and reprinted from* Liberty. *Several articles by Dietrick appeared in* Liberty.

If Cardinal Gibbons had but considered the original meaning of the word "wife," he would not have fallen into the error embodied in his statement that "Ancient Greece counted women of elementary education proper material for wives, while clever women of higher education enjoyed the license men accord their mistresses." The word "wife" literally means "woman," nothing else. Among the ancient Greeks the original form of marriage made the mother sole owner of the children. She lived with her kinspeople, and her husband had no authority either over her or over her children. Property descended entirely through the line of female ancestors. Matrimony meant, literally, the status of motherhood, and was highly honorable and dignified long before civilized people thought of such a thing as patrimony.

The father lived in his mother's or sister's or cousin's or aunt's house all of his life, visiting the mother of his children when she wished to receive him,—as a guest. His property or earnings all descended to his sisters' children, or to the children of his other female relatives. Women and men were perfect legal equals, and each sex followed what occupation it chose and could succeed in. Women were ecclesiastics, judges, rulers, sovereigns, etc., not only in ancient Greece, but also in ancient Israel (see Old Testament).

After some thousands of years of such customs, man left the house of his mother and cleaved to that of his wife's mother (reference to which is found in "Genesis," ch. 11, verse 24, though the author speaks at a late date, and makes an error in assuming that the first man who took that step left his *father* and mother). But he did not find his position sufficiently independent there to suit him. Leaving the house of his own mother for that of his mother-in-law was out of the frying-pan into the fire. Doubtless the bitter jests against the mother-in-law, which still point the wit of such comic papers as "Life," "Puck," "Judge," etc., are traces of lingering memory of the undignified position man long had to suffer as a subordinate in his mother-in-law's family. The distinguished missionary, Livingstone, who, in this century, visited a people where the custom is still in vogue, represents the condition of man therein as very humiliating. He is little more than a servant of the household, and has to pay adject deference to both the mother of his children and to his mamma-in-law. If he sits down in the presence of the latter, he has to be very careful not to sprawl his feet out towards here, but to tuck them back respectfully under his chair, in order not to seem to take too free and easy an attitude.

All this, of course, was annoying. So, afer a few thousand years of such custom, man made an effort to get the lady of his affections to go off from her people and live alone with him. When such effort failed among the ladies of his own race, sometimes man went off on a raid, stole a beautiful captive from a neighboring race, made her his "wife," and thus became the head of a household of his own. The slave "wife," of course, among strangers whose speech even was unknown to her, was at a great disadvantage. She had no brothers or cousins to take her part, and the poor alien was thus easily subjugated. Thus began the subjection of woman. The children of the slave wife were owned and ruled by their father. They took his name, inherited his property, and paid him allegiance. In such families the same undue prominence was given the eldest son that had, in the other, been given the eldest daughter. In short, patrimony flew to the opposite extreme from matrimony. Gradually such slave mothers as had married rich men lost the love of independence which was natural to women, and in time such mothers voluntarily sold their young daughters to other rich men, and the class of women thus living in ease and comparative idleness, uneducated in the knowledge possessed by free women, corrupted the morals of society, and succeeded in persuading public opinion that marital slavery and ignorance were actually superior to womanly independence and knowledge!

Then a silly world began to condemn such splendid women as Aspasia, Diotima, Corinna, Sappho, and the long line of glorious ancestresses, simply because they had been free wives instead of slave wives. But I wish to call Cardinal Gibbon's attention to the undoubted fact that Greece rose rapidly to its intellectual, artistic, and scientific glory under the *régime* of the free wives, and sank into corruption and decadence under the sway of the slave wives and slave mothers of its later days.

One or two of the fathers of the early Christian Church were men who had sense enough to appreciate the grandeur of character of the educated women of Greece. But the Parkhurst-spirited, narrow, and ignorant fathers of the third and fourth centuries used their utmost endeavor to divide wives into two classes,—respectable and non-respectable. Thus Father Clement of Alexandria, exhorted the women of his congregation to emulate the knowledge loving, independent, and active women of Greece and other parts of the antique world. He held up to them as a model Telesilla, the poetess, of Greece, who "produced fearlessness of death" in all the women who were her followers. He stimulated them to seek learning by preaching to them of Themisto, a celebrated student of philosophy; of Arete, another distinguished philosopher, whose son was famous as the "Mother-taught"; of Lastheneia and of Axiothea, both of whom studied with Plato, "besides Aspasia of Miletus, who was trained by Socrates in philosophy and by Pericles in rhetoric," and a host of others.

Not until the third century of our era did such ignorant bigots as Tertullian begin to advocate among Christians the same slavish conditions which had ruined the intellectual youth of Greece, and, ultimately, through these conditions, Christendom fell into the long night of the dark ages. Ignorant and subjected wives and mothers necessarily degrade the race. The process was hastened in Christendom by the fact that such brilliantly educated women as Paula, Marcella, and others (the first of whom helped Jerome to translate the Old Testament into Latin for the use of Catholic clergy) foolishly went into convents, and persuaded scores of other rich and educated women to do likewise. This left motherhood to the ignorant women, and ignorant women generally fasten superstition, bigotry and folly upon their offspring before the poor little victims are cut loose from their apron-strings.

Now, we can easily perceive why Cardinal Gibbons is so violent in his denunciations of educated womanhood. He says: "To place woman among men in universities that prescribe education without reference to the heart and soul debases womanhood through developing woman's intellect," (!) and, referring to countries where female infants have been drowned, he says: "Men may be obliged to return to this method, if the advancing New Woman goes to much greater lengths in enforcing her theories on society."

Now, as a friend, I should advise the cardinal to pause right here in his mad career against the "New Woman." The day has gone by when a monk can tear a Hypatia from the pursuit of philosophy and throw her to a rabble of insane monastics to be dragged to a violent death. The "heartful and compassionate" qualities which he eulogizes as "womanly" had very little manifestation under the system which Roman Catholicism persistently tried for over a thousand years in Europe,—the system of convent-educated, meagrely-educated womanhood. Society will be far wiser to trust itself to the "New Woman" than to the womanhood whose type was Isabella of Castile, an obedient daughter of the Church, an obedient wife and a fond mother (even the tigress can be a fond mother), but an ecclesiastical tool who ruined Spain, broke hundreds of thousands of hearts, and drove millions to despair and premature death.

The policy of Christendom has too long been that of making knowledge a special preserve of the priests,—Catholic and Protestant,—who assume to decide just who may know what is to be known, and how much of it these privileged ones shall know. I believe the time has come to tell the people—the whole people, male and female, young and old—all the facts which priests are trying to cover up and suppress; the chief of which facts is that there is no such thing as "authority" outside of ourselves. Cardinal Gibbons's opinion is Cardinal Gibbons's opinion, as the opinion of Moses or Ezra or Peter or Paul was their opinion,—nothing more. Any my opinion is that any man who wants to curb the intellect, to check the freedom of vocation-choosing, to retard the pursuit of knowledge, to gag the lips and bind the hand which seek to publish fullest, freest thought, is a most pestiferous enemy of society, *especially* when his efforts are directed against such development in woman.

There is a certain horrible species of cold-blooded animal which seeks to cover up its own plans and movements by showering forth a black liquid to embarrass those whom it desires to confound. That is precisely the mode which certain clergymen have pursued in seeking to perpetuate the subjugation of womankind. Hurling names, showering insinuations against character, stabbing in the back with innuendo, holding up false models of "womanliness," and crying aloud against the courageous few who dare to reject ecclesiastical models, are favorite tactics with such human cuttle-fish. Of course, they can't help their nature, but we must recognize it, and be on our guard against them. A truly manly man despises these cowardly efforts to limit and bind and curb and regulate woman. Man has made himself a law unto himself, publishing it in his pretended "heavenly" revelations, dogmas, and statutes. Woman is now constructing a law unto herself, and she is putting it forth, not on a pretendedly supernatural, but on a natural, basis. She is thoroughly sick of supernaturalism every time she looks at Spain and Italy, especially at Roman Italy.

Cardinal Gibbons might just as well make up his mind that women are slipping out of the clutches of the priest. And, in so doing, they are, for the first time in the history of the world, becoming truly religious, for they are learning what is religion,—the tie that binds; they have discovered that it is nothing but the common tie of our common humanity, the brotherly and sisterly love of a world-wide family.

XXVI. The Economic Tendency of Freethought

Voltairine de Cleyre

Freethought in America was an anti-clerical, anti-Christian movement which sought to separate the church and state in order to leave religious matters to the conscience and reasoning ability of the individual involved. Voltairine de Cleyre (1866–1912), whose essay "Anarchism and American Traditions" appears elsewhere in this anthology, was prominent both as a feminist and as a freethinker. The following article, reprinted from Liberty, *was originally delivered by de Cleyre as a lecture before the Boston Secular Society. It is an excellent example of the interrelationship between the individualist-feminist view of the church and of the state. In her essay "Sex Slavery," de Cleyre reiterated this two-pronged attack. She wrote: "Let every woman ask herself, 'Why am I the Slave of Man?' . . . There are two reasons why, and these are ultimately reducible to a single principle—the authoritarian supreme power GOD-idea, and its two instruments—the Church—that is, the priests—and the State—that is, the legislators."*

FRIENDS,—On page 286, Belford-Clarke edition, of the "Rights of Man," the words which I propose as a text for this discourse may be found. Alluding to the change in the condition of France brought about by the Revolution of '93, Thomas Paine says:

> The mind of the nation had changed beforehand, and a new order of things had naturally followed a new order of thoughts.

Two hundred and eighty-nine years ago, a man, a student, a scholar, a thinker, a philosopher, was roasted alive for the love of God and the preservation of the authority of the Church; and as the hungry flames curled round the crisping flesh of martyred Bruno, licking his blood with their wolfish tongues, they shadowed forth the immense vista of "a new order of things": they lit the battle-ground where Freedom fought her first successful revolt against authority.

That battle-ground was eminently one of thought. Religious freedom was the rankling question of the day. "Liberty of conscience! Liberty of conscience! Non-interference between worshipper and worshipped!" That was the voice that cried out of dungeons and dark places, from under the very foot of prince and ecclesiastic. And why? Because the authoritative despotisms of that day were universally ecclesiastic despotisms; because Church aggression was grinding every human right beneath its heel, and every other minor oppressor was but a tool in the hands of the priesthood; because Tyranny was growing towards its ideal and crushing out of existence the very citadel of Liberty,—individuality of thought; Ecclesiasticism had a corner on ideas.

But individuality is a thing that cannot be killed. Quietly it may be, but just as certainly, silently, perhaps, as the growth of a blade of grass, it offers its perpetual and unconquerable protest against the dictates of Authority. And this silent, unconquerable, menacing thing, that balked God, provoked him to the use of rack, thumb-screw, stock, hanging, drowning, burning, and other instruments of "infinite mercy," in the seventeenth century fought a successful battle against that authority which sought to control this fortress of freedom. It established its right to be. It overthrew that portion of government which attempted to guide the brains of men. It "broke the corner." It declared and maintained the *anarchy*, or non-rulership, of thought.

Now you who so fear the word *an-arche*, remember! the whole combat of the seventeenth century, of which you are justly proud, and to which you never tire of referring, was waged for the sole purpose of realizing anarchism in the realm of thought.

It was not an easy struggle,—this battle of the quiet thinkers against those who held all the power, and all the force of numbers, and all of the strength of tortures! It was not easy for them to speak out of the midst of faggot flames, "We believe differently, and we have the right". But on their side stood Truth! And there lies more inequality between her and Error, more strength for Truth, more weakness for Falsehood, than all the fearful disparity of power that lies between the despot and the victim. So theirs was the success. So they paved the way for the grand political combat of the eighteenth century.

Mark you! The seventeenth century made the eighteenth possible, for it was the "new order of thoughts," which gave birth to a "new order of things". Only by deposing priests, only by rooting out their authority, did it become logical to attack the tyranny of kings: for, under the old régime, kingcraft had ever been the tool of priestcraft, and in the order of things but a secondary consideration. But with the downfall of the latter, kingcraft rose into prominence as the pre-eminent despot, and against the pre-eminent despot revolt always arises.

The leaders of that revolt were naturally those who carried the logic of their freethought into the camp of the dominant oppressor; who thought, spoke, wrote freely of the political fetich, as their predecessors had of the religious mockery; who did not waste their time hugging themselves in the camps of dead enemies, but accepted the live issue of the day, pursued the victories of Religion's martyrs, and carried on the war of Liberty in those lines most necessary to the people at the time and place. The result was the overthrow of the principle of king-craft. (Not that all kingdoms have been overthrown, but find me one in a hundred of the inhabitants of a kingdom who will not laugh at the farce of the "divine appointment" of monarchs.) So wrought the new order of thoughts.

I do not suppose for a moment that Giordano Bruno or Martin Luther foresaw the immense scope taken in by their doctrine of individual judgment. From the experience of men up to that date it was simply impossible that they could foresee its tremendous influence upon the action of the eighteenth century, much less upon the nineteenth. Neither was it possible that those bold writers who attacked the folly of "hereditary government" should calculate the effects which certainly followed as their thoughts took form and shape in the social body. Neither do I believe it possible that any brain that lives can detail the working of a thought into the future, or push its logic to an ultimate. But that many who think, or think they think, do *not* carry their syllogisms even to the first general conclusion, I am also forced to believe. If they did, the freethinkers of today would not be digging, mole-like, through the substratum of dead issues; they would not waste their energies gathering the ashes of fires burnt out two centuries ago; they would not lance their shafts at that which is already bleeding at the arteries; they would not range battalions of brains against a crippled ghost that is "laying" itself as fast as it decently can, while a monster neither ghostly nor yet like the rugged Russian bear, the armed rhinoceros, or the Hyrcan tiger, but rather like a terrible anaconda, steel-muscled and iron-jawed, is winding its horrible folds around the human bodies of the world, and breathing its devouring breath into the faces of children. If they did, they would understand that the paramount question of the day is not political, is not religious, but is economic. That the crying-out demand of today is for a circle of principles that shall forever make it impossible for one man to control another by controlling the means of his existence. They would realize that, unless the freethought movement has a practical utility in rendering the life of man more bearable, unless it contains a principle which, worked out, will free him from the all-oppressive tyrant, it is just as complete and empty a mockery as the Christian miracle or Pagan myth. Eminently is this the age of utility; and the freethinker who goes to the Hovel of Poverty with metaphysical speculations as to the continuity of life, the transformation of matter, etc.; who should say, "My dear friend, your Christian brother is mistaken; you are not doomed to an eternal hell; your condition here is your misfortune and can't be helped, but when you are dead, there's an end of it," is of as little use in the world as the most irrational religionist. To him would the hovel justly reply: "Unless you can show me something in freethought which commends itself to the needs of the race, something which will adjust my wrongs, 'put down the mighty from his seat,' then go sit with priest and king, and wrangle out your metaphysical opinions with those who mocked our misery before."

The question is, does freethought contain such a principle? And right here permit me to introduce a sort of supplementary text, taken, I think, from a recent letter of Cardinal Manning, but if not Cardinal Manning, then some other of the various dunce-capped gentlemen who recently "biled" over the Bruno monument.

Says the Cardinal: "Freethought leads to Atheism, to the destruction of social and civil order, and to the overthrow of government." I accept the gentleman's statement; I credit him with much intellectual acumen for perceiving that which many freethinkers have failed to perceive: accepting it, I shall do my best to prove it, and then endeavor to show that this very iconoclastic principle is the salvation of the economic slave and the destruction of the economic tyrant.

First: does freethought lead to Atheism?

Freethought, broadly defined, is the right to believe as the evidence, coming in contact with the mind, forces it to believe. This implies the admission of any and all evidence bearing upon any subject which may come up for discussion. Among the subjects that come up for discussion, the moment so much is admitted, is the existence of a God.

Now, the idea of God is, in the first place, an exceeding contradiction. The sign God, so Deists tell us, was invented to express the inexpressible, the incomprehensible and infinite! Then they immediately set about defining it. These definitions prove to be about as self-contradictory and generally conflicting as the original absurdity. But there is a particular set of attributes which form a sort of common ground for all these definitions. They tell us that God is possessed of supreme wisdom, supreme justice, and supreme power. In all the catalogue of creeds, I never yet heard of one that had not for its nucleus unlimited potency.

Now, let us take the deist upon his own ground and prove to him either that his God is limited as to wisdom, or limited as to justice, or limited as to power, or else there is no such thing as justice.

First, then, God, being all-just, wishes to do justice; being all-wise, knows what justice is; being all-powerful, *can* do justice. Why then injustice? Either your God can do justice and won't or doesn't know what justice is, or he can not do it. The immediate reply is: "What appears to be injustice in our eyes, in the sight of omniscience may be justice.—God's ways are not our ways."

Oh, but if he is the all-wise pattern, they should be; what is good enough for God ought to be good enough for man; but what is too mean for man won't do in a God. Else there is no such thing as justice or injustice, and every murder, every robbery, every lie, every crime in the calendar is right and upon that one premise of supreme authority you upset every fact in existence.

What right have you to condemn a murderer if you assume him necessary to "God's plan"? What logic can command the return of stolen property, or the branding of a thief, if the Almighty decreed it? Yet here, again, the Deist finds himself in a dilemma, for to suppose crime necessary to God's purpose is to impeach his wisdom or deny his omnipotence by limiting him as to means. The whole matter, then, hinges upon the one attribute of authority of the central idea of God.

But, you say, what has all this to do with the economic tendency of freethought? Everything. For upon that one idea of supreme authority is based every tyranny that was ever formulated. Why? Because, if God is, no human being no thing that lives, ever had a *right!* He simply had a *privilege*, bestowed, granted, conferred, gifted to him, for such a length of time as God sees fit.

This is the logic of my textator, the logic of Catholicism, the only logic of Authoritarianism. The Catholic Church says: "You who are blind, be grateful that you can hear: God could have made you deaf as well. You who are starving, be thankful that you can breathe; God could deprive you of air as well as food. You who are sick, be grateful that you are not dead: God is very merciful to let you live at all. Under all times and circumstances take what you can get, and be thankful." These are the beneficences, the privileges, given by Authority.

Note the difference between a right and a privilege. A right, in the abstract, is a fact; it is not a thing to be given, established, or conferred; it *is*. Of the exercise of a right power may deprive me; of the right itself, never. Privilege, in the abstract, does not exist; there is no such thing. Rights recognized, privilege is destroyed.

But, in the practical, the moment you admit a supreme authority, you have denied rights. Practically the supremacy has all the rights, and no matter what the human race possesses, it does so merely at the caprice of that authority. The exercise of the respiratory function is not a right, but a privilege granted by God; the use of the soil is not a right, but a gracious allowance of Deity; the possession of product as the result of labor is not a right, but a boon bestowed. And the thievery of pure air, the withholding of land from use, the robbery of toil, are not wrongs (for if you have no rights, you cannot be wronged), but benign blessings bestowed by "the Giver of all Good" upon the air-thief, the landlord, and the labor-robber.

Hence the freethinker who recognizes the science of astronomy, the science of mathematics, and the equally positive and exact science of justice, is logically forced to the denial of supreme authority. For no human being who observes and reflects can admit a supreme tyrant and preserve his self-respect. No human mind can accept the dogma of divine despotism and the doctrine of eternal justice at the same time; they contradict each other, and it takes two brains to hold them. The cardinal is right: freethought does logically lead to atheism, if by atheism he means the denial of supreme authority.

I will now take his third statement, leaving the second for the present; freethought, he says, leads to the overthrow of government.

I am sensible that the majority of you will be ready to indignantly deny the cardinal's asseveration; I know that the most of my professedly atheistic friends shrink sensitively from the slightest allusion that sounds like an attack on government; I am aware that there are many of you who could eagerly take this platform to speak upon "the glorious rights and privileges of American citizenship"; to expatiate upon that "noble bulwark of our liberties—the constitution"; to defend "that peaceful weapon of redress, the ballot"; to soar off rhapsodically about that "starry banner that floats 'over the land of the free and the home of the brave.'" We are so free! and so brave! We don't hang Brunos at the stake any more for holding heretical opinions on religious subjects. No! But we imprison men for discussing the *social* question, and we *hang* men for discussing the economic question! We are so very free and so very brave in this country! "Ah"! we say in our nineteenth century freedom (?) and bravery (?), " it was a weak God, a poor God, a miserable, quaking God, whose authority had to be preserved by the tortuous death of a creature!" Aye! the religious question is dead, and the stake is no longer fashionable. But is it a strong State, a brave State, a conscience-proud State, whose authority demands the death of five creatures? Is the scaffold better than the faggot? Is it a very free mind which will read that infamous editorial in the Chicago "Herald": "It is not necessary to hold that Parsons was legally, rightfully, or wisely hanged: he was mightily hanged. The State, the sovereign, need give no reasons; the State need abide by no law; the State is the law!"—to read that and applaud, and set the Cain-like curse upon your forehead and the red "damned spot" upon your hand? Do you know what you do?—Craven, you worship the fiend, Authority, again! True, you have not the ghosts, the incantations, the paraphernalia and mummery of the Church. No: but you have the "precedents," the "be it enacteds," the red-tape, the official uniforms of the State; and you are just as bad a slave to statecraft as your Irish Catholic neighbor is to popecraft. Your Government becomes your God, from whom you accept privileges, and in whose hands all rights are vested. Once more the individual has no rights; once more intangible, irresponsible authority assumes the power of deciding what is right and what is wrong. Once more the race must labor under just such restricted conditions as the law—the voice of the Authority, the governmentalist's bible—shall dictate. Once more it says: "You who have not meat, be grateful that you have bread; many are not allowed even so much. You who work sixteen hours a day, be glad it is not twenty; many have not the privilege to work. You who have not fuel, be thankful that you have shelter; many walk the street! And you, street-walkers, be grateful that there are well-lighted dens of the city; in the country you might die upon the roadside. Goaded human race! Be thankful for your goad. Be submissive to the Lord, and kiss the hand that lashes you!" Once more misery is the diet of the many, while the few receive, in addition to their rights, those rights of their fellows which government has wrested from them. Once more the hypothesis is that the Government, or Authority, or God in his other form, owns all the rights, and grants privileges according to its sweet will.

The freethinker who should determine to question it would naturally suppose that one difficulty in the old investigation was removed. He would say, "at least this thing Government possesses the advantage of being of the earth,—earthy. This is something I can get hold of, argue, reason, discuss with. God was an indefinable, arbitrary, irresponsible something in the clouds, to whom I could not approach nearer than to his agent, the priest. But this dictator surely I shall be able to meet it on something like possible ground." Vain delusion! Government is as unreal, as intangible, as unapproachable as God. Try it, if you don't believe it. Seek through the legislative halls of America and find, if you can, the Government. In the end you will be doomed to confer with the agent, as before. Why, you have the statutes! Yes, but the statutes are not the government; where is the power that made the statutes? Oh, the legislators! Yes, but the legislator, *per se*, has no more power to make a law for me than I for him. I want the power that gave him the power. I shall talk with him; I go to the White House; I say: "Mr. Harrison, are you the government?" "No, madam, I am its representative." "Well, where is the principal?—Who is the government?" "The people of the United States." "The whole people?" "The whole people." "You, then, are the representative of the people of the United States. May I see your certificate of authorization?" "Well, no; I have none. I was elected." "Elected by whom? the whole people?" "Oh, no. By *some* of the people,—*some* of the *voters*." (Mr. Harrison being a pious Presbyterian, he would probably add: "The majority vote of the whole was for another man, but I had the largest electoral vote.") "Then you are the representative of the electoral college, not of the whole people, nor the majority of the people, nor even a majority of the voters. But suppose the largest number of ballots cast had been for you: you would represent the majority of the voters, I suppose. But the majority, sir, is not a tangible thing; it is an unknown quantity. An agent is usually held accountable to his principals. If you do not know the individuals who voted for you, then you do not know for whom you are acting, nor to whom you are accountable. If any body of persons has delegated to you any authority, the disposal of any right or part of a right (supposing a right to be transferable), you must have received it from the individuals composing that body; and you must have some means of learning who those individuals are, or you cannot know for whom you act, and you are utterly irresponsible as an agent.

"Furthermore, such a body of voters can not give into your charge any rights but their own; by no possible jugglery of logic can they delegate the exercise of any function which they themselves do not control. If any individual on earth has a right to delegate his powers to whomsoever he chooses, then every other individual has an equal right; and if each has an equal right, then none can choose an agent for another, without that other's consent. Therefore, if the power of government resides in the *whole people*, and out of that whole all but one elected you as their agent, you would still have no authority whatever to act for the *one*. The individuals composing the minority who did not appoint you have just the same rights and powers as those composing the majority who did; and if they prefer not to delegate them at all, then neither you, nor any one, has any authority whatever to coerce them into accepting you, or any one, as their agent—for upon your own basis the coercive authority resides, not in the majority, not in any *proportion* of the people, but in the whole people."

Hence "the overthrow of government" as a coercive power, thereby denying God in another form.

Upon this overthrow follows, the Cardinal says, the disruption of social and civil order!

Oh! it is amusing to hear those fellows rave about social order! I could laugh to watch them as they repeat the cry, "Great is Diana of the Ephesians!" "Down on your knees and adore this beautiful statue of Order," but that I see this hideous, brainless, disproportion idol come rolled on the wheels of Juggernaut over the weak and the helpless, the sorrowful and the despairing. Hate burns, then, where laughter dies.

Social Order! Not long ago I saw a letter from a young girl to a friend; a young girl whose health had been broken behind a counter, where she stood eleven and twelve hours a day, six days in the week, for the magnificent sum of $5. The letter said: "Can't you help me to a position? My friends want me to marry a man I do not like, because he has money. Can't you help me? I can sew, or keep books. I will even try clerking again rather than that!" Social Order! When the choice for a young girl lies between living by inches and dying by yards at manual labor, or becoming the legal property of a man she does not like because he has money!

Walk up Fifth Avenue in New York some hot summer day, among the magnificent houses of the rich; hear your footsteps echo for blocks with the emptiness of it! Look at places going to waste, space, furniture, draperies, elegance,—all useless. Then take a car down town; go among the homes of the producers of that idle splendor; find six families living in a five-room house,—the sixth dwelling in the cellar. Space is not wasted here,—these human vermin rub each other's elbows in the stifling narrows; furniture is not wasted, —these sit upon the floor; no echoing emptiness, no idle glories! No—but wasting, strangling, choking, vicious human life! Dearth of vitality there—dearth of space for it here! This is social order!

Next winter, when the "annual output" of coal has been mined, when the workmen are clenching their hard fists with impotent anger, when the coal in the ground lies useless, hark to the cry that will rise form the freezing western prairies, while the shortened commodity goes up, up, up, eight, nine, ten, eleven dollars a ton; and while the syndicate's pockets are filing, the grave-yards fill, and fill. Moralize on the preservation of social order!

Go back to President Grant's administration, —that very "pure republican" administration; —see the settlers of the Mussel Slough compelled to pay thirty-five, forty dollars an acre for the land reclaimed from almost worthlessness by hard labor,—and to whom? To a corporation of men who never saw it! whose "grant" lay a hundred miles away, but who, for reasons of their own, saw fit to hire the "servants of the people" to change it so. See those who refused to pay it shot down by order of "the State"; watch their blood smoke upward to the heavens, sealing the red seal of Justice against their murderers; and then — watch a policeman arrest a shoeless tramp for stealing a pair of boots. Say to your self, this is civil order and must be preserved. Go talk with political leaders, big or little, on methods of "making the slate," and "railroading" it through the ward caucus or the national convention. Muse on that "peaceful weapon of redress," the ballot.

Consider the condition of the average "American sovereign" and of his "official servant," and prate then of civil order.

Subvert the social and civil order! Aye, I would destroy, to the last vestige, this mockery of order, this travesty upon justice!

Break up the home? Yes, every home that rests on slavery! Every marriage that represents the sale and transfer of the individuality of one of its parties to the other! Every institution, social or civil, that stands between man and his right; every tie that renders one a master, another a serf; every law, every statute, every be-it-enacted that represents tyranny; everything you call American privilege that can only exist at the expense of international right. Now cry out, "Nihilist—disintegrationist!" Say that I would isolate humanity, reduce society to its elemental state, make men savage! It is not true. But rather than see this devastating, cankering, enslaving system you call social order go on, rather than help to keep alive the accursed institutions of Authority, I would help to reduce every fabric in the social structure to its native element.

But is it true that freedom means disintegration? Only to that which is bad. Only to that which ought to disintegrate.

What is the history of free thought?

Is it not so, that since we have Anarchy there, since all the children of the brain are legitimate, that there has been less waste of intellectual energy, more cooperation in the scienctific world, truer economy in utlizing the mentalities of men, than there ever was, or ever could be, under authoritative dominion of the church? Is it not true that with the liberty of thought, Truth has been able to prove herself without the aid of force? Does not error die from want of vitality when there is no *force* to keep it alive? Is it not true that natural attractions have led men into associative groups, who can best follow their chosen paths of thought, and give the benefit of their studies to mankind with better economy than if some coercive power had said, "You think in this line—you in that"; or what the majority had by ballot decided it was best to think about?

I think it is true.

Follow your logic out; can you not see that *true economy lies in Liberty*,—whether it be in thought or action? It is not slavery that has made men unite for cooperative effort. It is not slavery that produced the means of transportation, communication, production, and exchange, and all the thousand and one economic, or what ought to be economic, contrivances of civilization. No—nor is it government. It is *Self-interest*. And would not self-interest exist if that institution which stands between man and his right to the free use of the soil were annihilated? Could you not see the use of a bank if the power which renders it possible for the national banks to control land, production and everything else, were broken down?

Do you suppose the producers of the east and west couldn't see the advantage of a railroad, if the authority which makes a systematizer like Gould or Vanderbilt a curse where swept away? Do you imagine that government has a corner on ideas, now that the Church is overthrown; and that the people could not learn the principles of economy, if this intangible giant which has robbed and slaughtered them, wasted their resources and distributed opportunities so unjustly, were destroyed? I don't think so. I believe that legislators as a rule have been monuments of asinine stupidity, whose principal business has been to hinder those who were not stupid, and get paid for doing it. I believe that the so-called brainy financial men would rather buy the legislators than be the legislators; and the real thinkers, the genuine improvers of society, have as little to do with law and politics as they conveniently can.

I believe that "Liberty is the mother, not the daughter, of Order."

"But," some one will say, "what of the criminals? Suppose a man steals." In the first place, a man won't steal, ordinarily, unless that which he steals is something he can not as easily get without stealing; in liberty the cost of stealing would involve greater difficulties than producing, and consequently he would not be apt to steal. But suppose a man steals. Today you go to a representative of that power which has robbed you of the earth, of the right of free contract of the means of exchange, taxes you for everything you eat or wear (the meanest form of robbery),—you go to him for redress from a thief! It is about as logical as the Christian lady whose husband had been "removed" by Divine Providence, and who thereupon prayed to said Providence to "comfort the widow and the fatherless." In freedom we would not institute a wholesale robber to protect us from petty larceny. Each associative group would probably adopt its own methods of resisting aggression, that being the only crime. For myself, I think criminals should be treated as sick people.

"But suppose you have murderers, brutes, all sorts of criminals. Are you not afraid to lose the restraining influence of the law?" First, I think it can be shown that the law makes ten criminals where it restrains one. On that basis it would not, as a matter of policy merely, be an economical institution. Second, this is not a question of expediency, but of right. In *ante-bellum* days the proposition was not, Are the blacks good enough to be free? but, Have they the right? So today the question is not, Will outrages result from freeing humanity? but, Has it the right to life, the means of life, the opportunities of happiness?

In the transition epoch, surely crimes will come. Did the seed of tyranny ever bear good fruit? And can you expect Liberty to undo in a moment what Oppression has been doing for ages? Criminals are the crop of depots, as much a necessary expression of the evil in society as an ulcer is of disease in the blood; and so long as the taint of the poison remains, so long there will be crimes.

"For it must needs that offences come, but woe to him through whom the offence cometh." The crimes of the future are the harvests sown of the ruling classes of the present. Woe to the tyrant who shall cause the offense!

Sometimes I dream of this social change. I get a streak of faith in Evolution, and the good in man. I paint a gradual slipping out of the *now*, to that beautiful *then*, where there are neither kings, presidents, landlords, national bankers, stockbrokers, railroad magnates, patent-right monopolists, or tax and title collectors; where there are no over-stocked markets or hungry children, idle counters and naked creatures, splendor and misery, waste and need. I am told this is farfetched idealism, to paint this happy, povertyless, crimeless, diseaseless world; I *have* been told I "ought to be behind the bars" for it.

Remarks of that kind rather destroy the white streak of faith. I lose confidence in the slipping process, and am forced to believe that the rulers of the earth are sowing a fearful wind, to reap a most terrible whirlwind. When I look at this poor, bleeding, wounded World, this world that has suffered so long, struggled so much, been scourged so fiercely, thorn-pierced so deeply, crucified so cruelly, I can only shake my head and remember:

The giant is blind, but he's thinking: and his locks are growing, fast.

Suggested Readings

Gage, Metilda Josly. *Woman, Church and State* (1893). Watertown, Mass.: Persephone Press, 1980.

Hall, David D. *The Antinomian Controversy, 1636-1638: A Documentary History*. Middletown, Conn.: Wesleyan University Press, 1968.

Stanton, Elizabeth Cady. *The Woman's Bible* (1895). New York: Arno Press, 1972 (under the title *The Original Feminist Attack on the Bible*).

WOMEN AND VOTING

XXVII. A Right to Make Laws?

Lysander Spooner

Women's suffrage created more division among individualist feminists than any other issue. Many libertarians shared the moral reservations of Lysander Spooner (1808-1887) concerning political action, whether pursued by men or women. Others believed it was an injustice for women to have fewer legal rights than men. The following article by Spooner was published both in Liberty *and in J.M.L. Babcock's* The New Age. *As the foremost libertarian theorist of the 19th century, Spooner wrote in depth on the relationship of the individual to the state. Although he did not believe, as some, that voting was a form of sanctioning the state, he did maintain that it was a form of imposing one's will upon others—a practice in direct opposition to libertarian principles. Virtually all of the circle around* Liberty *condemned suffrage for men or for women.*

Women are human beings, and consequently have all the natural rights that any human beings can have. They have just as good a right to *make laws* as men have, and no better; AND THAT IS JUST NO RIGHT AT ALL. No human being, nor any number of human beings, have any right to *make laws,* and compel other human beings to obey them. To say that they have is to say that they are the masters and owners of those of whom they require such obedience.

The only law that any human being can rightfully be *compelled* to obey is simply the law of justice. And justice is not a thing that is *made,* or that can be unmade, or altered, by any human authority. It is a *natural* principle, inhering in the very nature of man and of things. It is that natural principle which determines what is mine and what is thine, what is one man's right or property and what is another man's right or property. It is, so to speak, the line that Nature has drawn between one man's rights of person and property and another man's rights of person and property.

But for this line, which Nature has drawn, separating the rights of one man from the rights of any and all other men, no human being could be said to have any rights whatever. Every human being would be at the mercy of any and all other human beings who were stronger than he.

This natural principle, which we will call justice, and which assigns to each and every human being his or her rights, and separates them from the rights of each and every other human being, is, I repeat, not a thing that man has *made,* but is a matter of science to be learned, like mathematics, or chemistry, or geology. And all the *laws,* so called, that men have ever *made,* either to create, define, or control the rights of individuals, were intrinsically just as absurd and ridiculous as would be laws to create, define, or control mathematics, or chemistry, or geology.

Substantially all the tyranny and robbery and crime that governments have ever committed—and they have either themselves committed, or licensed others to commit, nearly all that have ever been committed in the world by anybody—have been committed by them under the pretence of *making laws.* Some man, or some body of men, have claimed the right, or usurped the power of *making laws,* and compelling other men to obey; thus setting up their own will, and enforcing it, in place of natural law, or natural principle, which says that no man or body of men can rightfully exercise any arbitrary power whatever over the persons or property of other men.

There are a large class of men who are so rapacious that they desire to appropriate to their own uses the persons and properties of other men. They combine for the purpose, call themselves governments, *make what they call laws,* and then employ courts, and governors, and constables, and, in the last resort, bayonets, to enforce obedience.

There is another class of men, who are devoured by ambition, by the love of power, and the love of fame.

They think it a very glorious thing to rule over men; to make laws to govern them. But as they have no power of their own to compel obedience, they unite with the rapacious class before mentioned, and become their tools. They promise to *make such laws* as the rapacious class desire, if this latter class will but authorize them to act in their name, and furnish the money and the soldiers necessary for carrying their laws, so called, into execution.

Still another class of men, with a sublime conceit of their own wisdom, or virtue, or religion, think they have a right, and a sort of divine authority, for *making laws* to govern those who, they think are less wise, or less virtuous, or less religious than themselves. They assume to know what is best for all other men to do and not to do, to be and not to be, to have and not to have. And they conspire to *make laws to compel* all these other men to conform to their will, or, as they would say, to their superior discretion. They seem to have no perception of the truth that each and every human being has had given to him a mind and body of his own, separate and distinct from the minds and bodies of all other men; and that each man's mind and body have, by nature, rights that are utterly separate and distinct from the rights of any and all other men; that these individual rights are really the only *human* rights there are in the world; that each man's rights are simply the right to control his own soul, and body, and property, according to his own will, pleasure and discretion, so long as he does not interfere with the equal right of any other man to the free exercise and control of his own soul, body and property. They seem to have no conception of the truth that, so long as he lets all other men's souls, bodies, and properties alone, he is under no obligation whatever to believe in such wisdom or virtue, or religion as they do, or as they think best for him.

This body of self-conceited, wise, virtuous, and religious people, not being sufficiently powerful of themselves to *make laws* and enforce them upon the rest of mankind, combine with the rapacious and ambitious classes before mentioned to carry out such purposes as they can all agree upon. And the farce, and jargon, and babel they all make of what they call government would be supremely ludicrous and ridiculous, if it were not the cause of nearly all the poverty, ignorance, vice, crime, and misery there are in the world.

Of this latter—that is, the self-conceited wise, virtuous and religious class—are those woman suffrage persons who are so anxious that woman should participate in all the falsehood, absurdity, usurpation, and crime of *making law*, and enforcing them upon other persons. It is astonishing what an amount of wisdom, virtue and knowledge they propose to inflict upon, or force into, the rest of mankind, if they can but be permitted to participate with the men in *making laws*. According to their own promises and predictions, there will not be a single natural human being left upon the globe, if the women can but get hold of us, and add their power to that of the men in making such laws as nobody has any right to make, and such as nobody will be under the least obligation to obey. According to their programme, we are all to be put into their legislative mill, and be run through, ground up, worked over, and made into some shape in which we shall scarcely be recognized as human beings. Assuming to be gods, they propose to make us over into their own images. But there are so many different images among them, that we can have, at most, but one feature after one model, and another after another. What the whole conglomerate human animal will be like, it is impossible to conjecture.

In all conscience, is it not better for us even to bear the nearly unbearable ills inflicted upon us by the laws already made,—at any rate is it not better for us to be (if we can but be permitted to be) such simple human beings as Nature made us,—than suffer ourselves to be made over into such grotesque and horrible shapes as a new set of lawmakers would make us into, if we suffer them to try their powers upon us?

The excuse which the women offer for all the laws which they propose to inflict upon us is that they themselves are oppressed by the laws that now exist. Of course they are oppressed; and so are all *men*—except the oppressors themselves—oppressed by the laws that are *made*. As a general rule, oppression was the only motive for which laws were ever *made*. If men wanted justice, and only justice, no laws would ever need to be *made*; since justice itself is not a thing that can be *made*. If men or women, or men and women, want justice, and only justice, their true course is *not to make any more laws, but to abolish the laws—all the laws—that have already been made*. When they shall have abolished all the laws that have already been *made*, let them give themselves to the study and observance, and, if need be, the enforcement, of that one universal law—the law of Nature—which is "the same at Rome and Athens"—in China and in England—and which *man did not make*. Women and men alike will then have their *rights; all their rights; all the rights that Nature gave them*. But until then, neither men nor women will have anything that they can call their *rights*. They will at most have only such liberties or privileges as the laws that are *made* shall see fit to allow them.

If the women, instead of petitioning to be admitted to a participation in the power of *making more laws*, will but give notice to the present lawmakers that they (the women) are going up to the State House, and are going to throw all of the existing statute books in the fire, they will do a very sensible thing,—one of the most sensible things it is in their power to do. And they will have a crowd of men—at least all the sensible and honest men in the country to go with them.

But this subject requires a treatise, and is not to be judged of by the few words here written. Nor is any special odium designed to be cast on the woman suffragists; many of whom are undoubtedly among the best and most honest of all those foolish people who believe that laws should be *made*.

XXVIII. Perpetual Vassalage

Ezra H. Heywood

The following defense of women's suffrage is extracted from Ezra H. Heywood's Uncivil Liberty *and incorporates one of the best arguments in favor of suffrage: specifically, that the denial of enfranchisement was a statement of men's right to rule women. Since women were bound by laws and taxed to support them, it was nothing short of "tyranny" to withhold from them a voice in the political process. Moreover, along with the majority of suffrage advocates, Heywood envisioned a time when the votes of women would purify society.*

The protesting indignation of some women who had the honor to be, at least, rebellious slaves, widespread and increasing unrest broke out in the first formal declaration of independence, issued in 1848, from Seneca Falls, N.Y., by Elizabeth Cady Stanton, Lucretia Mott, and others. It enumerated grievances equal in number and seriousness to those set down in the famous manifesto of '76, and is destined to work a more extended and beneficent revolution. Current objections to woman's enfranchisement can hardly be accounted for, except on the supposition that the sexes, even husbands and wives, are not yet personally acquainted with each other or truth. Justice unites persons widely remote; injustice separates infinitely those standing side by side. Men reputed to know something of the nature of liberty, so-called radicals who have ceased to represent the moral sense, or even the intelligence of the hour, talk flippantly of "universal suffrage" while shutting out one-half of human-kind. A wit believed in universal salvation, provided he could pick the men; so perhaps these recreant "radicals" will conquer their prejudices against impartial suffrage, when assured the new comers will vote their party ticket. The right of man to political freedom appears in the fact that he is a sentient being, capable of reason and choice, looking before and after. To rule adult citizens against their will is tyranny; women are adult citizens, hence those who deny them the ballot are tyrants. A dozen years ago or more, the writer, with other specimens of sophomoric assurance, one morning at breakfast, questioned the propriety of Lucy Stone's refusal to pay taxes, allowing her furniture to be sold in preference; the combined, college-learned, male wisdom thinking it a great ado about a small matter. A lady opposite, who first called his attention practically to peace and anti-slavery reform, flung over the table, "No taxation without representation. Did you ever hear of Sam. Adams and John Hampden?" It was the first and last argument he ever attempted to make against woman's suffrage. To justify himself, her oppressor must class her psychologically with brutes, deny her a soul, prove either that she has no functions equal with man, or that she is incapable of exercising them—neither of which can be done. Boys who toss their empty heads at this reform, use freely that epithet which reveals so much contempt for the human understanding—"strongminded." Men are thought to personate reason, and women sentiment; but generally male objectors to this claim are noted for nothing more than their plentiful lack of logic and super abundance of mulish prejudice. Notwithstanding these disparaging exceptions, men yield to reason; and, at no distant day, physical strength will rally under the banner of moral beauty.

Whether suffrage is a right or privilege, natural or conventional, its denial to woman is equally indefensible. Minors become of age, slaves are emancipated, lunatics regain reason, idiots are endowed with intelligence, criminals are pardoned, traitors amnestied, disfranchised males of every class shed their disabilities and are restored to liberty; but the fact of sex—the crime of womanhood—dooms one to perpetual vassalage! Not the ability to drink, chew, smoke, lie, steal and swear, votes—though election day too often indicates these vices to be important conditions of membership in the male body politic—but intellect, conscience, character, are supposed to vote; and the boy proudly becoming "a man before his mother," is crowned a sovereign at twenty-one, because in thought and discretion he ceases to crawl as an animal, and stands an upright intelligence. Is she who endowed him with these royal qualities less capable of exercising them? If the admission fee to franchise is not age, but property, why are poor men received and rich women excluded? If the door swings open to integrity and courage, why are these turned away in women while their absence is welcomed in men? Simply because his booted, spurred and whiskered thing called government is a usurpation, and men choose to have it so. Since, then, custom not reason, fraud not justice, prejudice not good sense, object, this is a question not for argument, but for affirmation. Those who acknowledge the validity of existing government, by increasing its numerical power, not merely drop a stitch in their logic, but surrender the flag of impartial suffrage to its enemies. The negro certainly has quite as good a right to vote as his late masters. If ignorant, they made it a penal offence to teach him to read; if poor, they robbed him of his earnings by law. But who are negro men and Chinese that we should confer irresponsible power on them? To admit any man, be he black, red, yellow or a minor—our curled, white darling just come of age—to the franchise, who is not pledged to share it with women, is treason to liberty, a desertion of the logical duty of the hour.

A cruel kindness, thought to be friendly regard, assumes to "protect" those who, by divine right of rational being, are entitled, at least, to be let alone. We are not among wild beasts; from whom, then, does woman need protection? From her protectors. While making marriage almost her only possible means of permanent subsistence, and working for a living unpopular, custom forbids her to "propose," to seek a husband; hence this vicarious theory of government owes her, what Socrates claimed for himself, a support at the public expense. If in the old law phrase, "the husband and wife are one person, and he that one"; if, married or unmarried, her personality is buried in his, man should also embody her responsibility—be taxed for her food, clothing, leisure, pleasure, and punished for her sins. But, in practice, he does not recognize this obliging doctrine; for, while reserving the hottest corner of his future hell for her, in this life his responsibility ends with the gratification of his personal desires, and she is "abandoned"—thrown upon the tender mercies of public censure and charity. If there is hanging to be done, it is her head which goes through the noose; if imprisonment is decreed her body is locked up; if starvation ensues, she perishes, while he lives on fat, and free to protect new victims of this loving kindness. If she is to be restrained, can one inferior in rectitude and continence be her keeper? It is said that beauty leans on strength; that Venus rides on a lion, now as the old fable; but evidently the protector will despoil, unless she is armed with self-supporting and self-defending weapons.

Suggested Readings

Goldman, Emma. *Anarchism and Other Essays* (1911). New York: Dover Reprints, 1969, pp. 201-217.
Grimes, Alan P. *The Puritan Ethic and Woman Suffrage*. New York: Oxford University Press, 1967.
Kraditor, Aileen S. *Ideas of the Woman Suffrage Movement, 1890-1920*. New York: Columbia University Press, 1965.

WOMEN AND WAR

XXIX. Patriotism: A Menace to Liberty

Emma Goldman

The inclusion of Emma Goldman (1869-1940) within an individualist-feminist anthology may seem incongruous to those who correctly identify Goldman as a socialist-anarchist. Despite her differences with libertarianism, however, Goldman's adamant opposition to state interference in the life of the individual made her a valuable fellow traveler on many issues. "[Woman's] development," wrote Goldman, "her freedom, her independence, must come from and through herself. First, by asserting herself as a personality, and not as a sex commodity. Second, by refusing the right to anyone over her body; by refusing to bear children, unless she wants them; by refusing to be a servant to God, the state, society, the husband, the family." Because of her clear and often brilliant attacks on the state, Goldman has made lasting contributions to the literature of individualist feminism.

Besides exemplifying many strengths of 19th-century individualist feminism, she exemplified some of its weaknesses. Like most radical movements, individualist feminism carried over prejudice and intolerance from the surrounding society into its own movement. Thus, Goldman's condemnation of the "sexual perversion" engendered by military service—a passage which mars this fine essay—is partially understood, though not excused, by reference to the social context in which it was made. It is ironic that a radical movement seeking to liberate the individual from the state and its laws could not liberate itself from the attitudes which fostered these laws.

The following essay from Anarchism and Other Essays *(1911) is a ringing indictment of the sentiments which prompt men to make war. In 1917, when war fever gripped America, Emma Goldman and Alex Berkman were arrested for organizing No Conscription Leagues and sentenced to two years in jail, after which they were deported to Russia. Goldman's essay,* Patriotism, *is a call for universal brotherhood.*

What is patriotism? Is it love of one's birthplace, the place of childhood's recollections and hopes, dreams and aspirations? Is it the place where, in childlike naivety, we would watch the fleeting clouds, and wonder why we, too, could not run so swiftly? The place where we would count the milliard glittering stars, terror-stricken lest each one "an eye should be," piercing the very depths of our little souls? Is it the place where we would listen to the music of the birds, and long to have wings to fly, even as they, to distant lands? Or the place where we would sit at mother's knee, enraptured by wonderful tales of great deeds and conquests? In short, is it love for the spot, every inch representing dear and precious recollections of happy, joyous, and playful childhood?

If that were patriotism, few American men of today could be called upon to be patriotic, since the place of play has been turned into factory, mill, and mine, while deafening sounds of machinery have replaced the music of the birds. Nor can we longer hear the tales of great deeds, for the stories our mothers tell today are but those of sorrow, tears, and grief.

What, then, is patriotism? "Patriotism, sir, is the last resort of scoundrels," said Dr. Johnson. Leo Tolstoy, the greatest anti-patriot of our times, defines patriotism as the principle that will justify the training of wholesale murderers; a trade that requires better equipment for the exercise of man-killing than the making of such necessities of life as shoes, clothing, and houses; a trade that guarantees better returns and greater glory than that of the average workingman.

Gustave Hervé, another great anti-patriot, justly calls patriotism a superstition—one far more injurious, brutal, and inhumane than religion. The superstition of religion originated in man's inability to explain natural phenomena. That is, when primitive man heard thunder or saw the lightning, he cold not account for either, and therefore concluded that back of them must be a force greater than himself. Similarly he saw a supernatural force in the rain, and in the various other changes in nature. Patriotism, on the other hand, is a superstition artificially created and maintained through a network of lies and falsehoods; a superstition that robs man of his self-respect and dignity, and increases his arrogance and conceit.

Indeed, conceit, arrogance, and egotism are the essentials of patriotism. Let me illustrate. Patriotism assumes that our globe is divided into little spots, each one surrounded by an iron gate. Those who have had the fortune of being born on some particular spot, consider themselves better, nobler, grander, more intelligent than the living beings inhabiting any other spot. It is, therefore, the duty of everyone living on that chosen spot to fight, kill, and die in the attempt to impose his superiority upon all the others.

The inhabitants of the other spots reason in like manner, of course, with the result that, from early infancy, the mind of the child is poisoned with blood-curdling stories about the Germans, the French, the Italians, Russians, etc. When the child has reached manhood, he is thoroughly saturated with the belief that he is chosen by the Lord himself to defend *his* country against the attack or invasion of any foreigner. It is for that purpose that we are clamoring for a greater army and navy, more battleships and ammunition. It is for that purpose that America has within a short time spent four hundred million dollars. Just think of it—four hundred million dollars taken from the produce of *the people*. For surely it is not the rich who contribute to patriotism. They are cosmopolitans, perfectly at home in every land. We in America know well the truth of this. Are not our rich Americans Frenchmen in France, Germans in Germany, or Englishmen in England? And do they not squandor with cosmospolitan grace fortunes coined by American factory children and cotton slaves? Yes, theirs is the patriotism that will make it possible to send messages of condolence to a despot like the Russian Tsar, when any mishap befalls him, as President Roosevelt did in the name of *his* people, when Sergius was punished by the Russian revolutionists.

It is a patriotism that will assist the arch-murderer, Diaz, in destroying thousands of lives in Mexico, or that will even aid in arresting Mexican revolutionists on American soil and keep them incarcerated in American prisons, without the slighest cause or reason.

But, then, patriotism is not for those who represent wealth and power. It is good enough for the people. It reminds one of the historic wisdom of Frederick the Great, the bosom friend of Voltaire, who said: "Religion is a fraud, but it must be maintained for the masses."

That patriotism is rather a costly institution, no one will doubt after considering the following statistics. The progressive increase of the expenditures for the leading armies and navies of the world during the last quarter of a century is a fact of such gravity as to startle every thoughtful student of economic problems. It may be briefly indicated by dividing the time from 1881 to 1905 into five-year periods, and noting the disbursements of several great nations for army and navy purposes during the first and last of those periods. From the first to the last of the periods noted the expenditures of Great Britain increased from $2,101,848,936 to $4,143,226,885, those of France from $3,324,500,000 to $3,455,109,900, those of Germany from $725,000,200 to $2,700,375,600, those of the United States from $1,275,500,750 to $2,650,900,450, those of Russia from $1,900,975,500 to $5,250,445,100, those of Italy from $1,600,975,750 to $1,755,500,100, and those of Japan from $182,900,500 to $700,925,475.

The military expenditures of each of the nations mentioned increased in each of the five-year periods under review. During the entire interval from 1881 to 1905 Great Britain's outlay for her army increased fourfold, that of the United States was tripled, Russia's was doubled, that of Germany increased 35 per cent, that of France 15 per cent, and that of Japan nearly 500 per cent. If we compare the expenditures of these nations upon their armies with their total expenditues for all the twenty-five years ending with 1905, the proportion rose as follows:

In Great Britain from 20 per cent to 37; in the United States from 15 to 23; in France from 16 to 18; in Italy from 12 to 15; in Japan from 12 to 14. On the other hand, it is interesting to note that the proportion in Germany decreased from about 58 per cent to 25, the decrease being due to the enormous increase in the imperial expenditures for other purposes, the fact being that the army expenditures for the period of 1901-5 were higher than for any five-year period preceding. Statistics show that the countries in which army expenditures are greatest, in proportion to the total national revenues, are Great Britain, the United State, Japan, France, and Italy, in the order named.

The showing as to the cost of great navies is equally impressive. During the twenty-five years ending with 1905 naval expenditures increased approximately as follows: Great Britain, 300 per cent; France 60 per cent; Germany 600 per cent; the United States 525 per cent; Russia 300 per cent; Italy 250 per cent; and Japan 700 per cent. With the exception of Great Britain, the United States spends more for naval purposes than any other nation and this expenditure bears also a larger proportion to the entire national disbursements than that of any other power. In the period 1881-5, the expenditure for the United States navy was $6.20 out of each $100 appropriated for all national purposes; the amount rose to $6.60 for the next five-year period, to $8.10 for the next, to $11.70 for the next, and to $16.40 for 1901-5. It is morally certain that the outlay for the current period of five years will show a still further increase.

The rising cost of militarism may be still further illustrated by computing it as a per capita tax on population. From the first to the last of the five-year periods taken as the basis for the comparisions here given, it has risen as follows: In Great Britain from $18.47 to $52.50; in France from $19.66 to $23.62; in Germany, from $10.17 to $15.51; in the United States from $5.62 to $13.64; in Russia, from $6.14 to $8.37; in Italy, from $9.59 to $11.24, and in Japan from 86 cents to $3.11.

It is in connection with this rough estimate of cost per capita that the economic burden of militarism is most appreciable. The irresistible conclusion from available data is that the increase of expenditure for army and navy purposes is rapidly surpassing the growth of population in each of the countries considered in the present calculation. In other words, a continuation of the increased demands of militarism threatens each of those nations with a progressive exhaustion both of men and resources.

The awful waste that patriotism necessitates ought to be sufficient to cure the man of even average intelligence from this disease. Yet patriotism demands still more. The people are urged to be patriotic and for that luxury they pay, not only by supporting their "defenders", but even by sacrificing their own children. Patriotism requires allegiance to the flag, which means obedience and readiness to kill father, mother, brother, sister.

The usual contention is that we need a standing army to protect the country from foreign invasion. Every intelligent man and woman knows, however, that this is a myth maintained to frighten and coerce the foolish. The governments of the world, knowing each other's interests, do not invade each other. They have learned that they can gain much more by international arbitration of disputes than by war and conquest. Indeed, as Carlyle said, "War is a quarrel between two thieves too cowardly to fight their own battle; therefore they take boys from one village and another village, stick them into uniforms, equip them with guns, and let them loose like wild beasts against each other."

It does not require much wisdom to trace every war back to a similar cause. Let us take our own Spanish-American war, supposedly a great and patriotic event in the history of the United States. How our hearts burned with indignation against the atrocious Spaniards! True, our indignation did not flare up spontaneously. It was nurtured by months of newspaper agitation, and long after Butcher Weyler had killed off many noble Cubans and outraged many Cuban women. Still, in justice to the American Nation be it said, it did grow indignant and was willing to fight, and that it fought bravely. But when the smoke was over, the dead buried, and the cost of the war came back to the people in an increase in the price of commodities and rent—that is, when we sobered up from our patriotic spree—it suddenly dawned on us that the cause of the Spanish-American war was the consideration of the price of sugar; or, to be more explicit, that the lives, blood, and money of the American people were used to protect the interests of American capitalists, which were threatened by the Spanish government. That this is not an exaggeration, but is based on absolute facts and figures, is best proven by the attitude of the American government to Cuban labor. When Cuba was firmly in the clutches of the United States, the very soldiers sent to liberate Cuba were ordered to shoot Cuban workingmen during the great cigarmakers' strike, which took place shortly after the war.

Nor do we stand alone in waging war for such causes. The curtain is beginning to be lifted on the motives of the terrible Russo-Japanese war, which cost so much blood and tears. And we see again that back of the fierce Moloch of war stands the still fiercer god of Commercialism. Kuropatkin, the Russian Minister of War during the Russo-Japanese struggle, has revealed the true secret behind the latter. The Tsar and his Grand Dukes, having invested money in Corean concessions, the war was forced for the sole purpose of speedily accumulating large fortunes.

The contention that a standing army and navy is the best security of peace is about as logical as the claim that the most peaceful citizen is he who goes about heavily armed. The experience of every-day life fully proves that the armed individual is invariably anxious to try his strength. The same is historically true of governments. Really peaceful countries do not waste life and energy in war preparations, with the result that peace is maintained.

However, the clamor for an increased army and navy is not due to any foreign danger. It is owing to the dread of the growing discontent of the masses and of the international spirit among the workers. It is to meet the internal enemy that the Powers of various countries are preparing themselves; an enemy, who, once awakened to consciousness, will prove more dangerous than any foreign invader.

The powers that have for centuries been engaged in enslaving the masses have made a thorough study of their psychology. They know that the people at large are like children whose despair, sorrow, and tears can be turned into joy with a little toy. And the more gorgeously the toy is dressed, the louder the colors, the more it will appeal to the million-headed child.

An army and navy represents the people's toys. To make them more attractive and acceptable, hundreds and thousands of dollars are being spent for the display of these toys. That was the purpose of the American government in equipping a fleet and sending it along the Pacific coast, that every American citizen should be made to feel the pride and glory of the United States. They city of San Francisco spent one hundred thousand dollars for the entertainment of the fleet; Los Angeles, sixty thousand; Seattle and Tacoma, about one hundred thousand. To entertain the fleet did I say? To dine and wine a few superior officers while the "brave boys" had to mutiny to get sufficient food. Yes, two hundred and sixty thousand dollars were spent on fireworks, theatre parties, and revelries, at a time when men, women, and children through the breadth and length of the country were starving in the streets; when thousands of unemployed were ready to sell their labor at any price.

Two hundred and sixty thousand dollars! What could not have been accomplished with such an enormous sum? But instead of bread and shelter, the children of those cities were taken to see the fleet, that it may remain, as one of the newspapers said, "a lasting memory for the child."

A wonderful thing to remember, is it not? The implements of civilized slaughter. If the mind of the child is to be poisoned with such memories, what hope is there for a true realization of human brotherhood?

We Americans claim to be a peace-loving people. We hate bloodshed; we are opposed to violence. Yet we go into spasms of joy over the possibility of projecting dynamite bombs from flying machines upon helpless citizens. We are ready to hang, electrocute, or lynch anyone, who, from economic necessity, will risk his own life in the attempt upon that of some industrial magnate. Yet our hearts swell with pride at the thought that America is becoming the most powerful nation on earth, and that it will eventually plant her iron foot on the necks of all other nations.

Such is the logic of patriotism.

Considering the evil results that patriotism is fraught with for the average man, it is as nothing compared with the insult and injury that patriotism heaps upon the soldier himself,—that poor, deluded victim of superstition and ignorance. He, the savior of his country, the protector of his nation,—what has patriotism in store for him? A life of slavish submission, vice, and perversion, during peace; a life of danger, exposure, and death, during war.

While on a recent lecture tour in San Francisco, I visited the Presidio, the most beautiful spot overlooking the Bay and Golden Gate Park. Its purpose should have been playgrounds for children, gardens and music for the recreation of the weary. Instead it is made ugly, dull and gray by barracks, barracks wherein the rich would not allow their dogs to dwell. In these miserable shanties soldiers are herded like cattle; here they waste their young days, polishing the boots and brass buttons of their superior officers. Here, too, I saw the distinction of classes: sturdy sons of a free Republic, drawn up in line like convicts, saluting every passing shrimp of a lieutenant. American equality, degrading manhood and elevating the uniform!

Barrack life further tends to develop tendencies of sexual perversion. It is gradually producing along this line results similar to European military conditions. Havelock Ellis, the noted writer on sex psychology, has made a thorough study of the subject. I quote: "Some of the barracks are great centers of male prostitution. . . . The number of soliders who prostitute themselves is greater than we are willing to believe. It is no exaggeration to say that in certain regiments the presumption is in favor of the venality of the majority of the men. . . . On summer evenings Hyde Park and the neighborhood of Albert Gate are full of guardsmen and others plying a lively trade, and with little disguise, in uniform or out . . . . In most cases the proceeds form a comfortable addition to Tommy Atkins' pocket money."

To what extent this perversion has eaten its way into the army and navy can best be judged from the fact that special houses exist for this form of prostitution. The practice is not limited to England; it is universal. "Soldiers are no less sought after in France than in England or in Germany, and special houses for military prostitution exist both in Paris and the garrison towns."

Had Mr. Havelock Ellis included America in his investigaton of sex perversion, he would have found that the same conditions prevail in our army and navy as in those of other countries. The growth of the standing army inevitably adds to the spread of sex perversion; the barracks are the incubators.

Aside from the sexual effects of barrack life, it also tends to unfit the soldier for useful labor after leaving the army. Men, skilled in a trade, seldom enter the army or navy, but even they, after a military experience, find themselves totally unfitted for their former occupations. Having acquired habits of idleness and a taste for excitement and adventure, no peaceful pursuit can content them. Released from the army, they can turn to no useful work. But it is usually the social riff-raff, discharged prisoners and the like, whom either the struggle for life or their own inclination drives into the ranks. These, their military term over, again turn to their former life of crime, more brutalized and degraded than before. It is a well-known fact that in our prisons there is a goodly number of ex-soldiers; while, on the other hand, the army and navy are to a great extent supplied with ex-convicts.

Of all the evil results I have just described none seems to me so detrimental to human integrity as the spirit patriotism has produced in the case of Private William Buwalda. Because he foolishly believed that one can be a soldier and exercise his rights as a man at the same time, the miliary authorities punished him severely. True, he had served his country fifteen years, during which time his record was unimpeachable. According to Gen. Funston, who reduced Buwalda's sentence to three years, "the first duty of an officer or an enlisted man is unquestioned obedience and loyalty to the government, and it makes no difference whether he approves of that government or not." Thus Funston stamps the true character of allegiance. According to him, entrance into the army abrogates the principles of the Declaration of Independence.

What a strange development of patriotism that turns a thinking being into a loyal machine!

In justification of this most outrageous sentence of Buwalda, Gen. Funston tells the American people that the soldier's action was "a serious crime equal to treason." Now, what did this "terrible crime" really consist of? Simply in this: William Buwalda was one of fifteen hundred people who attended a public meeting in San Francisco; and oh, horrors, he shook hands with the speaker, Emma Goldman. A terrible crime indeed, which the General calls "a great military offense, infinitely worse than desertion."

Can there be a greater indictment against patriotism than that it will thus brand a man a criminal, throw him into prison, and rob him of the results of fifteen years of faithful service?

Buwalda gave to his country the best years of his life and his very manhood. But all that was as nothing. Patriotism is inexorable and, like all insatiable monsters, demands all or nothing. It does not admit that a soldier is also a human being, who has a right to his own feelings and opinions, his own inclinations and ideas. No, patriotism can not admit of that. That is the lesson which Buwalda was made to learn; made to learn at a rather costly, though not at a useless price. When he returned to freedom, he had lost his position in the army, but he regained his self-respect. After all, that is worth three years of imprisonment.

A writer on the military conditions of America, in a recent article, commented on the power of the military man over the civilian in Germany. He said, among other things, that if our Republic had no other meaning than to guarantee all citizens equal rights, it would have just cause for existence. I am convinced that the writer was not in Colorado during the patriotic regime of General Bell. He probably would have changed his mind had he seen how, in the name of patriotism and the Republic, men were thrown into bull-pens, dragged about, driven across the border, and subjected to all kinds of indignities. Nor is that Colorado incident the only one in the growth of military power in the United States. There is hardly a strike where troops and militia do not come to the rescue of those in power, and where they do not act as arrogantly and brutally as do the men wearing the Kaiser's uniform. Then, too, we have the Dick military law. Had the writer forgotten that?

A great misfortune with most of our writers is that they are absolutely ignorant on current events, or that, lacking honesty, they will not speak of these matters. And so it has come to pass that the Dick military law was rushed through Congress with little discussion and still less publicity, a law which gives the President the power to turn a peaceful citizen into a bloodthirsty man-killer, supposedly for the defense of the country, in reality for the protection of the interests of that particular party whose mouthpiece the President happens to be.

Our writer claims that militarism can never become such a power in America as abroad, since it is voluntary with us, while compulsory in the Old World. Two very important facts, however, the gentleman forgets to consider. First, that conscription has created in Europe a deep-seated hatred of militarism among all classes of society. Thousands of young recruits enlist under protest and, once in the army, they will use every possible means to desert. Second, that it is the compulsory feature of militarism which has created a tremendous antimilitarist movement, feared by European Powers far more than anything else. After all, the greatest bulwark of capitalism is militarism. The very moment the latter is underminded, capitalism will totter. True, we have no conscription; that is, men are not usually forced to enlist in the army, but we have developed a far more exacting and rigid force—necessity. Is it not a fact that during industrial depressions there is a tremendous increase in the number of enlistments? The trade of militarism may not be either lucrative or honorable, but it is better than tramping the country in search of work, standing in the bread line, or sleeping in municipal lodging houses. After all, it means thirteen dollars per month, three meals a day, and a place to sleep. Yet even necessity is not sufficiently strong a factor to bring into the army an element of character and manhood. No wonder our military authorities complain of the "poor material" enlisting in the army and navy. This admission is a very encouraging sign. It proves that there is still enough of the spirit of independence and love of liberty left in the average American to risk starvation rather than don the uniform.

Thinking men and women the world over are beginning to realize that patriotism is too narrow and limited a conception to meet the necessities of our time. The centralization of power has brought into being an international feeling of solidarity among the oppressed nations of the world; a solidarity which represents a greater harmony of interests between the workingman of America and his brothers abroad than between the American miner and his exploiting compatriot; a solidarity which fears not foreign invasion, because it is bringing all the workers to the point when they will say to their masters, "Go and do your own killing. We have done it long enough for you."

This solidarity is awakening the consciousness of even the soldiers, they, too, being flesh of the flesh of the great human family. A solidarity that has proven infallible more than once during past struggles, and which has been the impetus inducing the Parisian soldiers, during the Commune of 1871, to refuse to obey when ordered to shoot their brothers. It has given courage to the men who mutinied on Russian warships during recent years. It will eventually bring about the uprising of all of the oppressed and drowntrodden against their international exploiters.

The proletariat of Europe has realized the great force of that solidarity and has, as a result, inaugurated a war against patriotism and its bloody spectre, militarism. Thousands of men fill the prisons of France, Germany, Russia, and the Scandinavian countries, because they dared to defy the ancient superstition. Nor is the movement limited to the working class; it has embraced representatives in all stations of life, its chief exponents being men and women prominent in art, science, and letters.

America will have to follow suit. The spirit of militarism has already permeated all walks of life. Indeed, I am convinced that militarism is growing a greater danger here than anywhere else, because of the many bribes capitalism holds out to those whom it wishes to destroy.

The beginning has already been made in the schools. Evidently the government holds to the Jesuitical conception, "Give me the child mind, and I will mould the man." Children are trained in military tactics, the glory of military achievements extolled in the curriculum, and youthful minds perverted to suit the government. Further, the youth of the country is appealed to in glaring posters to join the army and navy. "A fine chance to see the world!" cries the governmental huckster. Thus innocent boys are morally shanghaied into patriotism, and the military Moloch strides conquering through the Nation.

The American workingman has suffered so much at the hands of the soldier, State and Federal, that he is quite justified in his disgust with, and his opposition to, the uniformed parasite. However, mere denunciation will not solve this great problem. What we need is a propaganda of education for the soldier: antipatriotic literature will enlighten him as to the real horrors of his trade, and that will awaken his consciousness to his true relation to the man to whose labor he owes his very existence.

It is precisely this that the authorities fear most. It is already high treason for a soldier to attend a radical meeting. No doubt they will also stamp it high treason for a soldier to read a radical pamphlet. But then has not authority from time immemorial stamped every step of progress as treasonable? Those, however, who earnestly strive for social reconstruction can well afford to face all that; for it is probably even more important to carry the truth into the barracks than into the factory. When we have undermined the patriotic lie, we shall have cleared the path for the great structure wherein all nationalities shall be united into a universal brotherhood,—a truly FREE SOCIETY.

Suggested Readings

De La Ramee, Louise. *English Imperialism*. New York: Tucker Publishing Co., 1900.

Hirst, Margaret E. *The Quakers in Peace and War*. New York: George H. Doran Co., 1923.

Walters, Ronald G. *American Reformers, 1815-1860*. New York: Hill and Wang, Inc., 1978.

SOURCES

"Human Rights Not Founded on Sex" is from Angelina Grimké, *Letters to Catherine E. Beecher, in Reply to an Essay on Slavery and Abolitionism*, pp. 62–66.

"Anarchism and American Traditions" is from *Selected Works of Voltairine de Cleyre*, pp. 118–135.

"Give Me Liberty" is extracted from the book by that name, pp. 18–31.

"Antigone's Daughters" appeared in the April 1982 issue of *Democracy*.

"Government Is Women's Enemy" was first published as a discussion paper by the Association of Libertarian Feminists.

"An 'Age of Consent' Symposium" appeared in *Liberty*, February 9, 1895.

"Irrelevancies" appeared in *Liberty*, February 1905.

"Prostitution" was first published as a discussion paper by the Association of Libertarian Feminists.

The Marriage Contract of Lucy Stone and Henry Blackwell was published in *History of Woman Suffrage, I*, pp. 260–261.

"Legal Disabilities of Women" is from Sarah Grimké, *Letters on the Equality of the Sexes and the Condition of Women*, pp. 74–83.

"Cupid's Yokes" is extracted from the book by that name, pp. 3–15.

"Love, Marriage and Divorce" is from *Love, Marriage and Divorce and the Sovereignty of the Individual*, pp. 115–123.

"Body Housekeeping" appeared in *The Word*, March 1893.

"The Persecution of Moses Harman" appeared in *Lucifer the Light Bearer*, May 24, 1906.

"If You Liked Gun Control, You'll Love the Antiabortion Amendment" appeared in *Reason*, May 1977.

"Relations Between Parents and Children" appeared in *Liberty*, September 3, 1892.

"Speech of Polly Baker" appeared in *The Word*, June 1873.

"Some Problems of Social Freedom" was published by the publishers of *The Adult*, 1898.

"Are Feminist Businesses Capitalistic?" was first published as a discussion paper by the Association of Libertarian Feminists.

"The Economic Position of Women" is from Suzanne La Follette, *Concerning Women*, pp. 157–206.

"Trade Unionism and Women's Work" is from Susan Anthony, *Women's Place in Industry and Home*, pp. 91–126.

"Protective Labor Legislation" was first published as a discussion paper by the Association of Libertarian Feminists.

"State Aid to Science" is from *Liberty*, September 10, 1888.

"Women and the Rise of the American Medical Profession" is from Barbara Ehrenreich and Deirdre English, *Witches, Midwives and Nurses*, pp. 21–41.

"Cardinal Gibbons's Ignorance" is from *Liberty*, April 20, 1895.

"The Economic Tendency of Freethought" is from *Liberty*, February 15, 1890.

"A Right to Make Laws?" is from *Liberty*, June 10, 1882.

"Perpetual Vassalage" is from E. H. Heywood, *Uncivil Liberty*, pp. 11–13.

"Patriotism: A Menace to Liberty" is from Emma Goldman, *Anarchism and Other Essays*, pp. 133–150.

INDEX

ABOUT THE EDITOR

Wendy McElroy writes and lectures on political theory and feminism. As a fellow of the Center for Libertarian Studies, she compiled an index (Dandelion Press, 1982) to *Liberty*, a periodical edited by Benjamin Tucker from 1881 to 1908, and she is now compiling an anthology and index of Ezra Heywood's *The Word*. She has served as an editor of *Reason* and of *The Castalian* and has published in *Literature of Liberty* and *The Journal of Libertarian Studies*. She has also written poetry and short stories for various publications, and is a member of the Association of Libertarian Feminists.

The Cato Institute

The Cato Institute is named for the libertarian pamphlets *Cato's Letters*. Written by John Trenchard and Thomas Gordon, *Cato's Letters* were widely read in the American colonies in the eighteenth century and played a major role in laying the philosophical foundation for the revolution that followed.

The erosion of civil and economic liberties in the modern world has occured in concert with a widening array of social problems. These disturbing developments have resulted from a failure to examine social problems in terms of the fundamental principles of human dignity, economic welfare, freedom, and justice.

The Cato Institute aims to broaden public policy debate by sponsoring programs designed to assist both the scholar and the concerned layperson in analyzing questions of political economy.

The programs of the Cato Institute include the sponsorship and publication of basic research in social philosophy and public policy; publication of the *Cato Journal*, an interdisciplinary journal of public policy analysis, and *Policy Report*, a monthly economic newsletter; "Byline," a daily public affairs radio program; and an extensive program of symposia, seminars, and conferences.

CATO INSTITUTE
224 Second St., S.E.
Washington, D.C. 20003